UNTANGLING
THE
COLD WAR

UNTANGLING
THE
COLD WAR

A STRATEGY FOR TESTING RIVAL THEORIES

William A. Gamson
THE UNIVERSITY OF MICHIGAN

Andre Modigliani
HARVARD UNIVERSITY

LITTLE, BROWN AND COMPANY   Boston

FIRST PRINTING

Printed simultaneously in Canada by
Little, Brown & Company (Canada) Limited

PRINTED IN THE UNITED STATES OF AMERICA

To Zelda and Kathy

PREFACE

This book treats the Cold War as an interaction — as a concrete sequence of actions and reactions generated by two coalitions over a specific historical period. Our aim is to test a number of competing theories of why this interaction took the course it did. The theories to be tested are based on the writings of historians, political scientists, and other analysts of the Cold War, such as Robert Strausz-Hupé, Marshall Shulman, Adam Ulam, George Kennan, Charles Osgood, David Horowitz, D. F. Fleming, Ronald Steel, and Carl Ogelsby.

The method used to test these theories is new. Unlike the typical approach of historians and political scientists, interweaving description and explanation into a running interpretive account, our own approach makes a sharper separation between description and theory. Based on a daily monitoring of Cold War events, we begin by constructing a description of the interaction between the Soviet and Western coalitions as it unfolded over the period from 1946 to 1963. Next, drawing on writers such as those noted above, we delineate a number of alternative theories that might plausibly account for the observed interaction. Finally, we confront the theories with the data in order to determine which best explains the observed sequence of actions and reactions.

We view this book as making a contribution both to research strategy and to an understanding of the Cold War. The analytic framework developed in the first half of the book could be applied to any bipolar conflict that meets the general specifications discussed in Chapter One. We believe it represents a novel way of utilizing historical data to study conflicts between large social units. If the framework is valid, and if it has been properly applied to the Cold War, then the conclusions drawn from it should contribute to our understanding of this particular historical conflict.

The first two chapters of the book describe our analytic framework and the research strategy based upon it. The third and fourth chapters discuss the theories to be tested and the predictions each would make about the coalitions' pattern of interaction. The fifth and sixth chapters contain the bulk of our findings: the results of pitting the theories against the data. The last chapter utilizes these findings to analyze distinct phases in the Cold War interaction and proposes an outline for interpreting the details of this historical period.

Collaborations take many different forms and a word about the nature of this one is in order. We employed no division of labor in this research. Each of us was fully involved in each stage — in the development of research strategy, in the problems of measurement, in the analysis, and in the presentation in this book.

Of course we had a good deal of help from others. The initial stimulus came from a five-week summer conference held at Craigville, Massachusetts, in 1962 on International Conflict and Behavioral Science, sponsored by the American Academy of Arts and Sciences. During most of the project, we were supported by a grant from the Carnegie Corporation of New York through the Center for Research on Conflict Resolution at the University of Michigan. William Barth, the associate director of the Center, did a variety of things that made life easier for us and enabled us to devote our energies to this research. During parts of the project, Mr. Modigliani was supported by a predoctoral fellowship from the National Institute of Mental Health (No. 5 F1 MH-24 346-03) and later by small grants from the Clark and Milton Funds at Harvard University.

A number of research assistants helped us, especially with the arduous task of coding daily Cold War interaction over an eighteen-year period. Rosemary K. Coffey did the bulk of this coding and worked on the comparison of the *New York Times* with French- and German-language newspapers. Antioch students George D. Keebler, Jan Smith, and Oliver Lock Holmes carried out a variety of tasks, working on this project as part of the Antioch co-op job program. Janet Goff typed the final draft with care and good humor.

A number of people read through the draft and made helpful suggestions and criticisms. We extracted this service from our wives and happily they responded good-naturedly to this form of involuntary servitude. Walter Corson and Craig Eisendrath took the time to give us helpful and detailed criticisms and suggestions.

CONTENTS

ix

Appendix E
MAJOR SOVIET AND WESTERN ACTIONS, 1946–63   196

Appendix F
BELLIGERENT/ACCOMMODATIVE SCORES
FOR 125 INTERACTIONS UNITS, 1946–63   204

LIST OF ILLUSTRATIONS

UNTANGLING
THE
COLD WAR

Chapter One

AN APPROACH
TO STUDYING THE COLD WAR

This is a study of the Cold War. We hope that it also has broader implications since our interests transcend the understanding of one particular historical conflict. More generally, we are interested in developing new ways to study conflicts between large social units such as nations. In the pages that follow, we develop a systematic procedure for analyzing and understanding the Cold War. Although our research strategy can be applied to other dyadic conflicts as well, here we concentrate exclusively on the Cold War as a prototype and intrinsically interesting special case.

The conflict that will concern us is a protracted one, punctuated by sporadic violence. Its protagonists are two coalitions of nations, one led by the United States, the other by the Soviet Union. We will treat this conflict as an interaction — that is, as a concrete sequence of actions and reactions by the two adversaries, spanning a specified historical period. Our aim is to understand this interaction sequence as fully as possible. To achieve this, we would need to know why each side behaved as it did on each occasion over the years. We will settle, however, for understanding why certain broad patterns of interaction occurred. We intend the terms of our understanding to be in a form that makes them applicable to these same patterns when they occur in other international conflicts. And we are certain that an understanding of these broader patterns provides a highly useful and necessary framework within which to pursue more detailed analyses.

HISTORICAL BOUNDARIES OF THE COLD WAR

We have designated January, 1946, as the beginning of the period we intend to study. In the years prior to this, the United States and the Soviet Union, later to become antagonists, were still partners in a wartime alliance. To be sure, there were many indications of serious conflict among the allies prior to 1946, but at least until 1945, the

1

overriding common goal of winning the war kept these conflicts under rein. The strains in the wartime Soviet alliance with Great Britain and the United States never approached the open hostility so characteristic of the Cold War.

1945 was the year of transition. The defeat of Germany removed the major cooperative incentive of the wartime alliance. In addition, the successful development of the atomic bomb reduced the dependence of the United States on the Soviet Union for a rapid ending of the war in the Pacific and hastened the erosion of the Soviet-Western entente. As attention shifted to the nature of the postwar world, divisive issues came to the fore and the two opposing coalitions began to take shape. A brief chronology of events illustrates the growing disagreement and changing relationship.

In March of 1945, the Soviet Union requested a revision of a treaty with Turkey in order to gain access to a port on the Mediterranean. But Turkey, with firm Western backing, refused. In April and May, a dispute over the composition of the provisional government of Poland led to the abrupt American cancellation of lend-lease to the Soviet Union. The situation improved briefly in late June when an agreement on Poland was reached and lend-lease was reinstated. But the Potsdam conference in July underlined the unresolved issues. By the end of August, Churchill was already denouncing "police governments" established in Eastern Europe and declaring that "a tragedy on a prodigious scale is unfolding itself behind the iron curtain which divides Europe in twain" (cf. Luard, 1964, p. 20). In September, Soviet requests for control of the Dodecanese and trusteeship of Libya were denied by the Western powers. Lend-lease was again canceled, and in October a foreign ministers' conference on peace treaties deadlocked and broke down. Although the year ended with a joint Allied recognition of two more Eastern European provisional governments, the basic lines of the Cold War had clearly been drawn.

The systematic collection of data for our study begins with January of 1946. Already in the first quarter of this year, the relationship had so changed that, for the first time, the possibility existed that a disagreement might end in a violent confrontation between the former allies. In January, Iran brought charges in the Security Council against the Soviet Union for failing to evacuate its troops from Azerbaidjan. These charges were immediately supported by the United States and Great Britain. The Soviet Union refused to discuss the question and issued a volley of countercharges against the presence of British and French troops in Lebanon, Syria, Greece, and Indonesia. In early March, an unexpected Soviet troop movement toward Teheran brought the crisis to a head. Acrimonious debates ensued in the newly formed

United Nations, resulting in a Soviet veto and walkout from the Security Council. Eventually, the Soviet Union reaffirmed its intention to evacuate its troops, but for some days the possibility that the dispute would lead to violence existed. This same possibility, made more menacing by the antagonists' possession of nuclear weapons, hung ominously in the background of Soviet-Western relations for most of the next two decades.

As early as 1946, then, three characteristic features of the Cold War were already discernible. First, the Cold War period was marked by a persistent and often extreme antagonism between the United States and the Soviet Union. Many disagreements brought these two powers and their allies to the brink of war. In the case of Korea, prolonged military conflict occurred although United States and Soviet troops did not face each other directly. In Berlin, they did face each other but fortunately things never went over the brink.

A second feature of the Cold War period was the strong bipolarity of the world alliance structure. In pursuing their conflicts, the United States and the Soviet Union were each supported by a relatively stable coalition of nations. Repeatedly these two coalitions stood united on opposite sides of international issues. On the Western side, the Anglo-American-French alliance rapidly expanded to include most of Western Europe as well as many other countries around the world. On the Soviet side, a small core of satellite countries expanded to include most of Eastern Europe as well as North Korea and eventually China. This bipolar coalition system was remarkably inclusive. No major power stood apart from it, and, until the time when numerous formerly colonial nations had gained their independence, no significant and coherent "third world" force existed.

The third feature of this period was the domination of the world stage by the major powers, most notably the Soviet Union and the United States, but also France, Great Britain, and China. The formalization of their leading roles in the structure of the United Nations Security Council was only one aspect of this broader phenomenon. More generally, international events could be treated and understood largely as major power confrontations. Conflicts involving the smaller nations (whether civil or otherwise) became noteworthy primarily insofar as they created cleavages among the major powers. Antagonisms which initially had little to do with the Cold War conflict were often rapidly appropriated and guided by the United States and the Soviet Union. It was rare for a conflict anywhere in the world to be largely out of the control of one or more of the principal Cold War protagonists.

If these three distinctive features mark the Cold War, their gradual abeyance marks its demise. During the early and mid 1960's, important changes occurred in the character of Soviet-American relations as well as in the broader international arena. These changes were of sufficient magnitude to make it no longer useful to view subsequent international events as a straightforward continuation of the Cold War. It is, of course, difficult and risky to pick a watershed for events so close to the present, but the end of the Kennedy administration in November, 1963, corresponding as it does to the establishment of a Soviet-Western detente in the summer and fall of that year, seems a sensible closing date for the period we intend to focus on in this study.

Since the detente of 1963, each of the characteristic features of the Cold War has become significantly less pronounced. First, the marked antagonism between the United States and the Soviet Union has, to a large degree, subsided. As Shulman notes, "the conflict relationship between the Soviet Union and the West has passed from a stark post-war confrontation to a more ambiguous stage in which the balance of conflicting and parallel interests is less clearly defined, and the conflict itself has a more diffuse character" (1966, p. 14). The manifestations of this relaxation of tension have been numerous. With the possible exception of a brief and highly circumscribed clash during the Arab-Israeli War of 1967, there has been no major hostile confrontation between the United States and the Soviet Union since the Cuban missile crisis of 1962.[1] Cultural exchanges have been expanding and arms-control agreements have been reached on nuclear testing, nuclear proliferation, and military uses of space. The most remarkable aspect of this detente is that it has continued to exist, and even to progress, despite the potentially highly divisive Vietnam issue. Both the United States and the Soviet Union have sought to tone down mutual recriminations over their respective roles in this war. Although there have been hostile exchanges, these have been restrained and frequently seem more designed for coalition partners or domestic consumption than acts of influence aimed at an opponent.

Second, since the early 1960's, the bipolar world alliance structure has been substantially eroded. The world is no longer divided into two cohesive and mutually hostile camps. As a consequence of the Sino-Soviet split, China has become a major power largely independent of either the Soviet or the Western coalition. France, too, has pursued an increasingly independent foreign policy, finally withdrawing from NATO altogether. Notable divisions have developed among the Warsaw Pact countries of Eastern Europe; and United States policy in

[1] The Soviet invasion of Czechoslovakia in the summer of 1968 is not an exception. The United States made it quite clear both before and after this event that, while it sympathized with the Czech position, it would not become a party in the conflict.

Vietnam has created further divisions in the Western coalition. Finally, considerable cohesion has developed among the countries of the Third World. In short, the international arena can no longer be described and analyzed in simple, bipolar terms; the old alliance structure has become too fragmented and fluid.

Third, during the last decade, conflicts involving the smaller nations (especially conflicts of a nationalistic or revolutionary nature) have come increasingly to the forefront of the world stage while the role of the great powers has receded. In part this has been the result of a rising tide of nationalism and anticolonialism, and in part it has been a consequence of the Soviet-American detente and the loosening of the bipolar alliance structure. Local conflicts have been less prone to be drawn into the East-West framework: major powers have been less motivated to exploit and to guide such conflicts, while smaller nations have been more wary of outside interference in their affairs. When the major powers have become involved, it has been more a matter of drifting entanglement than a matter of deliberate strategy. Shulman likens the situation to that of "two tired wrestlers whose ring is swirling with many former spectators, and whose main bout has become something of a free-for-all" (1966, p. 32). The Vietnam conflict illustrates the degree to which major powers can become captives of local forces and events over which they have little control. In general, it has become decreasingly useful to view international events as merely reflecting and affecting the strategy and tactics of the great powers.

In sum, the conflict we intend to study spans the time period from January, 1946, to November, 1963. It was marked by three distinctive characteristics: a persistent Soviet-American antagonism, a bipolar world alliance structure, and great power domination of international events. Thereafter, these features gradually receded, leaving a residual conflict sufficiently different from the original as to be no longer fruitfully characterized as the same conflict. As Shulman argues, "Whereas in its first post-war phase, the confrontation between the Soviet Union and the United States was the dominating fact of international politics . . . today this confrontation no longer holds the center of the stage. The conflict of purposes between these two systems has become caught up in the turbulent currents of international politics. . . . Not that the Cold War is over, but it has been transformed and merged into a larger and more complex setting" (ibid., pp. 31 and 109).

RESEARCH STRATEGY

History, it seems, can be everyone's handmaiden. A few dramatic events such as the attack on South Korea or the Soviet withdrawal of missiles from Cuba may serve to sustain dubious lessons against the force of much counterevidence. Different events will support different points of view, and by judicious selection many competing interpretations can be woven. Since facts and events do not speak for themselves, we cannot avoid imposing meaning on them; understanding necessarily involves organizing, selective emphasis, and other simplifications of an apparently incoherent jumble of events. Our own research strategy does not omit this necessary step in the process of analysis — indeed, it cannot — but it does seek to postpone it. That is, we shall seek to postpone interpretation until we have described as comprehensively and objectively as possible the universe of events that we wish to understand.

Our ultimate aims do not differ appreciably from those of other investigators concerned with understanding the Cold War. Historians and political scientists have also sought to analyze and understand the strategic objectives of the Cold War adversaries and their resultant interaction. However, these investigators have seldom made a systematic effort to separate description from interpretation. Instead, they have preferred to interweave the two to create a running, interpretive account of the interaction. Furthermore, in searching for explanations, these investigators have tended to focus directly on the decision-making processes of the adversaries, basing their analyses on such data sources as government documents, public speeches, proceedings and accounts of relevant policy-making bodies, memoirs, and diaries. Such historical documents do contain information on the objectives and strategy of the adversaries although there are often great methodological difficulties involved in obtaining, sampling, and interpreting them.

Different investigators using this approach frequently end up with dramatically different interpretations of the Cold War, as we shall see in detail in Chapter Three. Each man has his favorite events, speeches, or documents; and by featuring appropriate material, each can support his own point of view. There are, to be sure, more and less plausible interpretations, but the rules of inference are loose and place few restrictions on the ingenious investigator. Not being political scientists or historians, we have our own repertoire of methodologies. These, too, no doubt have their limitations, but then we feel more comfortable with the vices we know.

Our own methodological approach is distinguished by a sharp separation between description and interpretation. We begin by identifying and describing as clearly and systematically as possible the interaction sequence that we wish to explain. This account is "objective" in the sense that any observer following our rules of description could reproduce it. In constructing this account, we make no effort to obtain information that bears directly on a party's decision to engage in certain actions. Rather, we use as data only the outputs of such decisions — *only the concrete actions taken by a party*. Such data is largely a matter of public record and any good daily newspaper can provide most of it. There is usually little ambiguity about what a party has done; controversy arises over why it was done and whether it was justified.

After establishing the sequence of concrete actions generated by the two protagonists over the course of the Cold War, we shall then proceed to interpret this sequence or, more precisely, to test alternative interpretations. In constructing these alternatives, we borrow heavily from the conclusions of historians and political scientists, especially those who offer competing interpretations of the Cold War. But each theory must, in the end, confront the same set of data, and the proof of its usefulness is in explaining with parsimony the sequence of actions described by our data.[2]

THE INTERACTION FRAMEWORK

We shall treat the Cold War as a special case of *dyadic, mutually contingent, hostile interaction*. In discussing each of the above terms, we will clarify who the Cold War protagonists were and which of their many concrete actions are considered relevant data for our study.

The Cold War as Dyadic Interaction

Dyadic interaction is interaction involving two parties. These parties need not be monolithic. On the contrary, they may be quite complex and their degree of internal integration or strain may be an important variable which will affect the course of the interaction. The parties to the Cold War were such complex entities — they were coalitions of nations, each led by a major power. The term "coalition" implies the "joint use of resources to determine the outcome of a decision" (Gamson, 1964a, p. 82). Each party in the Cold War consisted of nations that, over some extended period, coordinated their resources in interaction with a common adversary. This coordination was achieved through a mixture of formal alliance and informal control or dominance by the coalition leader.

We call these parties to the Cold War the "Soviet" and the "Western" coalitions: the former term is intended as a shorthand for the USSR and its allies, while the latter term includes the United States

[2] Some theories of the Cold War may wish to emphasize phenomena that are not included in our description. In this sense, the description is not as comprehensive as these theories would wish. Rather it constitutes a minimal set of actions to which *any* theory of the Cold War must address itself. The exclusion of events that some theories might consider important raises issues that are discussed in the final section of this chapter.

and its allies. Ambiguities can easily arise over the precise boundaries of these coalitions at different periods. These boundaries are important because they have direct implications for which events we consider to be a part of the Cold War interaction. For example, the point at which Cuba became a member of the Soviet coalition determines the point at which we begin including Cuba-United States conflict.

The rules by which we determine membership in each coalition over time can be stated in fairly general terms that are applicable to both coalitions simultaneously. At any given time, each coalition can contain core members and temporary members. A *core* member is a country that clearly maintains a relationship of solidarity with the leader of one coalition and a relationship of conflict with the opposing coalition. There are essentially two ways of establishing such solidarity and many countries have made use of both. First, any country that participates in a military alliance with the coalition leader is considered a core member. Such alliances can be bilateral (e.g., the United States and Japan) or multilateral (e.g., the NATO countries and the Warsaw Pact countries). Second, even if a country is not involved in such a formal military alliance, it qualifies for core membership if it establishes its solidarity in other ways — for example, through proclamations of support for the coalition and opposition to its adversary. In effect, by this second criterion, a nation is treated as a core member if it says publicly that it *considers* itself a core member.[3]

In addition to core members, any normally "nonaligned" country can become a *temporary* member of a coalition, for a circumscribed period, if it is explicitly supported by core members of that coalition in a conflict against members of the opposing coalition. Thus, although Egypt is not normally treated as a member of the Soviet coalition, it was a temporary member during the Suez crisis of 1956 when it had the explicit backing of the Soviet Union in its conflict with Great Britain and France. Similarly, despite India's long-run policy of neutrality, it is considered a temporary member of the Western coalition at the time it accepted United States support during its conflict with China. The actions of any nation, then, can temporarily

[3] Clearly, under the above definition, core membership changes to some degree over time. Thus, Thailand did not become a core member of the Western coalition until it agreed to participate in the SEATO alliance in 1954; China did not become a core member of the Soviet coalition until the Moscow conference of 1949 with its series of bilateral agreements and proclamations of solidarity. Conversely, a core member of a coalition loses this status whenever an open break occurs with the coalition leader marked by expressions of neutrality (or mutual recrimination) and the implicit or explicit severance of military alliance. Thus, France left the Western coalition when it withdrew from NATO, and Yugoslavia left the Soviet coalition when its leaders were expelled by the Cominform.

become a part of the Cold War if that nation is acting in concert with core members on an issue that divides the coalitions.

We should make clear that our designation of the Cold War as a conflict between two coalitions does not represent any effort to describe the world from 1946 to 1963 as divided into two completely monolithic camps. Rather, this assumption of dyadic conflict is a reasonable approximation based on the overall bipolarity of the Cold War alliance structure. It permits us to simplify our analysis by avoiding the unnecessary complexities of a multilateral interaction. Our strategy of analysis will afford ample opportunity to detect and to study the effects of internal dissension within a coalition. Although we *do* assume that the core members of a coalition will usually pursue a common foreign policy, we do *not* assume that they will do so at all times. Moreover, so long as a core member does not formally break with its coalition, we treat its actions as actions of the coalition even though the coalition leader may disapprove of them. For example, the Anglo-French attack on Egypt during the Suez crisis of 1956 is treated as a Western coalition activity even though the United States overtly disapproved of the attack. In such a case, the Western "actor" is inconsistent and our analysis will permit us to detect this and examine its consequences.

The Cold War as Mutually Contingent Interaction

Jones and Gerard (1967) make a series of distinctions among types of interaction situations centering around the concept of contingency. They assume two basic determinants of any party's behavior in a dyadic interaction situation: the plans it brings into the situation, and the actions of the other party toward it. The term "plans" refers both to the goals with which it enters the interaction and to its pattern of attitudes and expectations about the situation and other party. One may then ask, for any dyadic interaction situation, how much each party's responses are determined by its own plans, how much they are determined by the responses of the other party, and how much they are based on a genuine combination of the two.

We treat the Cold War as a mutually contingent interaction in which each coalition was influenced in important ways both by what the other coalition did and by its own goals and perceptions of the other side. We assume that each coalition had certain long-range goals or strategic objectives. These goals involve conceptions of what constitutes an international environment favorable to national security and general well-being. The successful pursuit of foreign policy implies the implementation of these goals. But since the goals of the two coalitions were partially incompatible, neither side could hope to implement its own objectives directly without regard to the responses of the other. Each had to deal with the actual or potential intransigence of the other and, hence, each necessarily became involved in a continuing effort to influence the other. This fact made their interaction a mutually contingent one.[4]

Not all actions by a coalition are contingent on what the adversary coalition is doing. Some may be contingent on what other nations outside the coalitions are doing, some on what its own members are doing, and some on purely domestic factors. Clearly, these types of contingent action are less relevant to the Cold War: they are not, strictly speaking, a part of Soviet-Western interaction. While they may have affected this interaction, they were actions taken in response to factors that were external to it. In viewing the Cold War as a mutually contingent interaction between two coalitions, we wish to treat the actions of each side *both as determinants and as consequences* of the actions of the other. Any action by a coalition that is in no way contingent on the behavior of the other cannot be treated in this fashion.

For these reasons, the present study will focus on those coalition actions that are *tactically contingent* on the behavior of the opposing coalition. By this we mean actions in which the decision calculus includes what the other side has done or might do as one important element; it need not be the only, or even the primary, element. For example, the Soviet decision to quell the Hungarian uprising of 1956 is considered a tactically contingent action. In making this decision, Soviet decision-makers had to consider the possible Western response as one important element. On the other hand, the first Soviet atomic test is not considered a tactically contingent action. The entire Soviet atomic development program can be seen as broadly contingent on the existence of an inimical Western coalition, but the timing of the

[4] Perhaps we should deal here with a possible objection to our language, which treats nations and coalitions as if they were conscious actors. Obviously, nations and coalitions interact through the actions of their foreign policy decision-makers. International conflicts may be viewed as interactions between sets of decision-makers. But it would be a mistake to treat interactions as if the decision-makers were free agents responding to one another. They are foreign policy decision-makers by virtue of the fact that they occupy certain institutionalized, national roles. Not only do these roles place definite constraints on an incumbent, but, more important, entrance into such roles implies acceptance of certain national goals which may or may not be perfectly congruent with the incumbent's personal values. Thus, to talk about nations and coalitions as actors is to employ a shorthand for sets of decision-makers representing their nation or coalition and acting on its behalf.

first test was determined by the internal pace of its own research and development.[5]

The Cold War interaction, then, will be described as a chronological sequence of tactically contingent actions generated by the two coalitions. In the process of trying to interpret and understand this sequence, we shall, of course, consider relevant events and factors which were external to it. If there is reason to believe that some non-contingent event (e.g., a change in leadership or a breakthrough in military capability) conditioned the observed pattern of interaction, we intend to explore and evaluate this possibility. We are interested in making more precise statements about the conditions under which different patterns of interaction occur. We may learn, for instance, that a particular pattern occurs only when there is evidence of power inequality and not when the two coalitions are approximately equal in power.

Apart from leading us to focus on tactically contingent actions, treating the Cold War as a mutually contingent interaction has other important implications — implications about the parameters needed to understand this conflict. However, we will defer the discussion of these relevant parameters until Chapter Two.

The Cold War as Hostile Interaction

Any dyadic relationship may be viewed as held together by certain integrative bonds which are subject to stress from disintegrative forces or disagreements. By *integrative bonds,* we mean (1) joint mechanisms for handling and resolving conflict (e.g., the Security Council, the hot line, regular diplomatic channels) and (2) joint mechanisms for the implementation of common goals (e.g., trade agreements, cultural exchanges, joint scientific programs, UNESCO).

By *disintegrative forces,* we mean a weighted sum of all outstanding disagreements between the two parties. The weighting should reflect the extent to which their respective positions are in conflict and the extent to which the issue is viewed as central, important, and requiring rapid solution by the parties involved. The magnitude of any disagreement will change with time and should *not* be viewed as an intrinsic property of the disagreement, but rather as a reflection of how much one or the other party wishes to make of it.

---

[5] There are, of course, situations in which nuclear testing can be a tactically contingent action, e.g., the Soviet high-yield test series in 1961 which broke the moratorium on atmospheric tests and came in the midst of a Berlin crisis. Here, it is apparent that the Soviet action was importantly contingent on the contemporary activity of the West.

A *hostile interaction* is characterized by a relatively high ratio of disintegrative forces to integrative bonds. Elsewhere, we have used this ratio to define the degree of tension in a relationship (Gamson and Modigliani, 1963). In these terms, a hostile interaction is simply one in which the average level of tension is relatively high.

Even in a hostile interaction such as the Cold War, each party engages in a range of behavior running from guarded cooperation to extreme belligerence. Such variation can be expected from the mutually contingent nature of their interaction. If the coalitions react to one another in some systematic way, a variation in the behavior of one should be associated with some (but not necessarily an identical) variation in the behavior of the other. Nothing in the definition of hostile interaction should be taken to imply uniformly hostile action by each side.

Although, in theory, the number and intensity of integrative bonds are an important aspect of a hostile interaction, the present study will focus exclusively on disintegrative forces — i.e., on those coalition actions which had the effect of either *increasing or decreasing disagreements between the two coalitions*. The reason for this restriction is largely an empirical one: integrative bonds between the Soviet and Western coalitions varied little during the course of the Cold War, although they did decrease sharply at its outset and increase gradually toward its end. It was the ebb and flow of disintegrative forces — of disagreement-relevant actions — that provided the volatile element in this hostile interaction. We focus, then, on disintegrative forces because these constituted the more variable, more explosive, more dramatic — in short, more interesting — facet of the Cold War interaction.

In sum, the interaction framework leads us to describe the Cold War as a chronological sequence of tactically contingent, disagreement-relevant actions by the Soviet and Western coalitions. We consider this sequence to be the raw material that any interpretation of the Cold War must explain.

SOME PROBLEMS IN STUDYING THE COLD WAR

We are not without a certain ambivalence about our decision to study the Cold War. These doubts stem from several sources. First, a great deal is still unknown about the interaction examined here. Fortunately, this is a less serious problem than it might first appear to be since, for our purposes, we do not need to know many things of critical interest to historians. However, we *do* need to know with considerable accuracy when certain specified Soviet and Western coalition actions took place.

Secret documents and memoirs of participants are important or even vital for building explanations of what happened but they rarely will alter our description of events. For example, we still lack much knowledge of the Cuban missile crisis of 1962. There are conflicting versions of whether the initiative for placing missiles was Soviet or Cuban and of what the Soviet Union hoped to achieve by placing missiles in Cuba. At the level of description, however, we know within a few days when the Soviet military build-up began, when the first missiles began arriving, when the United States instituted its "quarantine," and when the Soviet Union agreed to withdraw its missiles.

There are, we must admit, a few occasions about which even basic descriptive information is lacking. For example, we have no confidence that we know what transpired between American destroyers and North Vietnamese PT boats in the Bay of Tonkin during early August of 1964. We are fortunate that this episode lies outside of the scope of our study, but it is possible that some of the "facts" which we rely on in describing other incidents will prove to be false. For the most part, however, new discoveries are much more likely to affect the interpretation rather than the description of events, and insufficient information is not, therefore, a serious problem.

A second problem in studying the Cold War stems from our proximity to these events. It is difficult to maintain the sort of detached examination that this book attempts. The Cuban missile crisis may be history but it is difficult for us to reread the daily newspapers of that time without experiencing a great deal of intense emotion. We are and have been engaged in these events in our daily lives, not in any sense as participants who influenced the decisions but simply as observers who talked and argued about their meaning with friends in lengthy and often heated discussions. We have developed our own convictions about these events and cannot take it casually or kindly when our data suggest, as they sometimes do, that our views are false or at least limited to certain special conditions. There are certain advantages in studying older conflicts which we can approach with few preconceptions. At any rate, we must leave it to the reader to judge to what extent our biases are obtrusive in this study.

Another problem in studying the Cold War is a more subtle one. A large amount of international conflict in recent years — particularly in Africa, Asia, and Latin America — raises questions about the basic framework of this analysis. The actors in this study are major powers and their allies; the units are coalitions of nations. Our analysis treats of conscious decisions taken by the foreign policy decision-makers of one coalition in response to the conscious decisions taken by the foreign policy decision-makers of their adversary.

Yet this framework seems artificial and imposed when applied, for example, to events in the Congo or in Laos. While conscious decisions by national actors are still involved, these actors frequently become the captives of events which neither side in the conflict controls. Major power interaction is only one aspect, perhaps the least important one, of many conflicts. To treat such conflicts as if they were only major power confrontations would be to obscure their meanings in many cases.

While we accept the above argument, we do not feel it invalidates this study for two reasons. First, our framework applies to dyadic conflicts involving major powers because this is a basic feature of the Cold War period. The recession of this feature in recent years is one of the major reasons for terminating the period under study at November, 1963. The substantial majority of cases we deal with are unambiguously major power interactions involving conscious decisions by national actors. The Cuban missile crisis, the Berlin blockade, the successful negotiation of an Austrian treaty, the negotiation of a nuclear test ban treaty, and many other cases raise few problems of the sort described above.

Second, even when the interaction of major powers is confounded with the effects of indigenous movements, one may legitimately focus on the aspect we are interested in here. The Hungarian revolution of 1956 is a case in point. Its inception may be treated as a "natural" event, that is, one which was not the result of conscious decision by the protagonists in the Cold War. The stupidity and rigidity of a Gero and the brutality of a Rakosi are treated here as part of the terrain of Soviet-Western interaction. However, the Soviet decision to intervene and the Western response to this intervention were part of the interaction itself. They were conscious acts, contingent in part on what the other side was doing or was expected to do.

A final problem goes to the basic logic of this study. Is it possible to build a description of the Cold War that all would accept as a fair arena for testing their theories? Imagine, for example, a theorist who emphasizes the nature of capitalism as a fundamental cause of the Cold War. He might argue that the actions he is asked to account for were epiphenomena — distracting and superficial components among the many more important and subtle manifestations of imperialism. The real substance of the Cold War was in the quiet, daily acts of Western expansion that never got reported in the pages of the *New York Times*. The power of his theory, he might argue, is in explaining things that other theories of the Cold War ignore or treat as irrelevant. The test to which we put his theory is limited and unfair since it forces him to compete in explaining data that he does not regard as central. Similarly, a rival theorist might emphasize the nature of messianic world communism as a cause of the Cold War and deplore our failure to include in our description many cases of quiet and steady subversion of Western institutions.

This is an important but answerable argument. We grant that actions excluded from our description *might* give additional support to some theories. And we are happy to concede that the actions included may be the outgrowth of underlying socioeconomic, political, or ideological forces. But we do not admit that the included actions are trivial or irrelevant. On the contrary, they are fraught with important consequences for millions of people and, on occasion, have threatened to engulf the world in a major war. Any theory of the Cold War ought to be able to provide some explanation of these actions regardless of what else it may be able to explain.

CONCLUSION

It is worth making explicit some matters which will not concern us in this book. We are not interested in making a contribution to the rhetoric of the Cold War. We are not concerned with justifying the actions of any country or with allocating relative blame to one side or the other. Conceivably, our analysis could give ammunition to one or another partisan, just as it might also aid us in understanding the conditions most likely to keep conflicts from developing into war. While the latter objective is a more accurate reflection of our personal concern, its acceptance or rejection does not affect the validity of this study.

In discussing the problems in studying the Cold War, one should not lose sight of some of the compensating advantages. Involvement has its reward: the promise of immediate relevance. Because we are close to these events, because they threatened to affect all of us in a very direct way, we are eager to understand them and to draw lessons from them that may even have some influence on future policy.

Interaction between national actors does not become less important simply because nationalism and anticolonialism become more relevant. The Cold War offers us the twin advantage of studying a conflict of great intrinsic interest and importance and of using this conflict to study an extended special case of hostile interaction.

Chapter Two

RESEARCH TACTICS

Chapter One argued that the Cold War can be viewed as a chronological sequence of tactically contingent, disagreement-relevant actions. In Chapter Three, we examine a number of competing "belief systems" that generate differing explanations of this sequence. Before we can examine these belief systems and their associated theories of the Cold War, we need to clarify two aspects of our research framework:

1. The nature of the thing to be explained. How, in fact, do we propose to describe the Cold War as a "sequence of actions"? Concretely, what ought a theory of the Cold War be able to explain?

2. The nature of the explanation. What kinds of assumptions must a theory make in order to explain this sequence? Of what does any theory of the Cold War consist? What are its component parts?

DESCRIBING THE COLD WAR: AN OVERVIEW

In building a description of the Cold War interaction, we begin by classifying all tactically contingent, disagreement-relevant actions as either *refractory, conciliatory,* or *neutral.* Any action which had the effect of increasing disagreement between the two coalitions or making disagreement between them more salient is classified as *refractory.* Conversely, any action which had the effect of decreasing disagreement or of making it less salient is classified as *conciliatory.* Finally, a few residual actions with trivial or ambiguous affects on disagreement are classified as *neutral.*

It is critical for our research strategy that no interpretation be implied about the motive or justification for an action in classifying it as refractory or conciliatory. An action may be benignly motivated, but if it provokes a quarrel, it is considered refractory. Nor does this classification reflect any distinction between "aggressive" and "defensive" actions, for such words imply interpretations of the motive

16

behind a refractory action. If one coalition mobilized its troops in response to an armed attack by the other side, this mobilization is considered a refractory action as is the armed attack. No moral judgment is intended.

Furthermore, all actions are coded in terms of their immediate rather than their long-range impacts. If the Soviet Union objected to some Western action, the Western action is considered refractory — even if the Soviets later came to view it more favorably, or even if it stimulated a sequence of events that ultimately helped to reduce the conflict. History's ultimate judgment on whether an action may have contributed to conflict resolution is irrelevant for describing the interaction. What matters is the adversary's perception *at the time it had to consider a response*. Thus, a coalition's actions are considered refractory (or conciliatory) if they were viewed as such by the adversary at the time they occurred.

There are, to be sure, many practical problems involved in actually classifying as refractory or conciliatory the multitude of actions taken by each coalition over the course of the Cold War; and there are yet other problems involved in determining the magnitude (or intensity) of any given refractory or conciliatory action. These problems are dealt with in Appendix A where the coding rules are discussed. For the moment, allow us simply to assert that for every action taken by either coalition during the entire period under study, we do in fact have a score indicating how refractory or conciliatory that action was.[1]

The terms "refractory" and "conciliatory" are used to describe *single actions* taken by a coalition. Such actions are the building blocks of our analysis, but we also need terms to describe *sequences of actions* taken by a coalition over a period of weeks or months. For this purpose, we use the terms "belligerent," "accommodative," and "balanced." If, in a given period, a coalition engaged in many strongly refractory actions and few conciliatory ones, we classify this overall pattern of behavior as *belligerent*. On the other hand, if a coalition engaged in many strongly conciliatory actions but few refractory ones, we classify this overall pattern of behavior as *accommodative*. Finally, if a coalition engaged in an even mixture of both types of actions, we classify this overall pattern of behavior as *balanced*. The classification assigned to a particular sequence of actions depends, then, on the scores of the single actions that composed the sequence. Ultimately,

[1] This statement is not quite as all-encompassing as it sounds. Recall that we deal only with tactically contingent, disagreement-relevant actions. In addition, we exclude actions whose impact on disagreement is so minimal that they fail to meet a threshold requirement discussed in Appendix A (such actions are classified as neutral).

sequences of actions are assigned to one of nine possible classes. In order of decreasing belligerence, these classes are: extremely belligerent, quite belligerent, fairly belligerent, balanced firm, balanced, balanced flexible, fairly accommodative, quite accommodative, and extremely accommodative.[2]

In using the terms "belligerent" and "accommodative" to describe a sequence of actions, once again no judgment is intended about the motivation behind the sequence or about its justifiability. A belligerent sequence might have been motivated by an aggressive desire to exploit the adversary or by a defensive desire to resist the adversary's aggressiveness. Similarly, an accommodative sequence might have been motivated by weakness or laxity in the face of an aggressive challenge or by receptivity — by a desire to settle outstanding differences through mutual compromise. We leave it to the competing belief systems about the Cold War to place whatever interpretation they prefer on the behavior of each coalition.

The Basic Interaction Unit

Having introduced the terms needed to describe each coalition's behavior, we now turn to the issue of combining the two sides' behavior into "interaction units" that can be used to test rival theories of the Cold War. Our procedure for creating such interaction units begins with the identification of a number of *major* refractory and conciliatory actions taken by each coalition — such actions as landing Marines in Lebanon or lifting a blockade in Berlin. Each of these actions is assumed to have been partly contingent on the adversary's previous behavior. Thus, each major action by a coalition is treated as a "response" to its adversary's preceding pattern of behavior.[3]

The adversary's preceding pattern is coded into an appropriate category of belligerent, balanced, or accommodative behavior. When this is done for every major action taken by either coalition, we emerge with a large number of basic interaction units. Each unit contains a major action of one coalition (which can be either refractory or conciliatory), and the preceding pattern of behavior of its adversary (which can range from extremely belligerent to extremely accommodative).

Chart 2.1 illustrates a series of such interaction units for the period January, 1948, to December, 1949. Each unit is denoted by a pair of vertical lines that bracket a portion of the time axis. Every unit is

[2] Appendix A presents the precise rules for combining single-action scores into an overall score.

[3] A complete list of the major actions of each coalition can be found in Appendix E.

Chart 2.1

Interaction Units for a Selected Portion of the Cold War: January, 1948, to December, 1949

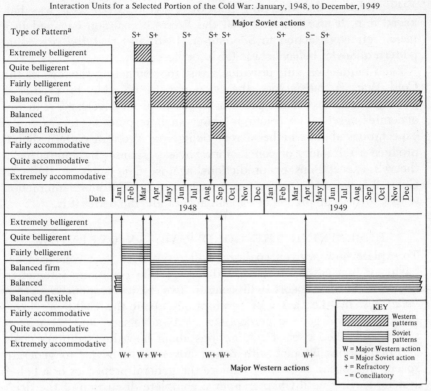

"Each category reflects a certain combination of refractory and conciliatory actions during a time period. The details of translating an array of single actions into an overall pattern are provided in Appendix A.

terminated by a major coalition action that is indicated by a vertical arrow pointing to the date on which it occurred. The adversary's pattern of behavior in the preceding time period is described by a horizontal bar whose elevation corresponds to a level of belligerence on the scale to the left of the chart.[4] For example, the chart indicates that

[4] The length of a bar indicates the length of the time period over which the adversary's behavior is assessed. As shown in the chart, time periods essentially run from one major action to the next. The question of just how long a time period should be is an important and complex one. If the period is too long, it may include actions that are irrelevant to the response being explained. The introduction of such "noise" will hinder any theory's efforts to explain the response. Conversely, if the period is too short, relevant actions may be excluded and, again, the likelihood of any theory's being able to explain the response is diminished. To be sure, in the long run the best theory still ought to do the best job with the available data. Appendix A discusses the precise rules by which we determine the lengths of time periods.

the Soviet coalition engaged in a major conciliatory action in April, 1949, and that the preceding pattern of Western behavior was balanced firm. It also indicates that the Western coalition engaged in a major refractory action in September, 1948, and that the preceding pattern of Soviet behavior was fairly belligerent.

Each interaction unit provides a test for competing theories of the Cold War. A satisfactory theory ought to be able to predict a coalition's response to the previous behavior of its adversary. A theory generates a set of expectations about such responses — for example, expectations about whether a very belligerent Western pattern should produce a refractory or conciliatory Soviet response. By comparing a theory's expectations or predictions against data such as those in Chart 2.1, we are in a position to evaluate it. The more interaction units a theory can predict or explain accurately, the better it is.

EXPLAINING THE COLD WAR: AN OVERVIEW

To explain how a given coalition will respond to its adversary's behavior, it is necessary to have a theory of that coalition's interactive behavior. Such a theory will contain two basic components: (1) a *belief system* — i.e., a set of assumptions about the coalition's long-range goals and general perceptions of its adversary; and (2) a *decision model* — i.e., a set of assumptions about how the coalition's goals and perceptions interact with recent adversary behavior to generate specific responses. Below, we explore the general properties of a belief system, leaving until Chapter Four a complete discussion of the decision model.

The assumptions about goals and perceptions that make up a belief system can be treated as the values of certain basic parameters. How many different parameters are needed before one can plug into a decision model and make predictions about a coalition's responses? We believe that three are necessary and that, while one can always increase precision by adding additional parameters, these three are *sufficient* to develop meaningful interpretations of a coalition's behavior:

1. The coalition's own strategic goals.
2. The coalition's image of how its own goals are perceived by the adversary.
3. The coalition's perception of its adversary's strategic goals.[5]

[5] The necessary and sufficient nature of these three parameters stems from two convergent lines of thought. On one hand, we found that we needed at least this many in order to treat the Cold War as a mutually contingent interaction. On the other hand, when we looked at the literature, we found these parameters quite

How do these parameters operate to influence a coalition's response? No precise answer can be given without introducing assumptions about the decision process, but the general idea ought to be clear. Arriving at a response to the adversary's recent behavior is a two-step process. First, a coalition interprets this recent behavior, seeking to decipher the information it contains about its adversary's immediate intentions. Second, it utilizes this information in choosing a course of action which at least protects and possibly advances its own strategic interests. The parameters are necessary, for there is no universally appropriate response to any given type of adversary behavior. Should one exploit the adversary's accommodative behavior because it is indicative of laxity or should one regard it as an indication of receptivity and an invitation to find mutually acceptable compromises? The answer depends on one's goals. Should one interpret an adversary's belligerent behavior as motivated by fear or by aggressive designs? The answer depends on one's perception of the adversary's goals and his perception of one's own goals. And what is the meaning and the appropriate response to an adversary's balanced behavior? These questions cannot be answered without specifying the values of the three parameters listed above.

Values for the Parameters

The three parameters have a useful common property: they are all stated in terms of strategic goals. This means that we can apply the same set of possible values to each parameter. Goals may be characterized in many ways but a useful simplification for international relations focuses on three values. A coalition's strategic goals may be:

1. CONSOLIDATION. Such a coalition is interested in holding on to what it has and in making its influence more secure in areas where it is already established. A consolidationist coalition does not engage in aggression nor does it attempt to exploit an adversary's weakness. However, this does not in any way imply that it will always be conciliatory. It may respond with extreme belligerence whenever it feels its security is being threatened by an adversary. Furthermore, if it views its security in global terms, it may well find itself resisting an adversary's attempted encroachments even in areas where it presently has no special influence. But it always stands ready to bargain and negotiate when this appears to be a fruitful path to the resolution of outstanding disagreements. Its characteristic orientation is defensive and nonexploitative.

---

sufficient to organize the many conflicting explanations of the Cold War. This latter point is the central theme of Chapter Three.

2. EXPANSION. Such a coalition is interested in expanding its influence into new areas or in increasing its influence in areas where its present influence is modest. Furthermore, it is willing to pursue its expansionist aims despite the likelihood that this will generate disagreements with its adversary. However, it is concerned with reducing its adversary's influence only where such influence serves as a constraint on its own ambitions.

In its own eyes, an expansionist coalition may feel that it is acting honorably and even nobly. It may see itself as protecting others against the possibility that these unfortunates will fall prey to the evil designs of some adversary. Or, it may see itself as bringing enlightenment and other benefits to those who are victims of oppression. Walewski, the French Foreign Minister in 1857, is supposed to have told Bismarck that it was the business of a diplomat to cloak the interests of his country in the language of universal justice. Whether or not one accepts such a cynical view, governments have been quite ingenious in convincing themselves of the moral justice of their own behavior.

The fundamental distinction between a consolidationist and expansionist coalition is that the latter may be refractory in the absence of any immediate provocation or threat from its adversary — although it will invariably believe that it has good and sufficient reasons for its action. However, it shares with a consolidationist coalition a willingness to negotiate and bargain when it sees a reasonable possibility of achieving its strategic objectives through such means. Its characteristic orientation is opportunistic.

3. DESTRUCTION. Such a coalition is interested in decreasing its adversary's influence as a means of eventually destroying its adversary as a serious competitor in the international arena. The reduction of its adversary's influence is not merely a way of removing a constraint on its own ambitions in a few limited areas. In fact, it is more the reverse: weakening its adversary in the adversary's strong areas will be more helpful to a destructionist coalition than merely increasing its own influence in areas of little concern to its adversary.

A destructionist coalition, like an expansionist coalition, may feel it is carrying out a mission in removing an evil influence from the international scene. But this goal does not imply that it will be perpetually refractory. A destructionist coalition will press its aims when it has good opportunity to do so, but it need not be reckless or unconcerned about the cost of its actions. Certain occasions are bound to be more to its advantage than others and it can afford to bide its time. Hence, it may be appropriate for it to be conciliatory sometimes to lull its adversary into a false sense of security or to buy time for a more auspicious moment. However, unlike either a consolidationist or an expansionist coalition, it can never achieve its ends through genuine bargaining and compromise. The only way in which negotiations may serve it is through ratifying and securing its gains and through reducing its adversary's vigilance so that it can take further aggressive action with fewer risks. Its characteristic orientation is exploitative.

FURTHER THOUGHTS ON GOALS. In speaking of strategic goals, we mean to distinguish a *politically operative objective* from an *abstract preference* for some ideal state of the world. For example, both the Soviet Union and Western coalitions would undoubtedly have preferred a world in which their antagonist was either fundamentally changed or no longer a serious competitor in the international arena. But the existence of such mutual animosity does not necessarily imply that destruction of the other was a real objective of either coalition's foreign policy. It is one thing to hope that one's adversary will drop dead; it is quite another to work actively for the achievement of that end. In using the term "strategic goals" here, we mean those end states that are operative and guiding elements in the choice of a course of action.

In addition, we view the three goals of consolidation, expansion, and destruction as arranged in a hierarchy of inclusiveness. A consolidationist is interested *only* in securing its current areas of influence. An expansionist is interested both in securing its current influence *and* in increasing it. Finally, a destructionist is interested in securing its current holdings, in expanding into new areas, *and* in destroying the adversary's influence. Such a hierarchy of inclusiveness is implied by the very nature of these three goals. An expansionist cannot hope to expand its influence if it does not protect what it already has. Similarly, a destructionist cannot hope to destroy the influence of its adversary if it does not both protect what it already has and expand its influence when good opportunities arise.

The definitions of destructionist, expansionist, and consolidationist may still seem somewhat vague, but this is not inappropriate at this point. Their more rigorous definition is contained in the assumptions made about how, for example, a destructionist and expansionist differ in interpreting and responding to an adversary's behavior. These assumptions are, in effect, the decision model presented in Chapter Four. However, it may be useful to anticipate this discussion with a few examples designed to show how the parameter values described above are used.

Consider, first, a coalition that is attempting to interpret belligerent behavior on the part of its adversary. If this coalition views its adversary as consolidationist, it will be unlikely to interpret the belligerence as aggressive. If, in addition, it believes that its adversary perceives it to be expansionist, then it will be even more likely to view the belligerence as resistant rather than aggressive. As a result, it would be more likely to reassure its adversary by some form of conciliatory action than to defend itself by acting in a refractory fashion.

As another example, consider a coalition that is attempting to decide on a response to its adversary's recent accommodative behavior. If the goals of this coalition are destruction, it will be likely to press forward aggressively, hoping to exploit the adversary's apparent laxity or unpreparedness. If, on the other hand, the goals of this coalition are consolidation, it will be uninterested in pressing forward and will instead be likely to match the adversary's accommodativeness in the hope of moving toward some mutually satisfactory resolution of outstanding disagreements.

SUMMARY

We have introduced a number of terms in this chapter — some to be used in describing the Cold War and others to be used in explaining it. Table 2.1 summarizes these terms. Refractory, conciliatory, and neutral are terms used to describe single actions; belligerent, accommodative, and balanced are used to describe patterns of action over a given time period. None of these terms implies anything about the motive or justification for the behavior being described.

Such behavior is subject to different interpretations. Belligerent behavior may be viewed as aggressive or resistant; accommodative behavior may be lax or receptive; and balanced behavior, depending on the circumstances, could be interpreted as any of the above. The key to making these interpretations are three parameters of a coalition: its goals, its image of how its goals are perceived by its adversary, and its perception of its adversary's goals. A belief system may assign a value of destruction, expansion, or consolidation to these parameters. Once one of these values is specified for each parameter, belligerent, accommodative, and balanced behavior can be interpreted, and an appropriate response can be designated. Thus, a complete theory of the Cold War must include assumptions about the values of six parameters — three for each coalition. These are: (1) Soviet goals; (2) Soviet image of how its goals are perceived by the West; (3) Soviet perception of Western goals; (4) Western goals; (5) Western image of how its goals are perceived by the Soviets; and (6) Western perception of Soviet goals.

In the next chapter, we turn to the abundant literature on the Cold

Table 2.1

Summary of Key Terms Used in Describing and Interpreting the Cold War Interaction

Category	Descriptive or observational language	Interpretive or explanatory language
Single actions	Refractory	—
	Conciliatory	—
	Neutral	—
Patterns of action over a given time period	Belligerent	Aggressive, resistant
	Accommodative	Lax, receptive
	Balanced	Any of above
Parameters and their possible values[a]	Own goals	Destruction, expansion, consolidation
	Image of how own goals are perceived by adversary	Expansion, consolidation
	Perception of adversary's goals	Expansion, consolidation

[a]*The reasons for excluding "destruction" as a possible value for the second and third parameter are discussed in Chapters Three and Four.*

War in order to examine a number of competing views on the true values of these parameters.[6]

[6] The reader who desires further information on our procedures for describing the Cold War — that is, for coding Soviet and Western actions and for creating interaction units — is referred to in Appendixes A and B. Appendix A presents our coding procedures in detail and Appendix B examines the validity of our data source.

Chapter Three

RIVAL BELIEF SYSTEMS
ABOUT THE COLD WAR

INTRODUCTION

Many historians, political scientists, journalists, and politicians have ventured opinions on the appropriate values for the parameters discussed in the preceding chapter. It makes sense to begin our search for plausible sets of values by examining the work of such commentators.

The various works we will examine all view the Cold War as a mutually contingent interaction. Some clearly sound that way. Alperovitz (1965) and Shulman (1963), for example, explicitly treat each side as reacting in significant ways to its adversary's behavior. Other writers, however, apparently treat the Cold War as an asymmetrically contingent interaction. In their perspective, the West always reacted to Soviet initiatives while the Soviet coalition followed a grand design. For example, MacIntosh argues that "the direction of Soviet foreign policy in the years 1944 to 1947 cannot . . . be attributed to any influence exerted by the Western powers" (1963, p. 17).

Even those who emphasize grand designs implicitly admit *tactical* contingencies. MacIntosh does not intend the statement quoted above to mean that specific Soviet actions were not influenced by specific Western actions. He suggests, for example, that "Mr. Winston Churchill's famous speech in Fulton in the United States in March, 1947,[1] played a part in clinching Stalin's argument that he now had to face a united Anglo-American front in the pursuit of his plans in the field of foreign strategy" (*ibid.*, p. 20). Our point is that even those who see the United States as a harried improvisor facing the challenge of a cool and ruthless grand strategist still offer explanations of a tactical level of the interaction.

[1] The date of the "famous speech" was actually March, 1946. The error is not trivial. By inadvertently placing the speech a year later, MacIntosh can more easily maintain his belief in the generally nonreactive nature of Soviet foreign policy.

Some Conventions
for Inferring Parameter Values

Few interpretations of the Cold War include clear statements of all of the parameter values. Typically, a few are mentioned explicitly and others must be inferred. The goals of each coalition are the most likely to draw explicit comment. However, we also need to know the values that a writer intends to assign to the perception parameters: each coalition's perception of the adversary's goals and each coalition's image of how the adversary perceives its own goals. (For the sake of brevity, we shall refer to this last parameter as the "reflected image" parameter for it represents a coalition's image of its own goals as reflected by the adversary.) Whenever these parameter values are not specifically suggested by a writer, we will rely on certain conventions or rules of inference.

The first convention enables us to handle cases in which a writer has failed to specify a coalition's perception of its adversary's goals. When no question is raised about such perceptions, we will infer that the author is assuming accurate or veridical perception. For example, if a writer states that Western goals were consolidationist and nowhere suggests that the Soviet coalition was unaware of this, we will infer that the writer believes the Soviet coalition *was* aware of this.

The second convention enables us to handle cases in which a writer has failed to specify a coalition's reflected image. Here we will examine what value the author has assigned to the coalition's goals and what value he has assigned to the adversary's perception of these goals. If the values assigned to these two parameters are identical, then we will infer that the reflected image parameter has the same value. For example, if a writer argues that the West was consolidationist and that the Soviet coalition perceived the West as consolidationist, but he makes no statement about whether the West was aware of this Soviet perception, we infer that the West's reflected image was also consolidationist since there is no discrepancy on the other two parameters.

The reasoning behind this convention needs some elaboration. A coalition is likely to rely on two sources in constructing an image of how its goals are perceived by the adversary: (1) knowledge of what its own goals actually are and (2) cues about how the adversary is actually perceiving its goals. To the extent that it relies on the former source, its image will be "autistic"; to the extent that it relies on the latter source, its image will be "realistic." Our second convention states that when an author sees the two sources as perfectly congruent, he must be assuming that the coalition's image is in agreement with both sources (unless, of course, he explicitly makes some statement to the contrary). If an author does *not* see the two sources as congruent, then we cannot tell what he may have in mind and we are forced to break the writer's theory into two alternative theories: one assumes the coalition's image is "autistic"; the other assumes the coalition's image is "realistic."

The third convention states that any belief system (i.e., set of parameter values) must be able to predict and interpret both the belligerent and the accommodative behavior of each coalition. This convention is based on the empirical observation that over the course of the Cold War, each coalition was, in fact, sometimes accommodative and sometimes belligerent. For example, if by the logic of its assumptions, a belief system predicts that the Soviet coalition will always be refractory no matter what the West does, it cannot possibly account for the observed variability.

In practice, this convention places two restrictions on the values that a writer may assign to the parameters: (1) a coalition cannot perceive its adversary as destructionist, for if it did it would never be accommodative toward this adversary; and (2) a coalition cannot believe that its adversary perceives it as destructionist, for if it did it could never make sense of the adversary's accommodative behavior. Fortunately, no writer clearly assigns the value "destructionist" to either of these parameters. A few are ambiguous in that their language could be taken to mean either "destructionist" or "expansionist." In all such cases, we will infer that the writer means "expansionist." [2]

THE BELIEF SYSTEMS

The many positions on the Cold War can be usefully divided into families based on the assumptions made about the true nature of Soviet and Western goals.[3] Within each family, there is a certain amount of variation on how each side perceives the other's goal and is perceived in turn. We will pick one member of each family as a starting point, and, where there are significant variations, we will include relatives by examining the particular parameter on which there is disagreement. Consanguinity, however, always means agreement on the true goals of the two coalitions.

Since both Soviet and Western goals theoretically may have been destructionist, expansionist, or consolidationist, there are nine logically

[2] Notice that this third convention does *not* restrict the assignment of "destructionist" as the value of a coalition's true goals. It merely prohibits this value with respect to a coalition's *perception of the adversary's goals* and *reflected image*.

[3] Levine's (1963) useful analysis and categorization of different positions on what American arms policy should be has many similarities to the discussion here.

possible families of belief systems. However, three of these can be eliminated for want of any serious support: the beliefs that two destructionists were confronting each other or that either was a destructionist facing an expansionist. This leaves us with six families that have been seriously discussed, and we will consider each of these in turn.

Soviet Destructionist vs. Western Consolidationist

The Soviet coalition, in this view, aimed not for the achievement of specific expansionist goals but for the destruction of the values and social system embodied by the United States and Western Europe. "There is in train today," writes Byron Dexter, a former managing editor in the journal *Foreign Affairs*, "a development without parallel in history — a war which has as its frank objective the overthrow of all the parliamentary governments of the world and their replacement by Communist dictatorships centrally controlled in Moscow" (1950). The basic goal according to Strausz-Hupé et al. was "world domination by the communist elite and destruction of that freedom of man that ennobles our civilization" (1961, p. 406).

Those who take such a view of Soviet goals take pains to distinguish it from the belief that the Soviet Union was merely expansionist, pursuing traditional Russian imperialist aims with some sensitivity to new opportunities that came their way. "We are engaged in a pervasive struggle with the forces of Communism — a conflict between two gigantic systems, each armed with massive military power, and both locked in a contest in which even a minor mistake may prove fatal. In this situation, we can find salvation neither in 'gimmick' solutions nor in the leaven of compromise. The sources of conflict are not arms races, clashes of interest or the 'unresolved issues' along the battle lines of the Cold War. The root causes of conflict are the closed monolithic society and revolutionary doctrine of an implacable adversary bent upon remaking the world in his own image" (*ibid.*, p. 252). "Different political systems can exist side by side, but not when one system is aggressive, geared to conflict, and bent upon conquest" (*ibid.*, p. 8).

The Western coalition, on the other hand, is tacitly or explicitly regarded as consolidationist. Strausz-Hupé and his colleagues take the United States to task for its failure to follow a "forward strategy." Among the reasons for this failure, they rank as most important "the *defensive* psychology of the West and the moral aversion of the free nations to employ force for purposes other than defense against physical aggression" (*ibid.*, p. 37). Similarly, Bouscaren suggests that the "international Communist movement" won many successes in the postwar period by "capitalizing on American demobilization and the western desire for peace" (1962, p. 133). In fact, Western goals are rarely discussed by those who hold these views; the rapid demobilization of Western armies following World War II is usually regarded as sufficient evidence that the West was consolidationist if, indeed, one need cite any evidence for such a self-evident and widely shared assumption.

Those who hold that the Soviet coalition was destructionist also hold that it was sometimes conciliatory, given that it faced a consolidationist but sometimes edgy adversary. They are anxious to make it clear that such accommodative behavior does not contradict their assumptions about destructionist goals. Triska writes, "The aim of Soviet ideology — domination of the world — does not change; strategy, operational direction, tactics, and propaganda do" (1958, p. 64). "The balance of power concept is foreign to a Soviet planner. All-out domination is the goal" (*ibid.*, p. 75). Similarly, Wolfe writes, "Between irreconcilable opponents, one of whom is destined by history to be destroyed, the other to conquer, agreement — like dialogue — can be only ostensible. . . . To them, lulls cannot conceivably or decently be preliminaries to all-out peace. Nor are separate issues really separate, except in the sense that they have been separated out for strategical or tactical convenience from the general context of struggle. Every negotiation, every issue, even every day's session they regard primarily as a move in that irreconcilable conflict" (1962, pp. 163–64).

The Soviet coalition made concessions because they did not want to take unnecessary risks in the pursuit of their goal. Triska quotes Molotov as telling a *New York Times* correspondent, "We should like the [global] change-over to communism to be as painless as possible" (1958), p. 72). Bouscaren writes, "The Communist strategy of protracted conflict seeks to avoid a general, direct, decisive encounter with the enemy unless and until overwhelming physical superiority sufficient to ensure the enemy's complete destruction — and his alone — has been acquired" (1962, p. 3).

The West, however, failed to perceive the true nature of Soviet destructionist goals, believing them to be merely expansionist. Strausz-Hupé et al. call attention to the "strange reluctance of the West to face the plain fact that the goals of the enemy are as fixed as his methods are flexible." Sometimes this fact was dimly perceived by the West but too often "Communist legerdemain" raised false hopes and blinded the West to the true destructionist goal of its adversary (1961, p. 37). Or, as Triska argues, "Soviet leaders, speaking to a world-wide audience, cannot afford to talk in terms of doctrinal or even strategical directives if such revelations would cause the failure of contemplated actions; they must emphasize the immediate minimum Soviet program and mislead, confuse and lull the suspicions of the world at large. Propaganda must be utilized to speed up action in a particular phase of short-range duration" (1958, p. 81).

Indeed, using the convention mentioned above, the West could not have perceived its adversary as destructionist since if it had, it would never have been conciliatory when in fact it sometimes was. For similar reasons, the Soviet coalition must have been aware that it was not recognized as destructionist but merely as expansionist; it could hardly have expected to completely fool Western leaders into viewing it as consolidationist.

How were Western goals perceived by the Soviet coalition? There is ambiguity here that will lead us to consider some variants within the family. In one view, Soviet perceptions of the West are not regarded as problematic — it is assumed that the Soviet leaders were cold-eyed realists and saw the West for what it was. Of course, peaceful Western intentions take on a different meaning in the Soviet mirror: the Western coalition was not friendly but weak-willed and preoccupied with its own problems. This is the meaning of the Soviet recognition that the West was consolidationist. As Wolfe asks, "What reason does a man looking with Khrushchev's eyes have for abandoning the view that 'capitalist-imperialism' is decadent when it is losing all its colonies, did not show the resolution to protect Hungary's freedom or complete the unification of Korea, failed to make the military moves to prepare its sort of peace during World War II, thereby letting maimed and bleeding Russia pick up all of Eastern Europe, half of Germany, win powerful allies and partners in Asia, expand the 'camp of Communism' from one-sixth of the earth to one-fourth, with one-third of the earth's population?" (1962, p. 167.) Nor is it anywhere suggested in this parent view that the West believed that its peaceful intent was misunderstood. In sum, the West was consolidationist, was perceived this way by the Soviet coalition, and recognized this fact.

Another view questions whether the Soviet coalition accurately perceived the West as consolidationist. Here, an effort is made to enter into the psychological world of the Soviet leaders and to uncover their "operational code" or belief system (see Leites, 1953, and George, 1967). Soviet leaders were, in this variant, less the cold-eyed realists of the parent view above and were quite capable of misperceiving their adversary. Viewing the world as divided into two hostile camps only one of which would survive, the Soviet leaders to some degree projected their goals onto the West. In spite of his earlier argument for Soviet perception of Western weakness, Wolfe argues that "the doctrine teaches that the enemy must surely be conspiring, subverting, striving to overthrow the system which spells its death" (1962, p. 168). There is no necessary inconsistency in perceiving a weak conspirator, but there is ambiguity in inferring Soviet perceptions of the West from such a combination. If weakness is the central emphasis, then the adversary is too preoccupied to carry out its malevolent aims; if conspiracy receives greater emphasis, then the adversary must be at least expansionist. Given the ambiguity, we will resolve it by treating both interpretations as viable variants.

Notice that the paranoia attributed to Soviet leaders cannot, under our conventions, be interpreted as a belief that the West was pursuing Soviet *destruction* as an operational goal. If this had been true, then conciliatory tactics would never have been appropriate; but such a paranoid leadership might easily have misperceived the West as expansionist instead of recognizing its consolidationist aims. Their operational code predisposed the Soviet leaders to expect and fear encroachments by their adversary. " 'Yielding' to an opponent is so worrisome a danger in the classical Bolshevik code (and, presumably, so anxiety-arousing a fantasy in the old Bolshevik psyche) that it gave rise to a strong injunction to be ultra-sensitive to encroachments of any kind. No matter how trivial they seem, the opponent's encroachments are to be opposed because failure to 'resist from the start' may encourage him to step up his attack" (George, 1967, p. 37).

Finally, if the Soviet coalition misperceived Western goals as expansionist, it is ambiguous whether or not the Western coalition was aware of this Soviet misunderstanding. One might quite plausibly argue either that the West assumed it was correctly perceived as consolidationist or that it recognized that it was misperceived as expansionist. We will include both variants. We will see in Chapter Four that it makes some difference which of these two arguments is correct in predicting how the West responded to various Soviet actions.

Table 3.1 summarizes the above discussion by outlining the value assigned to each of the six parameters for each of the positions discussed above.

Soviet Expansionist vs. Western Consolidationist

"Their goal is expansion and our goal is peace," Richard M. Nixon told the American Legion convention during the 1968 presidential campaign.[4] Mr. Nixon has much company in his belief that the Cold War pitted two major power blocs against each other — one vying for the preservation and the other for the expansion of its political influence and control. For Halle, the Cold War, like the two world wars, "has

---

[4] Quoted in the *Boston Globe,* September 13, 1968.

Table 3.1

Soviet Destructionist vs. Western Consolidationist

PARAMETERS

Soviet goal	Soviet image of how it was perceived	Soviet view of Western goal		Western goal	Western image of how it was perceived	Western view of Soviet goal
Destruction	Expansion	Consolidation		Consolidation	Consolidation	Expansion
Destruction	Expansion	Expansion		Consolidation	Consolidation	Expansion
Destruction	Expansion	Expansion		Consolidation	Expansion	Expansion

been a worldwide power contest in which one expanding power has threatened to make itself predominant, and in which other powers have banded together in a defensive coalition to frustrate it" (1967, pp. 8–9). In this view, the Soviet coalition planned to extend its control through the achievement of specific political goals, some of which conflicted with our own. Of course, they would have liked to see the Western social system replaced by one more consonant with Communist values, but they were not committed to the destruction of the West as an operative goal that influenced their specific actions.

This view distinguishes between the more limited objectives of an expansionist power and those of a destructionist. It holds that an expansionist power, unlike a destructionist one, concedes the adversary's influence as a fact of life but attempts to move into "gray" areas or power vacuums and to probe for "soft spots." Notice, for example, Shulman's tone in discussing the immediate postwar period: "The serious weakening of the British and French positions in Central and Eastern Europe and the destruction of German and Eastern European power led to a period of active probing by the Soviet Union to establish the outer periphery of its new sphere of control. The militancy with which this was done in the early Cominform period created the impression in the West that this constituted the revival of a world revolutionary drive. This impression was probably mistaken" (1963, p. 258).

Writing a few years later, Shulman draws the same conclusion less tentatively. He grants that conditions of Soviet expansion left "a residual ambiguity whether the thrust has been motivated primarily by national territorial aspirations or by a renewal of international revolutionary ambitions. It seems clearer in retrospect than it did at the time that the expansion into Eastern and Central Europe was, like most of Soviet foreign policy, an action of the Soviet state in pursuit of its national aspirations. The ideology of Communism undoubtedly shaped the perceptions of the Soviet leadership in the way it came to believe that Soviet security required the total domination of the satellite states, but it has become increasingly clear that the goal of international proletarian revolution was essentially symbolic language for the advancement of Soviet national interests" (1966, pp. 52–53).

Similarly, MacIntosh writes, "While Poland, Rumania, and Bulgaria were being turned into Soviet satellites, the new frontiers of the Soviet base were being tested for soft undefended spots where further penetration might succeed or protective zones set up" (1963, p. 9). But Soviet expansion was pursued cautiously. "No plans for the conquest or subversion of any major Western country were put in hand, notwithstanding the fact that in two of them, France and Italy, the local Communist parties were the largest single political parties. . . . Thus, while absorbing Eastern Europe, the Soviet leaders revealed no specific strategic plan for establishing Communism in France or Italy" (*ibid.*, p. 30). As Levine puts it, the expansionist view "substitutes a picture of aggressive Soviet opportunism for the [destructionist] . . . sketch of constant hard-eyed malevolence" (1963, p. 186).

Those who view the Soviet coalition as expansionist tend to see continuity in Russian goals from the Tsarist period through the Soviet regime. In this view, Soviet expansionism was essentially traditional Russian expansionism with a new rhetoric. Mamatey, for example, remarks that Soviet war aims "bore a striking resemblance to the Tsarist imperialist aims" (1964, p. 55). Ulam argues that "none of Russia's post-war moves can in all fairness be described as bolts from the blue. In most cases, they had ample precedent in age-long aspirations of Russian foreign policy" (1968, p. 429). Halle describes how Communist ideology "made those who were driven by terrible necessity to the perpetration of sinister deeds feel themselves morally justified. From the first, however, the deeds themselves were directed toward more limited and practical objectives that were not essentially different from the traditional objectives of the Russian state. While the nominal ideology had an influence that one could only regard as dangerous, what was determinative for action was the complex of considerations, representing power-politics, that stemmed from the self-interest of the Russian state" (1967, p. 158).

Lukacs is even more explicit in criticizing Americans for overemphasizing the importance of dogma as a determinant of Soviet behavior. In contrast, he argues that Stalin, for example, resembled the figure of a "tsar rather than any international Communist revolutionary figure, and [was a man] whose exhortations of Russian national pride had deep roots in Russian history but no source at all in Marx." Americans, he argues, missed this point by "concentrating on the dangers of international Communism rather than on the historical features of Russian aggressiveness" (1966, p. 77).

Communist ideology is not irrelevant in this view because, among other things, it colored the Soviet world view; but the Soviet coalition was too pragmatic to take it seriously as an operational goal. Kennan, in his famous article "The Sources of Soviet Conduct" (1947), tries to convey this by calling attention to the lack of time limit in the achievement of the ultimate Communist victory. The Soviet belief in the innate antagonism between capitalism and socialism means that "we are going to continue for a long time to find the Russians difficult to deal with. It does not mean that they should be considered as embarked upon a do-or-die program to overthrow our society by a given date. The theory of the inevitability of the eventual fall of capitalism has the fortunate connotation that there is no hurry about it." Sharp, in a symposium on the role of ideology in Soviet foreign policy (1960), argues against the view that the Soviet coalition was engaged in a messianic drive for world power: "Granted that the Soviet leaders aim at 'world power' . . . they have long since decided not to fix any specific time limit for the achievement of this ultimate aim. Certainly the present generation of leaders has acted to modify (perhaps 'refine' is a better word) the aggressive drive for power abroad at least to an extent which will allow some enjoyment at home of the tangible fruits of the revolution this side of the Communist heaven." Or as Aspaturian puts it, "The general tendency was for Soviet ideological goals to recede or to erode into ritualistic rhetoric, while the growth in Soviet power created greater opportunities for the pursuit of traditional great-power goals" (1968, p. 131).

As with the previous family of belief systems, Western goals are not usually treated explicitly. In one way or another, the author usually asserts or implies their consolidationist nature without an extended argument on the point. For example, Ulam, after describing Soviet fears of aggression and expansionism, anticipates the question that he presumes his readers might have: "Were the Soviets really capable of such fantastic misconstructions of their opponents' intentions?" (1968, p. 448.)

Halle and Hayter are among the few writers of this disposition who *explicitly* argue the view that Western goals were consolidationist. Halle comments, "It is not clear that Stalin wanted to extend the area of his dominion as far west as possible, since he was cautious of provoking an Anglo-American reaction and since he knew that the area over which he could maintain effective control was limited. There can be no doubt, however, that Britain and the United States, for their part, were averse to committing their power too far east. We quite mistake the situation, then, if we think that there was a simple competition . . . in which Moscow was trying to draw the line between the two sides as far west as possible while Britain and America were trying to draw it as far east as possible" (1967, p. 80). "The original Cold War," he observes, "had been set off by the sudden expansion of Russia in Europe. Consequently, there could be little doubt in any impartial mind that, when the West rallied under American leadership to halt that expansion, it was acting in its own legitimate defense rather than in a spirit of aggression" (*ibid.*, p. 416). Similarly, Hayter acknowledges that "there are people in the West, more particularly in the United States, who believe that the destruction of communism everywhere, and the overthrow of the Communist regime in the Soviet Union itself . . . are legitimate objectives of Western policy" (1964, p. 317). But "this thinking is so far, luckily, minority thinking; it has never entered into governmental doctrine, even in the Dulles era. . . . It seems unlikely that this minority view could ever become dominant in American politics. . . . In fact, the West is, and is likely to remain, on the defensive" (*ibid.*, p. 318).

What of Western perceptions of Soviet goals and Soviet recognition of this perception? Since, in this belief system, there are no questions raised on the perception of Soviet expansionist goals, we infer that they were perceived by the West as expansionist with Soviet recognition of that accurate perception.

The perception of Western goals is more problematic, and here we must distinguish three variants. In the first view, the Soviet coalition mistook the West to be expansionist rather than consolidationist. It was influenced in this regard by its ideology and "operational code" as well as by specific Western acts which were misconstrued as aggressive.

In this view, the Soviet Union felt vulnerable in the face of immense United States power, including an atomic monopoly in the immediate postwar period. Lukacs asks us to put ourselves in Stalin's position in 1947. Russia had won the war but "her cities were devastated, her armies bled white." The United States, on the other hand, had "emerged as the greatest and most powerful nation of the earth. . . . Now Stalin did not particularly contest American power: he did not challenge America's sphere; did it not seem to him, however, that the Americans were beginning to challenge *his* sphere. . . . When Churchill, at Potsdam, complained about Rumania, Stalin would retort that he fulfilled their bargain by not intervening in Greece. Why were . . . the Americans meddling in Eastern Europe? Had they not won enough in the war?" (1966, p. 81.)

Shulman makes a similar argument but gives greater emphasis to

Soviet ideology. Such measures as the Truman Doctrine and the Marshall Plan became ideologically distorted in Soviet eyes as "American efforts to challenge the Soviet position in Eastern Europe and to establish an American hegemony in Western Europe" (1966, p. 7). "The measures that were intended by the United States to stabilize and protect Western Europe and the Eastern Mediterranean area appear to have been construed in Moscow within the framework of its preconceptions of the inherent aggressiveness of what it defined and stereotyped as 'capitalist imperialism'" (ibid., p. 6).

Ulam also argues that Stalin "and his clique expected mounting pressure on the Soviet Union, economic and psychological in its character, to make her surrender some of her wartime gains" (1968, p. 438). After an extended discussion of both sides' exaggerated fears, he concludes, "The period 1947–49 thus marks a complete . . . lack of communication between the two super-powers. Both the United States and Russia became convinced of the other's essentially aggressive design" (ibid., p. 450).

Halle also emphasizes unrealistic fears as an essential part of the dynamics of the Cold War conflict. "What we see throughout this history is the dynamism of the self-fulfilling prophecy. Moscow, anticipating a threat from the West, expands its empire in that direction, thereby provoking a reaction that confirms its anticipation. Washington, reacting in fear of Moscow's spreading tyranny, provokes the spread and intensification of that tyranny by moving to contain it, thereby confirming the fear on which it had acted" (1967, p. 148).

Former Secretary of War Stimson seemed to recognize that the Soviet coalition might have felt threatened by what it misperceived as Western expansionist aims: "We do not yet know surely in what proportion unreasonable fears and twisted hopes are at the root of the perverted policy now followed by the Kremlin. Assuming both to be involved, we must disarm the fears and disappoint the hopes. We must no longer let the tide of Soviet expansion cheaply roll into the empty places left by war, and yet we must make it perfectly clear that we are not ourselves expansionist" (1947).

Again, it is ambiguous whether Western leaders had insight into the fact that their adversary misunderstood Western consolidationist goals. We will include two alternatives: in one view, the West had insight into Soviet fears and misconceptions; and in the other, the West lacked this insight and believed it was recognized as consolidationist.

A final very important variant in this family assumes all perceptions of goals to be accurate. For some writers, the possibility of misperceptions of goals is never given serious consideration. For example, the assumption of accurate perceptions is implicit in MacIntosh's discussion of Soviet tactical changes in 1947: "The origin of the new tactical approach was the final and firm decision by the Soviet leaders in 1946–47 that the United States, the only rival to the Soviet Union in the world, had decided to use its strength to defend the 'capitalist' system in Europe; that the Soviet Union and the Communist parties in Europe, in their campaign to exploit allied victory in the war, would have to face not only war-weary Britain, France, and Italy, but the tremendous power of the United States" (1963, p. 19).

Ball sees Stalin as amused by American naiveté rather than fearful of American expansion after the war. "Bemused by the wishful thought that we could get along with our wartime ally and driven by a reckless but understandable desire to enjoy the peace that had been so long in coming, we were in no mood to pick quarrels with a Soviet Union that should have its hands full repairing the devastation that disfigured such vast areas of its soil. To Stalin we must have seemed foolish indeed, since we wanted so much to discover in his policies the reflection of a purpose totally alien to him" (1968, p. 261).

In other words, the Soviet leaders had no particular misperceptions of Western goals: they recognized them as consolidationist and viewed Western refractory behavior as resistant. This simple variant, in which a consolidationist West confronted an expansionist Soviet coalition with both parties perceiving each other accurately, is perhaps the most widely held theory of the Cold War in the United States. The difference between the first variant and this one is at the heart of whatever strategic differences existed between Republican and Democratic United States policy toward the Soviet Union during the Cold War period: the first view is more characteristic of a Kennedy or a McNamara; the last variant is more characteristic of a Nixon or a Dulles.

This family is summarized in Table 3.2.

Soviet Consolidationist vs. Western Consolidationist

The vision of the Cold War which emerges in this view is of two blundering giants, each with a strong stake in the maintenance of the status quo, but set at each other's throats by a series of misunderstandings and misguided fears. Differences of interest might have been involved, but mutually advantageous compromises were available. However, the psychological atmosphere of mutual insecurity and fear made it difficult for either side to accept such settlements. "Today, probably more than ever before in history," Osgood writes, *mutual insecurity* rather than struggle for power is the major source of international tensions" (1962, p. 161).

The key to the Cold War, in this view, is the understanding that

Table 3.2
Soviet Expansionist vs. Western Consolidationist

PARAMETERS

Soviet goal	Soviet image of how it was perceived	Soviet view of Western goal	Western goal	Western image of how it was perceived	Western view of Soviet goal
Expansion	Expansion	Expansion	Consolidation	Expansion	Expansion
Expansion	Expansion	Expansion	Consolidation	Consolidation	Expansion
Expansion	Expansion	Consolidation	Consolidation	Consolidation	Expansion

despite its bluster, the Soviet coalition was consolidationist. "The Soviet Union," writes Fromm, ". . . is a conservative, state-controlled, industrial managerialism, not a revolutionary system; she is interested in law and order and anxious to defend herself against the onslaught of the revolution of the 'have-not' nations" (1964, p. 14). He goes on to argue that the Soviet regime was most interested in "the development of its system; the bureaucracy ruling in the Soviet Union is expanding and securing the good life for themselves, their children, and eventually for the rest of the population. Khrushchev neither believes in the possibilities for revolution in the West, nor does he want it; nor does he need it for the development of his system. What he needs is peace, a reduction in the armaments burden, and unquestioned control over his system" (*ibid.*, p. 137).

Levine, in discussing this position, points out that many of those who argue for it concede that the Soviet Union had interests in Europe outside of Soviet borders. "These interests, however, they see as primarily defensive and consolidationist, with the Soviet Union consolidating its East European and East German positions and protecting itself against West Germany" (1963, p. 113). Neal and Fleming argue strongly for the defensive motivation of many Soviet actions. "The fact is," Neal writes, "that Stalin's foreign policy was not only in his view defensive, but also non-expansive, except for the security zone of Eastern Europe" (1960). Similarly, Fleming urges us to understand that the Russians' "first driving and continuing motive was, and is, security. This is the cardinal, outstanding fact which explains the Cold War more than anything else put together. Unless this dominating consideration is not only understood but *felt* there can be no understanding of the Cold War" (1961, p. 252).

Communist ideology, in this view, played a special role which reinforced Soviet conservatism: it provided a convenient excuse and justification for inaction. Kautsky, building on Murray Edelman's concept of symbolic reassurance (1964), argues that "the significance of world communism . . . lies in its function as a myth rather than in its eventual realization. . . . The continued use of the symbols 'world communism' and 'revolution' satisfies the interest in symbols of those who desire whatever they think these symbols represent. It does reassure them that their interests (presumably in radical change) are taken care of, and it may fill their needs as adequately as or more than an actual realization of world communism and the revolution could. The use of these symbols also reassures those who manipulate them that they remain orthodox and faithful to their heritage. One of the functions of symbolization, as Edelman notes, is 'that it induces a feeling of well-being, the resolution of tensions.' What sounds like the call to action — the demand that world communism be realized and capitalism be buried — may well serve the purpose or at any rate the function of inducing quiescence" (1965, p. 11).

The United States confused the forces for radical change in much of the world with Soviet Communist expansionism; it mistook Soviet approval or moral support for Soviet action or instigation. "The Communists," Warburg argues, "have ruthlessly and skillfully exploited revolutionary change and have thereby magnified the danger, but communism did not initiate the mid-twentieth-century revolutions; nor would these revolutions cease if the Communist dictatorships were to be overthrown" (1962, pp. 49–50).

If the Soviet coalition was consolidationist, so was the Western coalition, although this is more typically assumed than stated. Fromm, in describing the immediate postwar period, writes of how "the West . . . disarmed and became suspicious of aggressive Russian designs on the whole Western world when Stalin, violating the Yalta agreements, installed his regimes in Poland, Hungary, Rumania, and Bulgaria" (1964, p. 101). Warburg concedes that "during these early postwar years the United States seemed dedicated to an affirmative purpose — the purpose of binding up the wounds of war, of building the machinery for the preservation of peace, of aiding and guiding the revolution of the underprivileged, and of directing the great newly discovered forces of atomic energy exclusively toward peaceful human betterment" (1962, p. 51). And Osgood asks, "What are our goals? . . . Certainly we have no expansionist ambitions in South America, Europe, or Asia; . . . nor do we even desire to impose our way of life on others, except as they observe our model, try it on for size, and find it good. But we do want to *preserve our own way of life* for ourselves and our progeny" (1962, p. 157). Finally, Fleming, who is more ambiguous on this point, grants that the Western coalition at Yalta had no intention of recreating a hostile *cordon sanitaire* [5] against the Soviet Union in Eastern Europe.

But with two consolidationists facing each other, why a hostile interaction? The answer lies in each coalition's misunderstanding and misperceptions of the other's goals. "United States policy and public opinion," Fromm argues, "are based on the premises that the Soviet Union is (a) a socialist state, and (b) a revolutionary and/or imperialist system with the aim of world conquest" (1961, p. 67). Fleming quotes Truman's belief in 1946 that "Russia intends an invasion of Turkey and the seizure of the Black Sea Straits to the Mediterranean" (1961, p. 339). And he emphasizes the importance of Churchill's Fulton, Missouri, speech in 1946 in launching "the United States openly upon a policy of dealing with Russia as an incorrigible menace" (1961, p. 356). Similarly, Neal acknowledges that "the fear in the West is of aggression to *expand* the area of Soviet power" (1960, p. 156).

The Soviet coalition, it is argued, had similar fears about Western designs. Neal reminds us that in the early postwar years, "the American air force controlled the skies. The American navy controlled the seas. American bases, together with those of our British ally, were firmly ensconced around much of the great periphery of the Soviet Union. And the United States, and it alone, possessed the atom bomb. The Russians, obsessed as they were with the fears of capitalist hostility, could only have felt in an exposed and dangerous situation" (*ibid.*, p. 151). And Fleming emphasizes the horrible and devastating impact on Russia of the two world wars: "Terrible memories of this kind, twice burned in, cannot die. They are bound to dominate all thinking, mounting even to a security neurosis and giving rise to a fierce, permanent resolve that this kind of thing shall *never* happen again. There are many people in our own South who still feel strongly about what General Sherman and others did there nearly a hundred years ago. How then can the Russians forget what they have suffered at Germany's hands through Eastern Europe, during the next century?" (1961, p. 253.)

If such a historical basis for fear were not enough, American leaders added further fuel with loose and flamboyant talk. After all, Etzioni points out, "the Russians find quotations in Dulles and Eisenhower speeches and writings that refer to a 'crusade' against the evil of Communism and to our intentions to 'liberate' China, Eastern Europe, and the Russian people — which translated into Russian terms, means that

[5] The *cordon sanitaire* refers to the system of anti-Communist buffer states on Russia's borders in Europe following World War I.

we are out to dissolve their bloc and imperil their security. . . . We are alarmed by the Russians' development of rocketry and by Communist 'subversions,' but we do not realize that the Russians feel quite as threatened by the ring of military bases the United States has set around their mainland. It is safe to generalize that whatever we feel about them they feel about us. . . . We must always remember that the Russian viewpoint is truly different from ours, and that in all likelihood, neither side sees things as they really are" (1962, pp. 93 and 110).

Fromm sums up the argument for the Cold War as an outgrowth of mutual insecurity. Stalin interpreted Western apprehensions of Soviet postwar moves as "the spectrum of a new Western alliance against the Soviet Union. This fear of a Western alliance against the Soviets had always dominated Stalin's mind. . . . On the other hand, the West was always suspicious of Russian schemes for world revolutionary conquests, and Stalin's actions after the war seemed to confirm the worst. Thus, based on mutual suspicions, which were mainly unrealistic at the time, the cold war started" (1961, p. 101).

Each side was consolidationist, then, but perceived the other side as at least expansionist. Were they aware of how their goals were misperceived? Apparently not. The peaceful intentions of the United States were typically regarded by our leaders as self-evident. No one need fear the United States with its atomic monopoly since, as Fleming quotes Truman, "because of our love of peace, the thoughtful people of the world know that that trust will not be violated, that it will be faithfully executed." Fleming goes on to say that "Mr. Truman's consciousness of rectitude was total" (1961, p. 326). On the other side, Neal suggests that, given the power differential at the end of World War II, "to the Soviet Union, Western fears of Soviet military aggression right after the end of the war must have appeared ridiculous as well as insincere" (1960, p. 151). Thus, each side misperceived the other's goals but was unaware that it was similarly misperceived.

This belief system is summarized in Table 3.3 below.

Table 3.3

Soviet Consolidationist vs. Western Consolidationist

PARAMETERS

Soviet goal	Soviet image of how it was perceived	Soviet view of Western goal	Western goal	Western image of how it was perceived	Western view of Soviet goal
Consolidation	Consolidation	Expansion	Consolidation	Consolidation	Expansion

Soviet Expansionist vs. Western Expansionist

In the previous position, the crux of the policy critique was the challenge to the common assumption of Soviet expansionist goals. In this next position, the focus is shifted and the equally common assumption of Western consolidationist goals is called into question.

Both sides were seeking new areas of hegemony. C. Wright Mills puts it bluntly: "Both Russia and America are 'imperialistic' in the service of their ideas and in their fears about military and political security" (1958, p. 63). Each imperialism had its own form. "The economic aim of Soviet imperialism is simply booty. Such imperialism consists of the political control of an area with the aim of (1) accumulating valuable capital goods or (2) extracting agricultural and other 'surpluses' — as in the Stalinist exploitation of Eastern Europe" (*ibid.*, pp. 63–64). And the United States was no better since Marines followed the dollar in an effort to protect expanding American economic interests. Both countries "are brutal; both display the inhuman lack of sensibility characteristic of underdeveloped men in overdeveloped societies, of men with rationality but without reason" (*ibid.*, p. 72).

Horowitz also argues for the mutually expansionist nature of the Cold War adversaries in spite of differences in the forms such expansionism took. He contrasts the different styles in the Iranian crisis of 1946, the first serious public confrontation of the postwar period. The Soviet Union delayed the withdrawal of its troops to exact oil concessions but finally withdrew them under pressure. But "as the Russians left, the Americans moved in — not with troops and revolution — 'but silently with dollars.' . . . If America did not yet have military bases there, she could have them anytime she wished" (1965, p. 89). He goes on to quote Smith on the differences in the overt symptoms of the two kinds of expansionism: "When Russia extends her security zone abroad, it almost inevitably requires an overthrow of the *status quo*, for the *status quo* of the world is capitalistic; which means a lot of noise and ugly scenes. If America extends her zone of influence abroad, for the same reason — that the rest of the world is capitalist — it involves only supporting the *status quo*: no scenes, no noise" (Smith, 1949, p. 93).

In spite of the connotations of the word "containment," Western policy went beyond simply holding the line in Western Europe. The minimum objective, Horowitz argues, "was to deny Russia the influence she had won in Europe as a result of her wartime victories. To accomplish this, the United States embarked on a course designed to *compel* Russia to relinquish her positions in East Europe, without any

compensation in the way of recognition of her security interests in the
Central and East European areas" (1965, p. 278). Similarly, Alperovitz concludes that "it is now evident that, far from following his
predecessor's policy of cooperation, shortly after taking office Truman
launched a powerful foreign policy initiative aimed at reducing or
eliminating Soviet influence from Europe" (1964, p. 13). The United
States actively challenged Soviet influence in Eastern Europe, demand-
ing "that the governments subservient to Soviet influence be removed.
. . . Secretary Byrnes began a campaign of direct intervention in the
internal politics of Hungary, Bulgaria, and Rumania" (*ibid.*, pp. 202
and 205). Defense of Western Europe was not the primary motivation
of American policy. "Byrnes has been quite explicit; his policy always
aimed at forcing the Russians to yield in Eastern Europe, and in mid-
1947 he still continued to argue that the United States had it in its
power to force the Russians to 'retire in a very decent manner' " (*ibid.*,
p. 234).

Soviet expansionism, in Horowitz's view, was more reactive and was
stimulated by Western initiatives. It was only after the "bombshell" of
the Truman Doctrine was exploded that the Soviets responded "by
subverting the non-Communist governments of Hungary and Czechoslovakia, and by taking swift steps to integrate fully the economies
and political structures of the Eastern European countries and to
reduce them to satellites in the service of their mobilization against the
West" (1965, p. 90). The Truman Doctrine proved to be a "self-fulfilling
prophecy: given the mentality of the Russian leaders, the whole postwar United States policy of facing the Soviets with an 'iron fist' and
'strong language,' while at the same time making it as difficult as
possible for them to carry out the work of reconstruction, virtually
ensured the 'expansion' that the policy, allegedly, had been designed
to prevent" (*ibid.*, pp. 95–96).

The view that both sides were expansionist is also represented by
some writers who are generally quite sympathetic to American foreign
policy. Spanier seems to take this view but makes the United States
the reluctant dragon: "In the sense that the United States exercised
global responsibilities, it acted as an 'imperial' power. The first characteristic of this 'empire' was America's political involvement in all areas
around the Sino-Soviet periphery. . . . The formerly isolationist nation which felt that no quarrels anywhere affected its security, became
the world power which could not avoid becoming involved everywhere" (1968, p. 258).

America's global role, Spanier argues, was necessary to meet the
challenge of its adversary's attempts at expansion. "To suggest that
America's role as world policeman is unnecessary is to forget the

militancy of the Soviet Union and China [and] to deny their foreign policy aims" (ibid., p. 259). The United States had little choice, he argues, but to respond to "Soviet and/or Chinese attempts to exploit power vacuums, intraregional conflicts, and differences between the new nations" (ibid., p. 258). Thus, the belief that both sides were expansionist may accompany the argument that either side was especially culpable; or the holder of such a view may, like Mills, wish a plague on both houses.

Each side had genuine fears about the other's expansionism, even when its own actions were a primary cause. For Horowitz, Soviet perception of Western expansion was obvious. Given the "scope and use of United States power in the initial post-war period, it can be seen that by early 1947 when the cold war became a public reality, the Russians had real cause for concern about United States intentions and the future employment of United States economic and military muscle" (1965, p. 90). Western perceptions of Soviet expansionism are more problematic for Horowitz because he does not believe that the West ever seriously feared Soviet military aggression against Western Europe. Still, the West feared Communist expansion through subversion and revolution. "In the early cold war years, . . . the distinction between containing expansion and containing revolution was not so easily made. Among the reasons for difficulty was the fact that the monolithic structure of the international Communist movement, subordinate as it was to the Soviet Politburo, lent substance to Western propaganda and made it seem as though potential Communist revolutions would, if victorious, mean Soviet control, and ipso facto made the containment of Communist revolution seem to be equivalent to the containment of Soviet expansion" (ibid., p. 413).

For Spanier, on the other hand, it is Soviet fears that require elucidation since Western perceptions of Soviet expansion are assumed. Spanier clearly recognizes that Western actions took on a different hue when viewed through Soviet eyes: "As Russians, they recalled the many invasions from the West; as Communists, their fear of a future enemy invasion was strengthened by the ideological faith that posited capitalist states as their implacable enemies, merely waiting for the opportunity to strike; hence, the establishment of anti-Communist regimes in Eastern Europe would have been intolerable, and the American insistence upon free elections was seen as an attempt to push the Soviet Union out of Europe" (1968, p. 27).

A variant of the view described above holds that righteousness leads to blindness about how one is perceived. In this view, each side was expansionist and viewed its adversary in the same manner. However, it was so convinced of its own noble purposes that it could not enter-

tain the thought that others might see it as expansionist. "Power tends
to confuse itself with virtue," Fulbright writes, "and a great nation is
peculiarly susceptible to the idea that its power is a sign of God's
favor, conferring upon it a special responsibility for other nations — to
make them richer and happier and wiser, to remake them, that is, in
its own shining image" (1966, p. 3).

Steel points out the discrepancy between self-perceptions and others'
perceptions of American foreign policy. "However deep and sincerely
felt these assumptions of American benevolence may be, they are not
often shared by the nations that feel the direct effects of American
power. Nor are they always consistent with our own behavior throughout the world. . . . The United States has intervened massively in the
affairs of other nations. She has done so, to be sure, for the most noble
motives and with the most generous impulses. But her high ideals have
not diminished the impact of her power, nor has her generosity necessarily convinced others that her ambitions are purely philanthropic"
(1967, p. vii). "The United States has become an interventionist power,
indeed the world's major interventionist power, without most Americans quite realizing how it happened or its full implications. . . . We
have intervened in the politics of other nations . . . trying to push
some into new alignments, trying to remake the social structure of
others, and helping to overthrow the governments of not a few" (*ibid.*,
pp. 5–7).

Noble aims underlie this policy of intervention. "Postwar America
would have been quite happy to withdraw from Europe once the Nazi
armies were defeated. But we could not leave the Continent to the
mercy of the Russians, who had installed communist dictatorships in
Eastern Europe to replace the mainly right-wing, and occasionally
fascist, ones of the prewar era, and who menaced the war-weakened
nations of Western Europe with various forms of blackmail and subversion" (*ibid.*, p. 51).

There was a similar combination of expansionism and a belief in
noble purposes on the Soviet side. Steel argues that "the Russians,
while behaving in ways that augment their status as a great power,
. . . believe in the mythology of communism and their duty to spread
it to nations oppressed by the 'imperialists.' The fact that they have
rarely let their belief in the promulgation of the communist faith inter-
fere with the security of Mother Russia does not diminish the fact that
they conceive of themselves as a basically messianic power" (1967,
p. 29).

Each side, feeling itself justified in expanding for its own protection
and for the protection of those threatened by its rival, saw nothing
but naked ambition in the similar expansion of its adversary. "Carried
away by the vocabulary of the cold war, we sought to combat com-

munism and preserve 'freedom' in whatever area, however unpromising or unlikely, the battle seemed to be joined. Confusing communism as a social doctrine with communism as a form of Soviet imperialism, we assumed that any advance of communist doctrine anywhere was an automatic gain for the Soviet Union. Thus we believed it essential to combat communism in any part of the globe, as though it were a direct threat to our security, even in cases where it was not allied to Soviet power" (*ibid.*, p. 19).

But others do not accept the view of the West as merely consolidationist and defensive. "In the eyes of much of the world, America is a nation possessed of an empire of nominally independent client states and pursuing ambitions consistent with those of a great imperial power" (*ibid.*, p. vii). In the end, neither the United States nor the Soviet Union succeeded in fooling anyone about its expansionist goals. But enveloped by righteous indignation, they were unaware of how others viewed them.

This family is summarized in Table 3.4 below.

Soviet Consolidationist vs. Western Expansionist

This position differs from the previous one primarily in its greater emphasis on the defensive and security-conscious nature of Soviet policy. Williams writes that "the sources of Russian conduct are the drives to conquer poverty and achieve basic security in the world of nation states. From these efforts developed, on the one hand, the practices and traditions of centralized power to force saving, allocate investment, and maintain security, and, on the other, the heightened domestic tension between collective action and individual identity and the ambivalence of a foreign policy at once militantly and suspiciously defensive yet characterized by a missionary and benevolent desire to help other men save themselves" (1959, p. 191).

Oglesby is similarly skeptical of the argument for Soviet expansionism: "To argue that Stalin was bent on conquest and so maneuvered

Table 3.4
Soviet Expansionist vs. Western Expansionist

PARAMETERS

Soviet goal	Soviet image of how it was perceived	Soviet view of Western goal	Western goal	Western image of how it was perceived	Western view of Soviet goal
Expansion	Expansion	Expansion	Expansion	Expansion	Expansion
Expansion	Consolidation	Expansion	Expansion	Consolidation	Expansion

for the hegemony in East Europe that Russia finally acquired is to substitute for a very rich reality a myth as troublesome as it is banal. Stalin seems to have been neither an imperialist nor even very much of a Marxist" (1967, pp. 40–41). Writing for an audience living in the ambience of Cold War rhetoric, Oglesby finds it necessary to disclaim any attempt to absolve Stalin from the "many unforgettable patches of shame in that man's story: the sorry spectacle of the purges; his slaughtering of the kulaks; his willingness to watch and even support the attempted destruction of the Chinese Revolution; his cynical manipulation of the Spanish Loyalists; his toleration of British and American dismemberment of the Greek Revolution" (*ibid.*, p. 43). But these sins remain irrelevant to the argument that "Stalin's record in the early Cold War is less that of a fairy-tale monster on the prowl for sadism's blood and imperialism's plunder than that of a small, cold, very practical nationalist in a tight, dangerous situation" (*ibid.*, p. 43).

In this view, if Russia was frightened, it was not without good reason. Williams argues that already by the Yalta conference in 1945, it had become apparent that American leaders "were not prepared to abandon, or even seriously to modify, the traditional policy for American expansion" (1959, p. 161). To be sure, this traditional policy "also carried with it the spirit of American idealism and the vision of a better life for foreign peoples. And in many specific cases these ideals had been realized to some extent in the process of American expansion. . . . [But] the Open Door Policy did not cease being a program of imperial expansion simply because it spurned territorial and administrative colonialism in favor of an empire of economics, ideology, and bases" (*ibid.*, p. 208).

Oglesby is even less charitable to American good intentions. He says that the United States promoted an image in which the "peace American leaders pursued was of a plain, unvarnished kind, a simple peace in which good-neighbor nations let each other alone. This is incorrect. We want peace, to be sure. All nations want peace. But we want a certain kind of peace, one which seems to have very little to do with letting good neighbors alone or with democracy or progress. Put it roughly: For us, peace finally exists when the world is finally safe for American businessmen to carry on their business everywhere, on terms as favorable as they can be made, in settings managed preferably by native middle-class governments, but if need be by oligarchic and repressive ones, by the old foreign grads of Fort Bragg, or if the panic hits in a pivotal place, by our own Marines" (1967, pp. 70–71).

It would have been miraculous in such a situation if Russia, with all her traditional insecurity, had failed to perceive the Western coalition as at least expansionist. "It is not possible," Williams argued, "to maintain seriously that Russia has no valid historical or present fears of foreign attack" (1959, p. 188). And Oglesby speculates about the "horror" an exhausted Russia must have felt "as she watched the New Germany come alive with steel and guns, the calculated assembly on her political frontiers of a totally encircling military alliance, and the growing influence in her enemy's camp of the very boldest advocates of 'rollback' and 'liberation' " (1967, p. 16). Nor is it suggested that the West was unaware of these Soviet fears and thus, by convention, we assume that in this view the West recognized that it was perceived as expansionist.

Unlike the official Soviet view which we will discuss below, Western leaders are given some credit for sincerity in their fears of Soviet expansion at the end of World War II. Fear of direct military aggression was not the issue. As Williams argues, "Far from being concerned about a Russian attack, American leaders emphasized the importance of denying any and all Soviet requests or overtures for a revised strategic agreement in the Middle East and stressed the importance of pushing the Russians back to their traditional borders in Eastern Europe" (1959, p. 165). But there was another sort of fear, as Oglesby points out: "The United States saw Soviet Communism as threatening Europe with another long revolutionary convulsion. . . . Over the next decade, the democratic West watched horrified as East Germany and Poland and Hungary stood up only to be crushed" (1967, pp. 15–16). But the belief in Soviet expansion also served a convenient function for the West — it palliated United States foreign policy. Western misperceptions of Soviet goals were motivated. "Maybe" Oglesby says, "our ideology of Cold War anticommunism is a beauty mark" (*ibid.*, p. 45).

It is unclear in this view whether Soviet leaders are credited with insight into these mistaken Western fears about Soviet expansion. We will include both assumptions — that the Soviet coalition thought it was correctly perceived as consolidationist and that it was aware that it was misperceived as expansionist.

A variant in this family is the official Soviet view that gives the West no credit for misunderstanding Soviet goals. Western protestations of fear of Soviet expansionism are regarded as having been cynically motivated. The language used to define Western goals might be interpreted to imply Western destructionism rather than expansionism except for the fact that the West is seen to have had its hands full with its own internal crises and contradictions. Furthermore, Soviet officials could not really have believed that the West was pursuing Soviet destruction as an operative goal, or it would never have made sense for them to have been conciliatory, as, in fact, they sometimes were.

The Soviet official view is promulgated in a number of different publications. In *Fundamentals of Marxism-Leninism* (Dutt, 1960), the new stage of "the general crisis of capitalism" is described. Among the factors outlined as characteristic of this crisis is the "development of new contradictions within the imperialist camp, primarily between the United States and other developed capitalist countries as a result of the intensified expansion of U.S. imperialism and its drive for world domination." The Western countries, refusing to accept the historical setbacks that they were experiencing as the socialist countries developed and grew stronger, "launched their 'cold war' against the socialist countries. The new state in the general crisis of capitalism became a period of intensified imperialist aggressiveness, of increased war danger for the world."

Another source of the Soviet view is a speech by Andrei Zhdanov at the establishment of the Cominform in September, 1947. Zhdanov argues that "the aggressive and frankly expansionist course to which American imperialism has committed itself since the end of World War II finds expression in both the foreign and home policy of the United States. . . . The strategical plans of the United States envisage the creation in peacetime of numerous bases and vantage grounds situated at great distances from the American continent and designed to be used for aggressive purposes, against the USSR and the countries of the new democracy. America has built, or is building, air and naval bases in Alaska, Japan, Italy, South Korea, China, Egypt, Iran, Turkey, Greece, Austria, and Western Germany. There are American military missions in Afghanistan and even in Nepal. Feverish preparations are being made to use the Arctic for purposes of military aggression" (reprinted in Bishop, 1952, pp. 87–88).

Soviet goals, in the official view, were not only consolidationist but the West knew this fact very well. In the same speech, Zhdanov says, "The principal purpose of the ideological part of the American strategical plan is to deceive public opinion by slanderously accusing the Soviet Union and the new democracies of aggressive intentions, and thus representing the Anglo-Saxon bloc in a defensive role and absolving it of responsibility for preparing a new war" (ibid., p. 89). The Soviet coalition, of course, disclaimed any aggressive intentions. Its goal, as defined in an official USSR statement on the North Atlantic Pact in January, 1949, was "the consolidation of universal peace and international security" (ibid., pp. 94–102).

Western expressions of fear about Soviet expansion are regarded as disingenuous — not confused. Zhdanov says that a main feature of the Truman Doctrine was "unintermittent pressure on the countries of the new democracy, as expressed in the false accusations of totalitarianism and expansionist ambitions, in attacks on the foundations of the new democratic regimes, in constant interference in their domestic affairs, in support of all anti-national, anti-democratic elements within these countries, and in the demonstrative breaking off of economic relations with these countries with the idea of creating economic difficulties, retarding their economic development, preventing their industrialization, and so on" (*ibid.*, p. 91).

No misperceptions are recognized in this official Soviet view. Like its American counterpart,[6] it sees a recognized consolidationist facing a recognized (despite its efforts at deception) expansionist.

This family is summarized in Table 3.5 below.

Soviet Consolidationist vs. Western Destructionist

It is difficult to find a clear-cut statement of this view. Such a position is necessarily *critical* of Soviet policy because, unless the Soviet coalition misperceived Western destructionist goals, it would never have behaved in a conciliatory manner. Criticisms of Soviet policy from the right can be found abundantly among pro-Western and neutral writers. But this position offers a critique from the left: it presents a Soviet coalition that was gulled by tactical Western shifts into believing that peaceful coexistence was possible with a mortal enemy. Until there was some open schism in the Soviet coalition, such views were not expressed openly.

This is not to deny that there may have been shifts in official Soviet thinking and fundamental policy debate in the Soviet Union. However, as Aspaturian writes, "foreign policy debates are largely secret. . . . While foreign policy is discussed much more widely in the Soviet Union than heretofore, there is still no criticism of a systematic character about Soviet policy. Soviet decision-makers still act without prior public discussion and need not render an accounting in public, al-

Table 3.5

Soviet Consolidationist vs. Western Expansionist

PARAMETERS

Soviet goal	Soviet image of how it was perceived	Soviet view of Western goal	Western goal	Western image of how it was perceived	Western view of Soviet goal
Consolidation	Consolidation	Expansion	Expansion	Expansion	Expansion
Consolidation	Expansion	Expansion	Expansion	Expansion	Expansion
Consolidation	Consolidation	Expansion	Expansion	Expansion	Consolidation

[6] See Table 3.2, p. 39, third variant.

though increasingly, reports on foreign policy are made to the Supreme Soviet. Foreign policy is too crucial a matter to debate in public, since it would alert the outside world to Soviet intentions. Thus, there is no political opposition which can publicly offer an alternative program or policy. Opposition does exist, but behind closed doors of higher party and state organs. These criticisms and alternative policies are sometimes revealed indirectly through denunciation, rejection, allusions to 'bourgeois thinkers,' 'metal eaters,' 'certain comrades,' 'some people,' 'anti-Marxists,' etc." (1966, p. 284). However, Keep reviews the period from 1945 to 1961 and concludes that "a search through the dark cupboards of recent Soviet writing has not disclosed any independent thinking on contemporary international problems; if heretical views existed, they did not seem to have been judged worthy of comment or censure in the columns of *Pravda* or *Kommunist*" (1964, p. 109). Similarly, Zimmerman reports that "prior to 1960, evidence of any major reappraisal of American foreign policy was almost totally absent from the specialized press" (1969, p. 211).

The left Soviet critic — if he existed — must have brooded in silence as he watched his leaders underestimate the true nature of the Western threat. Presumably, such a critic would have agreed with Strausz-Hupé et al. that "different political systems can exist side by side, but not when one system is aggressive, geared to conflict, and bent upon conquest" (1961, p. 8). Here, of course, Western imperialism is seen as the aggressor whom one cannot appease by compromise.

With the advent of an open Sino-Soviet split, this hypothetical Soviet critic began to find his views expressed in the pages of the *Peking Review*. Indeed, the Soviet Union was viewed as consolidationist but this was far from a virtue. "The Soviet leaders seek only to preserve themselves and would let other people sink or swim. They have repeatedly said that so long as they themselves survive and develop, the people of the world will be saved. The fact is they are selling out the fundamental interests of the people of the world in order to seek their own momentary ease" (Chinese government spokesman, 1963).

Grown comfortable and lazy, the Soviet coalition had allowed itself to underrate the virulent nature of Western goals. K'ang Sheng, in a speech delivered at a conference of Warsaw Pact states in February, 1960, says, "While being obliged to make certain peace gestures, the U.S. ruling circles are still pushing ahead with their arms expansion and war preparations . . . and actively trying to strengthen and patch up military blocs in an attempt to gain time to improve their inferior military position" (cited in Floyd, 1964). A writer in *Red Flag* in April, 1960, warns, "If we lose our vigilance against the danger of the imperialists launching a war, if we do not work to stir the people of all countries to rise up against imperialism, but tie the hands of the people, then imperialism can prepare for war just as it pleases, and the inevitable result will be an increase in the danger of the imperialists launching a war." [7] Soviet policy was wrong not only because it betrayed the interests of the downtrodden but also because, by underrating the destructionist nature of Western imperialism, it contributed to the downfall of the Soviet Union as well.

This final position is summarized in Table 3.6. Table 3.7 collects the entire set of belief systems about the Cold War.

SOME FINAL CLARIFICATIONS

We have reviewed and classified a large body of literature on the Cold War in terms of our six parameters. A number of questions arise in interpreting these positions. In this section, we deal with some of the issues involved in reducing complex discussions of the Cold War to the dimensions of six parameters.

Stability and Change of Parameters

Scholars who concentrate on interpreting Soviet behavior are likely to be much more focused on the variability and change in Soviet goals and perceptions than in their constancy.[8] If they are concerned with our parameters at all, it is usually to make a point about actual or apparent shifts, particularly those associated with shifts in leadership. For example, Aspaturian writes, "The Cuban missile debacle apparently convinced Khrushchev that Soviet interests could best be served by pursuing an essentially status quo foreign policy with residual traces of political and ideological revisionism" (1968, p. 140). The im-

Table 3.6
Soviet Consolidationist vs. Western Destructionist

PARAMETERS

Soviet goal	Soviet image of how it was perceived	Soviet view of Western goal	Western goal	Western image of how it was perceived	Western view of Soviet goal
Consolidation	Consolidation	Expansion	Destruction	Expansion	Consolidation

[7] Reprinted in the *China Quarterly,* 1961, p. 93.
[8] See, for example, Zimmerman (1969) and Aspaturian (1968).

Table 3.7
Summary of Belief Systems about the Cold War

PARAMETERS

Family name and members	Soviet goal	Soviet image of how it was perceived	Soviet view of Western goal	Western goal	Western image of how it was perceived	Western view of Soviet goal
Soviet destructionist/ Western consolidationist						
Variant I (e.g., Strausz-Hupé et al.)	Destruction	Expansion	Consolidation	Consolidation	Consolidation	Expansion
Variant II	Destruction	Expansion	Expansion	Consolidation	Consolidation	Expansion
Variant III	Destruction	Expansion	Expansion	Consolidation	Expansion	Expansion
Soviet expansionist/ Western consolidationist						
Variant I (e.g., JFK)	Expansion	Expansion	Expansion	Consolidation	Expansion	Expansion
Variant II	Expansion	Expansion	Expansion	Consolidation	Consolidation	Expansion
Variant III (e.g., Dulles)	Expansion	Expansion	Consolidation	Consolidation	Consolidation	Expansion

Soviet consolidationist/ *Western consolidationist*						
Variant I (e.g., Fromm)	Expansion	Consolidation	Consolidation	Expansion	Consolidation	Consolidation
Soviet expansionist/ *Western expansionist*						
Variant I (e.g., Mills)	Expansion	Expansion	Expansion	Expansion	Expansion	Expansion
Variant II (e.g., Steel)	Expansion	Consolidation	Expansion	Expansion	Consolidation	Expansion
Soviet consolidationist/ *Western expansionist*						
Variant I (e.g., Oglesby)	Expansion	Expansion	Expansion	Expansion	Consolidation	Consolidation
Variant II	Expansion	Expansion	Expansion	Expansion	Expansion	Consolidation
Variant III (e.g., Soviet officials)	Consolidation	Expansion	Expansion	Expansion	Consolidation	Consolidation
Soviet consolidationist/ *Western destructionist*						
Variant I (e.g., Chinese)	Consolidation	Consolidation	Destruction	Expansion	Consolidation	Consolidation

plication here is that the goal parameter has changed and perceptions of the other side's goals are likely to be even less stable.

Many scholars see changes from 1946 to 1963 — a period in which there were many shifts in leadership by both sides, many technological and weaponry developments, and many major crises which might have affected one or more of our six parameters. Furthermore, some commentators argue that a parameter is *conditional* on the presence of a given factor rather than a fixed property of the actor. For example, some feel that the Soviet coalition was consolidationist but only because of Western military strength; this parameter will change if and when the condition is not met. Granting these qualifications, how can we expect to do justice to any fine-grained discussion of the Cold War by inferring a single set of parameters from it for the entire period of study? Furthermore, how can we expect to explain the Cold War itself with a single theory in which the parameters remain fixed?

In answer to the first of these questions, we are not trying to capture the full richness and complexity of a good historical account of the Cold War. Rather, we are interested in identifying those sets of parameter values that someone seriously argues existed at one time or another. We want plausible interpretations of combinations of our parameters and if the same man contributes more than one interpretation that is just as useful as if different men supply such interpretations. Imagine, for example, that historian Smith believes that Soviet goals were expansionist until 1953 and consolidationist after that while historian Jones believes that Soviet goals were destructionist throughout. We treat this as three interpretations — early Smith, late Smith, and Jones. Our emphasis is on the interpretation, regardless of source, rather than on the men who hold them. By the same reasoning, it would be irrelevant to argue that some interpretation was insincere and was only argued for propaganda purposes. As long as it is possible to be sincere while being wrong and to be right in spite of manipulative intent, we will consider all interpretations without regard to their motives.

And we need not expect to do justice to the Cold War with a single theory. Certainly, as a first step, we will examine the entire Cold War period with predictions derived from each set of parameters. But the analysis only begins there, and we will go on to examine relative success during different periods of the Cold War. We view the parameters as relatively stable properties of the actors — more stable than their tactics — but not as immutable properties. We hope to discover what contributes to their change by examining the relative success of different sets of parameters at different times.

Internal Policy Differences

We are well aware of continuous debate in this country about the nature of some of the parameters. As Aspaturian points out, "The Soviet Union, like the United States, is involved in a continuous great debate over foreign policy and national security matters centering around the issue of whether the heightening of international tensions or the relaxation of international tensions best serves the 'national interests.' In both countries, there are important spokesmen on both sides, although in the Soviet Union those who may be interested in maintaining international tensions make their views known only behind closed doors or in the esoteric type of communication which has inspired the profession of 'Kremlinology'" (1966, p. 253).

If neither side had a unitary line on such matters as perceptions of their adversary's goals, how can we expect to make sense of their behavior by assigning a single value to a parameter? If there was so much oscillation in policy that the major thrust changed on a weekly or monthly basis, there would indeed be little hope of finding some consistent patterns of Soviet-Western interaction. But we do not believe that such oscillation is characteristic. In spite of the existence of criticism, foreign policy decision-makers arrive at some set of shared assumptions about the parameter values and continue to hold them until some major crisis or personnel change creates a discontinuity. If we are wrong in our assumptions about the stability and relative continuity of parameters, we will pay the price of our error by finding no coherent patterns of Soviet-Western interaction when we examine the results.

CONCLUSION

We have examined a series of views of the Cold War and drawn from them statements and assumptions about the appropriate values for a set of six parameters. In the next chapter, we will move from the parameters to specific predictions about the pattern of Cold War interaction. Once we have associated a set of parameter values with a set of predictions, we will be able to evaluate the relative validity of the theories presented in this chapter by examining their ability to make successful predictions.

Chapter Four

A DECISION MODEL
FOR DERIVING PREDICTIONS

A theory of the Cold War is a *belief system* about the values of six parameters coupled with a *decision model*. This latter component specifies how parameter values determine each coalition's responses to the preceding behavior of its adversary. In explaining the responses of any one coalition, we need consider only half the parameter values. (Each of the views of the Cold War described in the preceding chapter really contains two belief systems: one about the values of the Western parameters and another about the values of the Soviet parameters.) In predicting how the West should respond to a given pattern of Soviet behavior, we need consider only the Western parameters. Similarly, in predicting Soviet responses to Western behavior, we need consider only the Soviet parameters. Hence, it is possible for a theory of the Cold War to be half right: its belief system about the West may be vindicated but its belief system about the Soviet coalition may be a poor predictor, or vice versa. This means that we test a theory of the Cold War in halves, examining its predictions about Soviet and Western responses in turn, and putting these two halves together for a total evaluation of the theory.

In this chapter we present the decision model that allows us to translate belief systems into predictions. This decision model is the same for both coalitions. Hence, a given set of parameter values always yields the same predictions regardless of which coalition it belongs to. For example, if a coalition has consolidationist goals, a reflected image of consolidationist, and perceives its adversary as expansionist (i.e., CCE [1]), its responses can be predicted irrespective of whether this coalition happens to be Soviet or Western. Predic-

[1] Henceforth, we will use the following abbreviations: D for destructionist, E for expansionist, and C for consolidationist. The parameters are always listed in the order: the coalition's goals, the coalition's reflected image, the coalition's perception of its adversary's goals.

tions are derived by applying the decision model directly to the values of the parameters.

Since we need not consider which coalition the parameters belong to when establishing predictions, we need derive only one set of predictions for each combination of parameter values assigned to one or the other coalition. A look back at Table 3.7 of Chapter Three reveals that only seven combinations were, in fact, assigned: DEC, DEE, ECE, EEC, EEE, CCE, and CEE. All seven of these are assigned to the Soviet coalition by one or another view and six of the seven are assigned to the Western coalition.[2] Later in this chapter we will show that these seven are *exhaustive* once one applies the conventions and restrictions on parameter values described in Chapter Three.

Our task, then, is to match each of these seven belief systems about a coalition with a set of predictions indicating how the coalition should respond to its adversary's previous behavior. We hope that the sets of predictions will be different so that we will be in a position to test the relative validity of each belief system.

THE DECISION MODEL

Imagine that we had a good reading on a coalition's parameter values. What further assumptions would be needed in order to specify the process by which the coalition decided on its response to some given pattern of adversary behavior? We will present here a simple model of the coalition's decision process — a model that first links the parameter values to an interpretation of the adversary's behavior, and then links this interpretation to a specific response. The actual decision process utilized by any country is extremely complex and we deliberately ignore many aspects of it. The resulting model is so simple that it is likely to seem a caricature. But the issue of what constitutes useful simplification and what constitutes oversimplification is a subtle one. We ask the reader to suspend judgment on the usefulness of the model pending our discussion of appropriate and inappropriate simplification in the last section of this chapter.

An Overview

Our model assumes that a coalition faces a three-step decision problem in deciding how to react to its adversary's recent behavior. First, it must interpret the adversary's behavior in order to infer the adversary's

---

[2] No position assigns the combination DEE to the West. In such a view, the West not only would have had destructionist goals but also would have perceived its adversary as expansionist. For the sake of completeness, we will test this belief system about the West along with the others even though we could find no one who argued it.

current intentions. This is the most critical step. Based on this interpretation, it can set a tactical objective of its own. Finally, having set
its tactical objective, it can proceed to implement an appropriate response.

The parameters operate primarily at the first step of this decision
process: they determine the interpretation that a coalition will place
on its adversary's behavior. Each parameter plays a somewhat different role. The first parameter (goals) determines a coalition's interpretation and consequent response to *accommodative* behavior. The second
and third parameters (reflected image and perception of the adversary's goals) determine a coalition's interpretation and consequent
response to *belligerent* behavior.[3]

Consider, first, the case of accommodative behavior. To the responding coalition, such behavior might mean that the adversary is
receptive to mutual accommodations, or it might mean that the adversary is lax and can be taken advantage of. Which perspective prevails depends on the coalition's goals. If its goals are destructionist, it
will have no interest in the adversary's receptivity to mutual accommodation and instead will prefer to exploit the opportunities provided
by its adversary's temporary laxity. This calls for a refractory response. But if the coalition has consolidationist goals, it will have little
interest in exploitation and a distinct interest in the adversary's possible receptivity and therefore will prefer to "approach" its adversary in
the hope of resolving outstanding disagreements. This calls for a
conciliatory response.

In the case of belligerent behavior, the responding coalition must
decide whether the adversary is being aggressive or merely resistant.
The relevant parameters are the second and third (reflected image and
perception of the adversary's goals). If the coalition believes that it is
seen by its adversary as consolidationist, it will be unlikely to view
the adversary's behavior as resistant for the adversary would have no
reason to feel threatened. If, in addition, it believes the adversary's
goals are expansionist, it will be even more certain that the adversary
is being aggressive rather than defensive. Since aggression must be
turned back, a refractory response will be called for.

Other parameter values would lead to a different interpretation and
response. If the coalition believes that it is seen by its adversary as
expansionist, it will be much more likely to view the adversary's behavior as defensive and resistant. If it also believes the adversary has

---

[3] When the adversary's behavior is balanced, then all three parameters become
relevant and the problem becomes more complicated. The derivation of responses
to balanced behavior will not be discussed in this overview, but it is taken up in
Appendix C.

consolidationist goals, it can rule out the possibility of aggression. In this case, the adversary must be reassured and a conciliatory response will be in order.[4]

In our discussion thus far, we have deliberately avoided using examples in which certain parameters took the value "expansionist." In fact, special problems arise when the responding coalition's goals are expansionist, or when both of its other parameters simultaneously take the value "expansionist." To understand these problems and arrive at predictions, we must carefully examine the decision faced by such coalitions.

If a responding coalition with expansionist goals faces an accommodative adversary, selection of an appropriate response will be complicated by the fact that such a coalition has a flexible, opportunistic orientation: it is interested in making gains through both mutual accommodation and exploitation of an adversary's laxity. Unlike coalitions with destructionist or consolidationist goals, it cannot immediately reject one of these alternatives in favor of the other. It needs further information to determine which course will be most profitable in this case. Such information can be extracted from its *own* recent behavior (i.e., from its behavior in the same time period that includes the adversary's behavior). If it has been belligerent, then the adversary's accommodative behavior suggests a laxity that could profitably be exploited, and a refractory response will be in order. But if it has been nonbelligerent, then the quandary remains. The adversary might be lax, but he also might be warily responding in kind. Here the coalition must base its response on the degree of the adversary's accommodation. If the adversary has been extremely accommodative (suggesting laxity), then an exploitative, refractory response would remain appropriate. If the adversary has been only fairly accommodative (suggesting receptivity), then a conciliatory response would seem better.[5]

Finally, we turn to the case of a coalition that believes its adversary sees it as expansionist and, in turn, perceives its adversary as expansionist. When confronted with belligerent behavior, such a coalition

[4] Reassurance can be carried out with malevolent or benevolent intentions depending on the coalition's goals. A consolidationist coalition will be seeking to create an atmosphere in which bargaining and mutual accommodation can take place. A destructionist coalition will be seeking to reduce the adversary's vigilance so that it may carry on with its aggressive plans. The point is that an aroused and defensive adversary will be deleterious to either coalition's objectives.

[5] If the adversary's level of accommodation falls between these two extremes, it becomes impossible to predict the coalition's response. Faced with such a case, a belief system would be permitted to "pass" — i.e., to abstain from making any prediction. The conditions under which a belief system may pass are discussed in Appendix C, which contains a more comprehensive statement of our model.

faces a difficult task of interpretation. Since it knows the adversary sees it as expansionist, it might assume that its opponent is simply being defensive and resistant. But since it perceives this adversary as expansionist, it must also consider the possibility that its opponent is being aggressive. Once again, such a coalition must look to its own recent behavior for additional information. If it has been nonbelligerent, then in all probability its adversary is being aggressive, for the adversary would have no reason to resist at this time; to repel such aggression, a refractory response would be called for. But if the coalition has been belligerent, no simple conclusion can be drawn. Resistance becomes a more plausible interpretation, but aggression cannot be excluded. Here, again, the coalition must base its interpretation and response on the extent of the adversary's belligerence. If the adversary has been extremely belligerent, then aggression is the more prudent interpretation, and a resistant, refractory response would be called for. If the adversary has been only fairly belligerent, then resistance is the more likely interpretation, and a reassuring, conciliatory response would be best.

The discussion of these special cases involving expansionist parameter values indicates that we must derive two sets of predictions for certain belief systems: one set for periods of *responder-belligerence*, and another set for periods of *responder-nonbelligerence*.[6] Notice that a responder-belligerent period makes no reference to the adversary's behavior, which may run the gamut from extremely belligerent to extremely accommodative.

Summarizing the Assumptions

Tables 4.1 and 4.2 summarize our discussion by providing a concise statement of the central assumptions in our model. Table 4.1 indicates how particular parameter values, when coupled with patterns of responder belligerence or nonbelligerence, lead to specific interpretations of an adversary's behavior.[7] Table 4.2 completes the cycle from parameter values to specific responses by specifying the connection between each possible interpretation of an adversary's behavior and the resulting response. Most of these connections are straightforward,

---

[6] The operational definition of such periods is presented in Appendix A where coding procedures are discussed.

[7] Notice that the distinction between periods of responder belligerence and periods of responder nonbelligerence only affects interpretations in two special cases: when the responding coalition's goal parameter is expansionist, or when both of its remaining two parameters simultaneously are expansionist. For a more comprehensive discussion of these and other assumptions contained in Table 4.2, the reader is referred to Appendix C.

Table 4.1

How a Coalition Interprets Accommodative and Belligerent Behavior as a Function of Its Parameter Values

If a coalition's strategic goal is:	And if its own recent behavior has been:	Then it will view the adversary's accommodative behavior as:
Destruction	Anything	Lax
Expansion	Belligerent	Lax
	Nonbelligerent	Lax or receptive
Consolidation	Anything	Receptive

If a coalition's reflected image and perception of the adversary's goals are respectively:	And if its own recent behavior has been:	Then it will view the adversary's belligerent behavior as:
Expansion and consolidation	Anything	Resistant
Expansion and expansion	Belligerent	Resistant or aggressive
	Nonbelligerent	Aggressive
Consolidation and expansion	Anything	Aggressive

but the link between an interpretation of "resistant" and a response of "conciliatory" requires some brief justification.

A coalition's response to a resistant adversary would seem to depend on its goals as well as on its interpretation of the adversary's behavior. As it happens, however, all goals lead to the same response. If a coalition is bent on exploiting its adversary, it will not find opportunities to do so while the adversary is on guard and resisting. If a coalition is interested in negotiation and mutual accommodation, it will not make progress while the adversary is wary and frightened. Hence, irrespective of a coalition's goals, the appropriate tactic is reassurance via a conciliatory response.

The Issue of Capabilities

The preceding argument (and, indeed, much of Table 4.2) hinges on one crucial assumption: the coalition and its adversary must be roughly equal in strategic capabilities. Clearly, a coalition with unequivocal strategic superiority could ride roughshod over a resisting adversary

Table 4.2

How a Coalition Responds to Different Interpretations of an Adversary's Behavior

If a coalition interprets its adversary's behavior as:	Its tactical objective toward its adversary will be to:	And its response will be:
Aggressive	Resist	Refractory
Resistant	Reassure	Conciliatory
Receptive	Approach	Conciliatory
Lax	Exploit	Refractory
Uninterpretable	Wait	?

and would in no way be constrained by the need to reassure. Similarly, a coalition with an obvious strategic inferiority could not resist an aggressive adversary but would be forced to capitulate. For these reasons we require the assumption of strategic parity. However, we require no assumption of parity in *tactical* capabilities.[8]

By rough strategic parity we mean that neither side can inflict devastating losses on the other with impunity. In general, we feel this assumption is quite justified in the case of the Cold War. Throughout the conflict, the Soviet coalition had the capability of doing severe damage to Western Europe (with the possible exception of the first

[8] Tactical capabilities vary from situation to situation. The West was at a tactical disadvantage in West Berlin, a Western island in its adversary's sea. The Soviet coalition was at a tactical disadvantage in the Caribbean. Clearly, tactical considerations place some important constraints on a coalition's responses. However, we would argue that such constraints are irrelevant to the type of analysis in which we are engaged. Tactical capabilities determine only the content and locus of a response. If a coalition feels its adversary is engaged in aggressive behavior that must be resisted, tactical considerations will in part determine the form this resistance will take. If the perceived aggression occurs in an area where the adversary has a tactical advantage, then the refractory response will be undertaken elsewhere. In other words, the adversary's aggression will be resisted indirectly by means of a counterthreat. For example, although the United States's "quarantine" of Cuba during the 1962 missile crisis placed the Soviet Union at a tactical disadvantage in the Caribbean, the Soviet Union could still have resisted by taking action against West Berlin (indeed, the United States feared just such a response). In short, tactical capabilities determine *where* the resistance will take place; they do not determine *whether* it will take place.

The above argument underscores once again the necessity for assuming rough parity in strategic capabilities. If either coalition could inflict devastating losses on the other with impunity, then the other would have no basis for counterthreat: any tactical "advantage" it might be able to exploit would become essentially meaningless.

year or so, and we shall consider this exception in discussing our results in Chapter Six). Later, with the development of long-range bombers and finally ICBM's, its range extended to the United States as well. The Western coalition, of course, had a similar capability to inflict devastating losses on the Soviet coalition. Neither side destroyed its adversary not because it *could* not do so, but because it *chose* not to do so.

The reasons why both coalitions made this choice are imbedded in the values of the parameters. Some would argue that one or the other coalition was consolidationist, caring only about its own protection and having no desire to destroy the other. Others would argue that one or the other coalition was deterred by the resistance and vigilance of the other. These arguments are the essential subject matter of our study and an analysis of capabilities will not resolve them.

Summarizing the Belief Systems' Predictions

Having outlined our model and discussed some of its underlying assumptions, we can now summarize the predictions of each belief system. Table 4.3 presents such a summary for the seven belief systems that will be tested in this study. It indicates how a coalition with a given set of parameter values ought to respond to each of the nine possible patterns of adversary behavior — both in periods of responder-belligerence and in periods of responder-nonbelligerence. In this table, R means a refractory response, C a conciliatory response, and ? means an indeterminate response to an ambiguous adversary pattern. These ambiguous patterns are the "boundary patterns" for a belief system. Notice that no belief system shifts from a conciliatory to a refractory prediction without moving through such a boundary region of indeterminancy. This keeps the predictions from becoming artificial; we do not force the belief systems to split hairs by making predictions in ambiguous cases. Rather, they are allowed to "pass" on such patterns.

We have omitted from our overview of the model a discussion of several additional assumptions necessary to derive all the predictions in Table 4.3. Specifically, we have not discussed the rules for arriving at an interpretation of balanced behavior, nor have we discussed the boundary conventions that determine the placing of the question marks.[9] However, a different question may be raised. Why do we propose to test only the seven belief systems shown in Table 4.3? In part, this is because our review of the literature indicated that only these be-

---

[9] The complete model or set of rules is included in Appendix C for those readers who wish to know exactly how all the predictions in Table 4.3 were derived.

Table 4.3

A Summary of Predictions for the Seven Belief Systems

PARAMETER VALUES

Response in responder-belligerent periods

Adversary's behavior	DEC	DEE	ECE	EEC	EEE	CCE	CEE
Extremely belligerent	C	R	R	C	R	R	R
Quite belligerent	C	?	R	C	?	R	?
Fairly belligerent	C	C	R	C	C	R	C
Balanced firm	?	?	R	C	C	R	C
Balanced	R	R	R	C	C	R	C
Balanced flexible	R	R	?	?	?	?	C
Fairly accommodative	R	R	R	R	R	C	C
Quite accommodative	R	R	R	R	R	C	C
Extremely accommodative	R	R	R	R	R	C	C

Response in responder-nonbelligerent periods

Adversary's behavior	DEC	DEE	ECE	EEC	EEE	CCE	CEE
Extremely belligerent	C	R	R	C	R	R	R
Quite belligerent	C	R	R	C	R	R	R
Fairly belligerent	C	R	R	C	R	R	R
Balanced firm	?	?	R	C	?	R	?
Balanced	R	R	R	C	C	R	C
Balanced flexible	R	R	?	C	C	?	C
Fairly accommodative	R	R	C	C	C	C	C
Quite accommodative	R	R	?	?	?	C	C
Extremely accommodative	R	R	R	R	R	C	C

lief systems have been proposed as possible explanations of the Cold War. Still, there are twenty-seven possible belief systems (each of the three parameters can take on three different values), and it might seem reasonable to test the remaining twenty possibilities just in case. It turns out, however, that every one of the remaining twenty violates one of two basic requirements for a viable belief system, and such violations make it impossible to derive meaningful predictions.

The two requirements are based on two "facts" about the Cold War interaction. First, each coalition showed, over the years, a mixture of both accommodative and belligerent patterns of behavior. Second, each coalition responded to the other with a mixture of both refractory and conciliatory major actions. We require that a belief system be consistent with these two facts by allowing a coalition to expect a mixture of patterns from its adversary and to respond with a mixture of major actions. Specifically, we require that any belief system about a coalition:

1. Permit that coalition to make sense of — to interpret — *both* the accommodative *and* the belligerent patterns of its adversary.
2. Permit that coalition to respond to its adversary in *both* a refractory *and* a conciliatory manner.

Only the seven belief systems shown in Table 4.3 are consistent with both of these requirements.[10] Thus, it makes good sense that all of the

[10] Nine of the twenty logical possibilities that we exclude are of the type –D–, i.e., they contain a value of destructionist for the reflected image parameter. If a coalition thinks its adversary sees it as destructionist, it can make no sense of this adversary's accommodative behavior. Why should the adversary ever be accommodative toward an enemy that is actively pursuing its destruction? Hence, all nine of these possibilities violate requirement 1.

Six more are of the type – –D, i.e., they assume that the coalition perceives its adversary as destructionist. If a coalition perceives its adversary as destructionist, it should never respond in a conciliatory manner, for, even the most accommodative pattern by such an adversary can only be a ploy. Hence, all six of these logical possibilities violate requirement 2. If a coalition were uncertain about whether the goals of its adversary were *really* destructionist, it might make sense for it to risk an occasional conciliatory response. Such a policy amounts to an implicit belief that the adversary may be merely expansionist and therefore receptive to some compromise on outstanding disagreements. But this implies a – –E belief system, a type not excluded by our rules. Conciliatory responses simply make no sense if the coalition is certain that its adversary is destructionist.

Of the remaining five possibilities, three are of the type –CC, i.e., they assume that the coalition believes it is perceived as consolidationist by its adversary and that it perceives its adversary as consolidationist. Such an assumption makes many views of the Cold War found in the literature can be comfortably accommodated by one or more of these seven.

SIMILARITIES AND DIFFERENCES
AMONG THE BELIEF SYSTEMS' PREDICTIONS

How different are the predictions generated by the seven belief systems? Table 4.3 provides the basis for answering this question. For each pair of belief systems we can compute a *coefficient of similarity:* the number of prediction cells on which the pair agrees, minus the number on which the pair disagrees, divided by the total number of cells. This coefficient will range from -1.00 to $+1.00$, with higher positive values indicating greater similarity and higher negative values indicating greater disparity. For example, the pair of belief systems DEC and CCE make identical predictions in only two cells, opposite predictions in twelve cells, and one or the other passes while the other does not in four cells. Hence, their coefficient of similarity is $-10/18 = -.56$, indicating considerable disparity.

Note that this method of assessing similarity weighs every prediction cell equally. In point of fact, our data on the Cold War indicate that the various patterns of adversary behavior do not occur with anything like equal frequency. To the extent that two belief systems happen to agree on higher frequency patterns, their predictions about the Cold War interaction will be more similar than would be expected from their coefficient of similarity. The opposite holds true for belief systems that happen to disagree on high frequency patterns. In this section, however, we are not so much interested in how the belief systems differ in practice — we can discover that directly from our data — as we are in how they differ in theory. To this end, the coefficient

---

it impossible for the coalition to interpret its adversary's belligerent behavior. Why should an adversary that is itself concerned with only consolidating its present position ever need to be belligerent toward a coalition that it believes has no wish to challenge it? Such belligerence cannot be seen as aggressive or resistant and, hence, it is uninterpretable. Thus, all three of these possible belief systems violate requirement 1.

Only two possibilities remain: DCE and CEC. Both of these are more reasonable than the preceding eighteen in the sense that they lead to distinct and meaningful interpretations of an adversary's belligerent, balanced, and accommodative behavior. Despite this, both belief systems run afoul of requirement 2. A coalition with DCE parameter values will always respond to its adversary in a refractory manner, while a coalition with CEC parameter values will always respond in a conciliatory manner. The reader can easily verify that this is the case when the adversary is either belligerent or accommodative by examining Tables 4.1 and 4.2. An examination of Tables C.3 and C.4 (Appendix C) in combination with Table 4.2 will verify the argument for balanced behavior as well.

Table 4.4

Coefficients of Similarity between the Belief Systems

Belief system	DEC	DEE	ECE	EEC	EEE	CCE
DEE	+.50					
ECE	−.06	+.45				
EEC	+.33	−.17	−.17			
EEE	−.11	+.39	+.39	+.45		
CCE	−.56	−.06	+.50	−.67	−.11	
CEE	−.67	−.17	−.17	−.11	+.45	+.33

of similarity is a useful tool; it indicates how much alike belief systems are over the entire range of adversary behavior.

Table 4.4 shows the coefficients of similarity for every pair of belief systems. As may be seen, ECE/CCE and DEC/DEE are the most similar pairs, and EEC/CCE and DEC/CEE are the most discrepant pairs. EEE, having positive coefficients with four of the others and slight negative coefficients with only two, is the most "central" belief system.

These results point to an important principle: discrepancy in parameter values is not necessarily equivalent to discrepancy in predictions. (The converse is also true.) For example, DEC and CCE have the most nearly opposite parameter values, but they do not make the most discrepant predictions. Both agree that balanced behavior should bring a refractory response; the former because it views such behavior as lax, the latter because it views such behavior as threatening. Thus, different orientations reflected in the parameter values can lead to the same behavioral response.

Table 4.4 answers the question of differences in predictions posed at the beginning of this section, but it does not provide much of an overall picture. Why are some pairs of belief systems more dissimilar than others? Are there any basic, underlying dimensions that can be used to understand the differences?

To answer these questions we need to translate the coefficients of similarity into distance relations. Similarity can then be depicted as proximity in an n-dimensional space. The method we use to achieve this transformation is nonmetric, i.e., it seeks to preserve only the *rank order* of the similarities among belief systems.[11] Actually, more than two dimensions are required to satisfy simultaneously all the

[11] The computational procedure is a variant of the one developed by Coombs (1964) for "nonmetric multidimensional psychological scaling."

distance relations contained in Table 4.4, but two dimensions are quite sufficient to arrive at a general picture.

This picture is presented in Chart 4.1. Notice that two "belief systems" that were excluded from our study are entered in this chart. One (DCE) was excluded because it makes only refractory predictions; the other (CEC) was excluded because it makes only conciliatory predictions. Although of little value in understanding the Cold War, they help to clarify the space depicted in the chart.

As may be seen, two sets of orthogonal dimensions can be used to organize the space. Along the x-axis, the belief systems project in order from –CE to –EE to –EC. Clearly, this represents a dimension of "perceived threat," with –CE coalitions feeling most threatened (they perceive their adversary as expansionist and believe they are seen as consolidationist). Along the y-axis, the belief systems project in order from C–– to E–– to D––. Clearly, this represents a dimension of "exploitativeness" with D–– coalitions being the most exploitative (they always seek to take advantage of an adversary's accommodative behavior).

The x and y axes can be used to define two other orthogonal dimensions: a dimension of "refractoriness" (upper-right to lower-left) and a dimension of "offensiveness" (upper-left to lower-right). In the lower-left quadrant, then, coalitions are predominantly refractory because they both exploit and feel threatened. In the lower-right quadrant, coalitions are less refractory because they feel less threatened — they can afford to use concessions to lower the opponent's guard. Coalitions

Chart 4.1
Similarity among the Belief Systems Depicted as Spatial Proximity

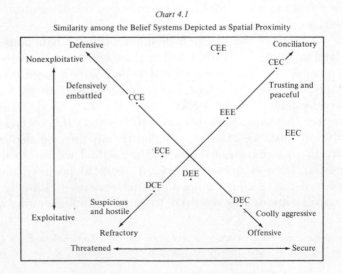

in the upper-right are predominantly conciliatory because they neither exploit nor feel threatened. Finally, coalitions in the upper-left are less conciliatory because they feel more threatened — they must use refractory actions to repel perceived aggression.

These, then, are the major dimensions that underlie the belief system predictions. These dimensions also give some insight into the total theories of the Cold War presented in Chapter Three. From the official Soviet and Western views of the Cold War, we can see that each side tended to see itself in the upper-left region (as nonexploitative and threatened) and its opponent toward the lower-right region (as more exploitative and secure). Hence, although both coalitions may have engaged in the same amount of refractory behavior, each attributed the opponent's behavior to motives other than its own. Right-wing critics of Western policy tend to further exaggerate the discrepancy, while left-wing critics tend to minimize or reverse it.

SIMPLIFICATION AND OVERSIMPLIFICATION

To evaluate different belief systems about the Cold War, we employ a large number of simplifying assumptions. It is not difficult to think of exceptions to many of them, and some readers might be tempted to reject our whole effort on the grounds that our model is oversimplified. We claim that it is not and that it is necessary for any critic to keep clearly in mind the distinction between useful simplification and oversimplification.

Useful simplifying assumptions meet three criteria:

1. They are unbiased.
2. They are not incorrect.
3. They are meaningful.

One may properly attack simplifying assumptions on the grounds of bias. Bias in this instance means that the assumption favors one belief system more than another, and if one finds results favorable to such a belief system, it may be because of this intrinsic bias rather than the greater worthiness of the successful belief system.

We have tried to make our simplifying assumptions unbiased with respect to the seven belief systems — that is, we claim that they do not help or hinder one belief system more than any other. A challenge to this claim can be checked and evaluated in most cases. We have made numerous such checks for bias and have, in the course of our research, changed some assumptions and coding rules to remove what we feared might be sources of bias. In many cases, we kept rules where the problem of bias proved insignificant because the questionable situation occurred rarely or affected all belief systems in an identical fashion.

Our major point here is that it is incumbent upon anyone who would attack a simplifying assumption as biased to indicate the way in which this bias might work to the advantage or disadvantage of one or more belief systems.

One may also attack simplifying assumptions on the grounds that they are incorrect. It is important to recognize that we make no claim that the assumptions are *always* correct. Thus, it is irrelevant to indicate known exceptions unless it is claimed that these exceptions are in fact more common than the assumption itself. This point may be illustrated by the assumption from Table 4.2 that a coalition will resist when it interprets its adversary's behavior as aggressive. Perhaps because of absorption in domestic concerns, a coalition might not resist on some occasions. But to claim the assumption is incorrect implies that there is no *tendency* for a coalition to resist what it perceives as aggression.

Finally, one may attack simplifying assumptions on the grounds that they are meaningless. The assumptions may not be biased or incorrect, but they may be trivial because they capture so little of reality or useless because their tendency to be right is so weak and marginal. The test of the claim that the simplifying assumptions described here are meaningful can be found only in the results of our analysis. If the assumptions, taken as a set, are meaningless and trivial then we should find no systematic differences among our belief systems in their ability to predict the Cold War interaction units. *Meaningless assumptions produce random results.* On this issue, the only proper posture toward our research strategy at this point is one of suspended judgment. And if we show that some belief systems can, with the assumptions made here, successfully explain the Cold War interaction, then our simplifying assumptions cannot be meaningless.[12]

---

[12] A charge of bias would still be quite legitimate but, as we argued above, the specific way in which the bias might have produced the results must be indicated.

Chapter Five

TESTING THE BELIEF SYSTEMS

A brief inventory is in order. In Chapter Two, we described the interaction units that any theory of the Cold War must explain. In Chapter Three, we reviewed and categorized rival belief systems about the values of certain basic parameters of the Soviet and Western coalitions. Each of seven different belief systems, together with a decision model (described in Chapter Four), yields a unique set of predictions.

We are ready to confront these predictions with our historical data on the interaction units that comprise the Cold War. Recall that every interaction unit is an ordered pair: a pattern of behavior by one coalition (which can range from extremely belligerent to extremely accommodative) followed by a single major action by the other coalition (which can be either refractory or conciliatory). Appendix E lists the 125 major actions that constitute the second part of our interaction units. Sixty-three of these are Soviet actions (60 percent refractory, 40 percent conciliatory) and 62 are Western actions (71 percent refractory, 29 percent conciliatory). Appendix F presents the belligerent-accommodative scores that constitute the first half of our interaction units. It shows that Western behavior prior to the major Soviet actions was belligerent 21 percent of the time, balanced 59 percent of the time, and accommodative 13 percent of the time, and that Soviet behavior prior to the major Western actions was belligerent 26 percent of the time, balanced 52 percent of the time, and accommodative 21 percent of the time.[1]

If a theory of the Cold War is any good, it ought to be able to tell us how the behavior of each coalition is related to the response of its adversary. It has 125 opportunities to do so. These 125 include 63 chances for a theory to test its assumptions about Soviet parameters by predicting Soviet responses to Western patterns, and 62 similar

[1] The prior behavior of the coalitions was "inconsistent" about 5 percent of the time. Inconsistent patterns are defined in Appendix A, p. 147.

chances for a theory to test its assumptions about Western parameters by predicting Western responses to Soviet patterns.

Each belief system confronts the same data. The most satisfactory way of evaluating its relative success is the simplest one: comparison of belief systems based on their number of correct predictions. The use of success rate, or percentage of correct predictions, as our basic measure makes the analysis that follows very straightforward. We take up in turn the separate tests of Soviet and Western belief systems.

TESTING THE SOVIET PARAMETERS

Table 5.1 shows the distribution of the 63 interaction units that are relevant to testing belief systems about the Soviet parameters. It combines the summary of predictions (Table 4.3, p. 66) with our actual empirical data on the interaction units. It tells us, for example, that following the 13 periods in which Western behavior was balanced flexible, the Soviet coalition was refractory 8 times and conciliatory 5 times. We can also discover by a glance at the prediction columns that (in responder-nonbelligerent periods) two belief systems expect refractory responses to this pattern (DEC and DEE), three expect a conciliatory response (EEC, EEE, and CEE), and two make no prediction (ECE and CCE).

Table 5.1, then, provides the basic data from which we can calculate overall success rates. Table 5.2 presents these calculations, and we can see that there are substantial differences in the relative success of rival belief systems. The belief system CCE — the view that the Soviet coalition was consolidationist, believed it was perceived as such, and saw the West as expansionist — scores highest at 73 percent. Just behind this at 69 percent is the belief system ECE which shares the final two parameter values but specifies an expansionist Soviet coalition. At the other extreme are the two belief systems closest to official American thinking about the Cold War — EEE and EEC. These belief systems differ from each other only in whether they think the Soviet coalition perceives the West as expansionist or consolidationist but they both trail all others with success rates of 37 percent and 36 percent respectively.[2]

Before we can simply award the honors to CCE and close the book on this half of the story, three possibilities must be considered.

[2] It is worth noting that there are no meaningful differences in success rates in responder-belligerent and responder-nonbelligerent periods. CCE, for example, scores 67 percent in one situation and 76 percent in the other; ECE scores 67 percent and 70 percent respectively. No other belief system scores above 54 percent in either responder belligerent or responder-nonbelligerent periods.

Table 5.1

Summary of Interaction Units for Testing Belief Systems about Soviet Parameters

	RESPONDER-BELLIGERENT PERIODS				RESPONDER-NONBELLIGERENT PERIODS			
	Predictions	Soviet responses			Predictions	Soviet responses		
Western patterns	D D E E E C C / E E C E E C E / C E E C E E E	Re-fractory	Con-ciliatory	Total	D D E E E C C / E E C E E C E / C E E C E E E	Re-fractory	Con-ciliatory	Total
Extremely belligerent	C R R C R R R	2	4	6	C R R C R R R	1	1[a]	2
Quite belligerent	C - R C - R -	2	0	2	C R R C R R R	0	0	0
Fairly belligerent	C C R C C R C	2	1	3	C R R C R R R	0	0	0
Balanced firm	- - R C C R C	2	0	2	- - R C - R -	10	3	13
Balanced	R R R C C R C	2	0	2	R R R C C R C	5	2	7
Balanced flexible	R R - - - - C	0	0	0	R R - C C - C	8	5	13
Fairly accommodative	R R R R R C C	0	0	0	R R C C C C C	1	5	6
Quite accommodative	R R R R R C C	0	0	0	R R - - C C	0	0	0
Extremely accommodative	R R R R R C C	0	0	0	R R R R R C C	0	2	2
Inconsistent		1	1	2		2	1	3
Total		11	6	17		27	19[a]	46

[a]This cell contains an interaction unit occurring in a responder-inconsistent period. Since all belief systems make identical predictions for the two types of responder period, this unit is placed in the responder-nonbelligerent category for convenience.

Table 5.2

Overall Success Rates for Belief Systems
about Soviet Parameters

Belief system	Number of predictions[a]	Number of correct predictions	Success rate[b]
CCE	45	33	73%
ECE	45	31	69
DEC	43	22	51
DEE	41	20	49
CEE	43	18	42
EEE	43	16	37
EEC	58	21	36

[a]*Excluding passes.*
[b]*Percentage of predictions correct.*

Random Factors

First, there is the factor of luck: perhaps CCE is favored by random error. We have granted the fact that Soviet responses are influenced by things other than Western behavior and the parameters included in the belief systems. These responses may be influenced, for example, by internal conflict in the Soviet coalition. There is no a priori reason to suspect that such factors will affect the success rates of the belief systems *differentially* but we cannot automatically exclude the possibility that their effects just happened to accumulate in favor of CCE.

How can we determine whether or not a success rate of 73 percent is due simply to luck? We cannot use conventional statistical tests. The random error of which we speak is not a sampling error since we claim to have the entire universe of major Soviet actions from 1946 to 1963. Moreover, there is no stochastic error in predictions — if the 63 interaction units were resubmitted to the belief systems a second time, they would make identical predictions. While we cannot say absolutely whether or not a belief system was lucky, we can ask a related question.

Imagine a simple-minded belief system that makes predictions by flipping a fair coin. Heads predict that the major Soviet action will be conciliatory, and tails predict it will be refractory. Certainly, before concluding that a belief system was adequate, we would want to know that it performed better than this. Thus we can ask what the probability is that a coin-flipper would obtain a success rate as high or higher than that obtained by each of the belief systems. Because the coin-flipper has a stochastic element built into its predictions, this is an answerable question.[3]

The answer is flattering only for CCE and ECE. A coin-flipper could be expected to equal or surpass them only once in a thousand tries and five times in a thousand tries respectively. For the rest of the belief systems, the coin-flipper would do better in predicting Soviet behavior most of the time. The probability figures for all seven belief systems are given in Table 5.3.

We suggested earlier that EEC and EEE are most characteristic of the official American theory of the Cold War. If this is true, we are tempted to conclude that the United States government could have been spared much anguish and expense in predicting Soviet behavior if they had, in 1946, simply replaced the State Department with a shiny quarter.

Table 5.3

Probabilities That a Coin-Flipper Would Equal or Surpass Belief System Success Rates

Belief system	Success rate[a]	Probability
CCE	73%	.001
ECE	69	.005
DEC	51	.50
DEE	49	.56
CEE	42	.86
EEE	37	.95
EEC	36	.97

[a]*These figures are repeated from Table 5.2 for convenience.*

[3] The probability (*P*) is given by the binominal formula:

$$P = \sum_{x=c}^{n} \binom{n}{c} (.5)^x (1 - .5)^{n-x}$$

where n is the total number of predictions made by the belief system and c is its number of correct predictions. Success rate is c/n. The expected value of the coin-flipper's success rate is .50. When n is large (>25), P may be accurately approximated from tables of the normal distribution where

$$z = \frac{c - .5n}{\sqrt{n(.5)(1 - .5)}}$$

is normally distributed with a mean of zero and a standard deviation of one (Siegel, 1956, p. 40).

Range of Success

The greater success rates of CCE and ECE are not likely due to luck, but perhaps their success is more limited than it appears. Each belief system must make predictions for a whole range of patterns of Western behavior. Yet Table 5.1 indicates that certain predictions — those corresponding to the high frequency patterns — are contributing disproportionately to success rates. For example, the balanced-firm pattern is one of the most frequent Western patterns, and the Soviet response to it tends to be heavily refractory. As it happens, only CCE and ECE correctly predict this outcome. Of course, they deserve credit for this, but we would feel more confident if we knew they were making correct predictions across the board rather than only in two or three such high-frequency prediction cells.

To investigate this problem, we use a second measure of success rate — one that gives equal weight to every prediction cell regardless of the number of cases it contains. Here, we ask not how often a belief system makes correct predictions but how often it can successfully predict the trend in each cell. In other words, how often can it successfully predict the prevailing Soviet response to each different pattern of Western behavior? Of the eighteen prediction cells in Table 5.1, seven are empty while ten show either a refractory or conciliatory trend. Since each of these ten contributes only one success or failure in this analysis, a belief system can obtain a high score only if it correctly predicts the prevailing responses to a wide range of patterns.

Table 5.4 contains the results of this analysis. Clearly CCE and ECE maintain their superiority at 88 percent and 78 percent respectively. Our coin-flipper would do as well as or better than CCE only about 2 percent of the time. Success cannot be explained by the limited contribution of a few patterns; in fact, the rank order among the belief systems remains virtually unchanged from Table 5.2.

Outside Help

A third argument against the relative success of CCE and ECE is an extremely important and subtle one. We considered above the possible effect of a variety of external factors affecting Soviet behavior other than the Soviet parameters and the preceding behavior of its adversary. These were considered "random" in the sense that there was no reason to think that they should help or hurt one belief system more than another.

However, the following closely related argument might be made by a partisan of, for example, EEE: "Although I had only 37 percent correct, I am actually doing better than CCE did with its 73 percent.

Table 5.4

Success Rates for Belief Systems about Soviet Parameters
for Pattern Trends

Belief system	Pattern trends to be predicted[a]	Number of correct pattern trends	Success rate	Probability[b]
CCE	9	8	88%	.02
ECE	9	7	78	.09
DEC	8	4	50	.64
DEE	7	3	43	.77
CEE	8	2	25	.96
EEC	10	2	20	.99
EEE	8	1	12	.996

[a]*Entries vary in magnitude because some belief systems pass on certain patterns.*
[b]*Probability that a coin-flipper would do as well or better.*

The analysis fails to reveal my superiority because the Soviet coalition was responding to some factor that is quite independent of Western behavior. This factor (for example, the Chinese challenge for leadership of the coalition), was *not* random but caused the Soviet Union to engage in many more major refractory actions than it would have if it had only been responding to Western action. CCE just happens to make a large number of refractory predictions and, thus, is able to capitalize on this outside refractory force to gain a grossly inflated success rate. My belief system, on the other hand, is hurt by such an outside influence."

If the above argument is valid, then *all* of the following things must be true:

1. The Soviet coalition must have engaged in a higher proportion of major refractory actions than EEE predicted. If this were not so, an advocate of EEE could not validly claim the existence of some outside refractory force.
2. EEE must have a higher success rate with its refractory predictions than with its conciliatory predictions. This must be so because, if some outside refractory force existed, it would only hurt conciliatory predictions while aiding or making refractory ones more certain.
3. EEE must have a higher success rate with its conciliatory predictions than its rival CCE has with its conciliatory predictions. If an external refractory force is upsetting conciliatory

predictions, it is a handicap that affects all belief systems. CCE may have fewer errors on conciliatory predictions simply because it makes fewer such predictions. But if the predictions it does make are really of poorer quality, then a larger *proportion* of them should prove wrong. Thus, if we compare belief systems only on conciliatory predictions, the effects of the hypothesized external influence are controlled and the underlying superiority of EEE should be visible.

4. EEE must have a higher success rate with its refractory predictions than CCE has with its refractory predictions. This follows from the previous reasoning. Here, the outside force should help all belief systems. While CCE may have a larger *number* of correct refractory predictions simply because it makes more of them, *proportionally* it should still lag behind EEE's less frequent but higher quality predictions.

For simplicity in presentation, we have stated the argument in terms of an external refractory force and a comparison between EEE and CCE. It applies equally, with appropriate adjustments, of course, to a hypothesized external conciliatory force as well and to comparisons between the success rates of any pair of belief systems. To explore the possibility in general, we must examine the success rates separately for refractory and conciliatory predictions for all belief systems (see Table 5.5).

How does the argument for EEE fare on our four criteria? EEE makes only ten refractory predictions, but the Soviet coalition engaged in thirty-eight major refractory actions. Thus, the first criterion is clearly met. However, EEE does even more poorly with its refractory predictions (30 percent) than with its conciliatory ones (39 percent). Thus, the argument already fails on the second criterion. This is sufficient, but it also fails on the third and fourth criteria: CCE scores 70 percent and 88 percent respectively against EEE's scores of 30 percent and 39 percent.

It is easy to see from Table 5.5 that no belief system could successfully maintain the external factor argument against CCE since this belief system is highest on both conciliatory and refractory predictions. In fact, the argument cannot be true for any comparison in Table 5.5 since the rank order for success on refractory predictions is the same as for overall success. This means that any comparison will necessarily fail on the fourth criterion.

Even if all four criteria are met, we cannot conclude that an external force is distorting the real success of the different belief systems. All that is established in such an event is the logical possibility or

Table 5.5

Success Rates for Refractory and Conciliatory Predictions
for Belief Systems about Soviet Parameters

Belief system	REFRACTORY PREDICTIONS			CONCILIATORY PREDICTIONS		
	Number of predictions	*Number of correct predictions*	*Success rate*	*Number of predictions*	*Number of correct predictions*	*Success rate*
CCE	37	26	70%	8	7	88%
ECE	39	26	67	6	5	83
DEC	30	16	53	13	6	46
DEE	38	19	50	3	1	33
CEE	8	3	38	35	15	43
EEE	10	3	30	33	13	39
EEC	2	0	0	56	21	38

plausibility of such a force. In this instance, an external force cannot even plausibly account for the greater success rate of CCE.[4]

Interpreting the Results

The superior performance of CCE does not seem to be due to an artifact. What, then, can we conclude about the values of Soviet parameters? Were they indeed predominantly CCE throughout the Cold War? What do we make of the fact that another belief system, ECE, performed nearly as well despite its different assumptions about the crucial Soviet goal parameter? Evidently, we can be reasonably confident about the second and third parameters: both of our leading belief systems agree on the values –CE. But what of the first parameter?

To pursue these questions, we make use of a property of the belief systems that was elaborated in Chapter Four — a property that links particular parameters to particular predictions. Essentially, the first or goal parameter is critical for predicting how a coalition will respond to its adversary's accommodative behavior; the second and third parameters are critical in predicting how a coalition will respond to its adversary's belligerent behavior; and all three parameters are important in the case of balanced behavior. Hence, if we break the predictions down by pattern of Western behavior, we gain more precise information about the role of individual parameters.

The breakdown is presented in Table 5.6. As expected, CCE and ECE hold a clear edge on belligerent and balanced patterns where the second and third parameters are critical to prediction. However, on accommodative patterns, CCE and CEE hold the edge. In other words, the two belief systems that share the assumption of Soviet consolidationist goals do best on those very patterns for which the goal parameter is crucial to prediction. This is the only point at which ECE diverges from CCE in its predictions, and it does so to its disadvantage.

A word of caution is in order here. There are only two interaction units about which CCE and ECE make different predictions. (Thus, we are clearly on much firmer ground in drawing conclusions about the second and third parameters about which the two most successful belief systems agree.) Although two in number, the cases are still quite suggestive about goals. They represent the two most extremely accommodative patterns in which the West engaged in the entire

[4] The effect of other factors besides the parameters is a complicated one and we will return to the same issue again in subsequent chapters. At this point, we merely wish to establish the fact that such external factors cannot account for the differential success rates of the belief systems.

Table 5.6

Success Rates for Belief Systems about Soviet Parameters by Type of Western Patterns

Belief system	BELLIGERENT PATTERNS			BALANCED PATTERNS			ACCOMMODATIVE PATTERNS		
	Number of predictions	*Number of correct predictions*	*Success rate*	*Number of predictions*	*Number of correct predictions*	*Success rate*	*Number of predictions*	*Number of correct predictions*	*Success rate*
CCE	13	7	54%	24	19	79%	8	7	88%
ECE	13	7	54	24	19	79	8	5	62
DEC	13	6	46	22	15	68	8	1	12
DEE	11	4	36	22	15	68	8	1	12
CEE	11	4	36	24	7	29	8	7	88
EEE	11	4	36	24	7	29	8	5	62
EEC	13	6	46	37	10	27	8	5	62

eighteen-year period. If an expansionist Soviet coalition had been
looking for an opportunity to exploit its adversary, it would have had
few better opportunities. Instead, it chose to respond in each case
with a major conciliatory action as one would expect of a consolidationist power.

We can tentatively conclude that *the Soviet coalition thought that
it was perceived as consolidationist and saw the West as expansionist;*
that *Soviet goals were clearly not destructionist;* and finally, and more
tentatively, that the few cases that bear on the matter suggest that
Soviet goals were consolidationist rather than expansionist.

There is much to gain by looking at the interaction units in a more
fine-grained manner, particularly with an eye to identifying possible
shifts in parameters over the eighteen-year period. But before turning
to this more detailed analysis in the chapter that follows, we will examine the other half of our interaction units to complete the general
picture.

TESTING THE WESTERN PARAMETERS

Table 5.7 shows the distribution of the 62 relevant interaction units;
from it we can calculate the overall success rates presented in Table
5.8. Again there are substantial differences in success and they are not
unlike those that occurred for the belief systems about Soviet parameters. The view that the West is consolidationist, believes it is seen
this way, and sees its adversary as expansionist (CCE) tops all others
with an impressive 82 percent, followed closely by ECE with 78 percent. The official Soviet view of the West (EEC), like its counterpart
in Washington, finishes last with a dismal success rate of 24 percent.[5]

As before, certain prediction cells contribute greatly to success rates.
Of the twenty-two cases in which Soviet behavior was balanced, the
West responded with a refractory action in all except three. We need
to be reassured that the success rates in Table 5.8 reflect across-the-
board performance. Table 5.9 provides the answer.

This time, the overall rank order is altered somewhat but not at all
to the disadvantage of the leader CCE. This redoubtable belief system
gets every one of its predicted trends correct — a feat that our coin-
flipper could be expected to duplicate slightly better than once in
10,000 tries. The most significant alterations from Table 5.8 are the
rise of CEE and the decline of DEE and DEC, but especially the
latter. DEC manages an overall success rate of 49 percent mainly by

---

[5] Again there are no meaningful differences between responder-belligerent and
responder-nonbelligerent success rates. CCE manages 82 percent in both types and
ECE scores 76 percent and 79 percent respectively.

Table 5.7

Summary of Interaction Units for Testing Belief Systems about Western Parameters

	RESPONDER-BELLIGERENT PERIODS				RESPONDER-NONBELLIGERENT PERIODS			
	Predictions	Western responses			Predictions	Western responses		
Soviet patterns	D E C / D E E / E C E / E E E / C C E / C E E	Re-fractory	Con-ciliatory	Total	D E C / D E E / E C E / E E E / C C E / C E E	Re-fractory	Con-ciliatory	Total
Extremely belligerent	C R C R R R	3	2	5	C R R C R R R	1	1[a]	2
Quite belligerent	C – R C – R –	1	0	1	C R R C R R R	1	0	1
Fairly belligerent	C C R C C R C	5	0	5	C R R C R R R	2	0	2
Balanced firm	– – R C C R C	2	0	2	– – R C – R –	4	0	4
Balanced	R R R C C R C	2	1	3	R R R C C C R C	17	2	19
Balanced flexible	R R – – – – C	0	0	0	R R – C C – C	1	3	4
Fairly accommodative	R R R R R C C	0	0	0	R R C C C C C	4	5	9
Quite accommodative	R R R R R C C	0	0	0	R R – – C C	0	2[a]	2
Extremely accommodative	R R R R R C C	0	1	1	R R R R R C C	0	1	1
Inconsistent		1	0	1		0	0	0
Total		14	4	18		30	14	44

[a] This cell contains an interaction unit occurring in a responder-inconsistent period. For all practical purposes, it can be treated as occurring in a responder-nonbelligerent period. The reason for this is that in the cases where this occurs, either a belief system makes identical predictions for both types of periods, or it passes in the responder-nonbelligerent case anyway.

Table 5.8

Overall Success Rates for Belief Systems about Western Parameters

Belief system	Number of predictions	Number of correct predictions	Success rate	Probability[a]
CCE	57	47	82%	<.001
ECE	55	43	78	<.001
DEE	54	31	57	.138
DEC	55	27	49	.556
CEE	56	22	39	.945
EEE	54	18	33	.992
EEC	59	14	24	>.999

[a]*We refer again to the probability that a coin-flipper would do as well or better.*

Table 5.9

Success Rates for Belief Systems about Western Parameters for Pattern Trends

Belief system	Pattern trends to be predicted	Number of correct pattern trends	Success rate	Probability
CCE	13	13	100%	.0001
ECE	12	10	83	.02
CEE	12	8	67	.19
EEE	11	5	45	.73
DEE	11	5	45	.73
DEC	12	2	17	.997
EEC	13	2	15	.998

getting the high-frequency balanced pattern correct. On virtually every other pattern, it does poorly.

Finally, we must examine refractory and conciliatory predictions separately to see if CCE's advantage can be attributed to some systematic outside force. Table 5.10 indicates that it clearly cannot. CCE and ECE continue to rank first and second on both refractory and conciliatory predictions.

There are additional points worth noting about Table 5.10. The fact that almost all belief systems have higher rates on refractory than conciliatory predictions suggests the possibility that some external

Table 5.10

Success Rates for Refractory and Conciliatory Predictions for Belief Systems about Western Parameters

Belief system	REFRACTORY PREDICTIONS			CONCILIATORY PREDICTIONS		
	Number of predictions	*Number of correct predictions*	*Success rate*	*Number of predictions*	*Number of correct predictions*	*Success rate*
CCE	44	38	86%	13	9	69%
ECE	46	38	83	9	5	56
CEE	10	7	70	46	15	33
DEE	49	31	63	5	0	0
DEC	39	24	62	16	3	19
EEE	12	7	58	42	11	26
EEC	2	0	0	57	14	25

refractory force might indeed be operating. It might account for the fact that in overall success rate DEC scores above CEE. In this comparison, CEE can meet all four of the criteria and can quite plausibly contend that it is doing better than either DEC or DEE. However, no belief system can maintain this argument against the two leaders.

Interpreting the Results

Again we wish to know which parameters are contributing to the success or failure of a given belief system. A sense of this is gained by examining success rates separately for belligerent, balanced, and accommodative patterns. This is done in Table 5.11. As before, only CCE is superior on all three types; on accommodative patterns CCE scores 69 percent against 45 percent for its rival ECE. CEE, the only other belief system that assumes Western consolidationist goals, shares the success of CCE in accommodative patterns.

The earlier discussion of Soviet parameters applies to Western parameters as well: we are on firmer ground drawing conclusions about the second and third parameters on which CCE and ECE agree. In this case, there are only four points at which CCE and ECE diverge. In each of these four, CCE makes a correct prediction while ECE is wrong twice and makes no prediction on the other two. Once again, these cases represent the most accommodative of all Soviet patterns. If the West was expansionist, we must ask why it chose to ignore its four best opportunities and, instead, responded with a major conciliatory action in each case.

In general, we conclude that *the Western coalition thought that it was perceived as consolidationist and saw the Soviet coalition as expansionist*. The few cases that bear on the matter suggest that *Western goals were consolidationist rather than expansionist and were definitely not destructionist*.

A Caveat

In suggesting that both the Western and Soviet coalitions were consolidationist, we are not making a judgment about their general virtue. Both sides may well have been involved in a "quiet expansionism" that increased their influence over third parties without increasing disagreements among themselves. Military and technical assistance, trade agreements, and foreign investments are potential vehicles for increasing influence. Whether such activities represent "expansion" is a matter of contention: some observers view foreign investment as imperialism, and technical assistance "to promote economic development" as a foothold for subversion. But whether one sees such activities as benign or malignant, the fact is that they elude our net.

Table 5.11
Success Rates for Belief Systems about Western Parameters
by Type of Soviet Pattern

Belief system	BELLIGERENT PATTERNS			BALANCED PATTERNS			ACCOMMODATIVE PATTERNS		
	Number of predictions	Number of correct predictions	Success rate	Number of predictions	Number of correct predictions	Success rate	Number of predictions	Number of correct predictions	Success rate
CCE	16	13	81%	28	25	89%	13	9	69%
ECE	16	13	81	28	25	89	11	5	45
DEE	15	7	47	26	20	77	13	4	31
DEC	16	3	19	26	20	77	13	4	31
CEE	15	7	47	28	6	21	13	9	69
EEE	15	7	47	28	6	21	11	5	45
EEC	16	3	19	32	6	19	11	5	45

The type of expansion we are geared to assess is an expansion that creates disagreements with the adversary. In other words, it is an expansion that proceeds through refractory activities. But the activities noted above typically involve some reciprocal agreement with the government of a third party and, as such, leave the adversary with little grounds for voicing an objection. Of course, if the adversary does challenge them, they become refractory actions and we then pick them up. More often than not, they proceed quietly precisely because the adversary, unable to do anything effective about them, chooses to remain silent.

Furthermore, activities associated with foreign aid are usually not tactically contingent in nature. Because such activities are unlikely to draw a reaction, a coalition can implement them without worrying about its adversary. Hence, we would not expect these activities to have any regular association with the behavior of an adversary.

In short, to assess the role of "quiet expansionism" would require a very different study from the one we have undertaken.[6] We reserve judgment for this reason and not because we belittle its potential significance. Certainly, the results of our own study should not be over-interpreted to imply the absence of overt or covert efforts by either coalition to extend its influence through non-conflict-producing means.

CONCLUSION

Most American international relations specialists take a highly skeptical view of the contributions of writers such as Charles Osgood and Erich Fromm. For those within the ambience of realpolitik, these psychologists, with their emphasis on misunderstanding and distrust, seem naive. But naiveté is double-edged. We all know the fable of the child who was insufficiently socialized to accept the "reality" of the emperor's "invisible" gown. Most fields have their intellectual blinders, and it may turn out that some of the assumptions about the Cold War, shared by the editors and readers of *Foreign Affairs*, have turned out to be handicaps in understanding events.

At least, this is what our results seem to suggest. Mutual misunderstanding and misperception were apparently an important part of the dynamics of this hostile interaction. They are not simply an additional

---

[6] Basically, such a study would entail examining the "control implications" of different forms of aid, trade, and investment. From the perspective of our own study, these implications might shed some light on the terrain of East-West interaction. For example, it might help to explain why certain countries join, and remain within, a particular coalition. Or, it might help to explain why certain countries are prone to revolutionary upheavals that become breeding grounds for East-West conflict.

consideration to provide a more complete picture of the essential conflict between a consolidationist West and its aggressive challenger.

But we do not mean to make this a contest between psychologists on the one hand and political scientists and historians on the other. Many things written on the Cold War by psychologists probably *are* naive, and nonpsychologists such as D. F. Fleming and Fred Warner Neal have emphasized the kind of theory of the Cold War suggested by our data. Increasingly, more orthodox writers such as Marshall Shulman are attempting to qualify and modify any simple belief in Soviet expansionism as the cause of the Cold War.

Some observers of the Cold War, by training or disposition, are predisposed to look for mutual insecurity as a root cause of conflict. Perhaps this disposition provides them with a distant early warning system, enabling them to react to clues in Soviet-Western conflict to which other observers are insensitive. Call it luck, then, that their favorite explanatory tools happen to work so well in this case.

Additional analysis of our data in the next few chapters will invariably complicate our conclusions. Furthermore, we recognize that our interaction units will not be universally accepted as the last word and ultimate test of a theory of the Cold War. But if one accepts them as a reasonable test, he must grant that the overall results are well explained by Fromm when he writes that the "fear of a Western alliance against the Soviets had always dominated Stalin's mind. . . . On the other hand, the West was always suspicious of Russian schemes for world revolutionary conquests. . . . Thus, based on mutual suspicions, which were mainly unrealistic at the time, the cold war started" (1961, p. 101).

Chapter Six

DID THE PARAMETERS
OF THE COLD WAR CHANGE?

Many things happened in the years from 1946 to 1963: heads of state changed, new weapons and delivery systems were developed, dramatic confrontations occurred. Changes took place in a steady, cumulative fashion. With such a shifting terrain for Soviet-Western interaction, isn't it likely that one or more of the parameters for the two coalitions changed? Perhaps our examination of overall performance obscures some significant shifts during parts of the total period.

We saw in Chapter Five that certain belief systems enjoy rather general success in predicting Soviet and Western responses: 73 percent and 82 percent, respectively, of the predictions made by the top two belief systems were correct. But even the most accurate belief system makes a number of errors. If these errors happen to be concentrated in one or two time spans during which rival belief systems are making fewer errors, then this would suggest that the parameters may have changed during certain parts of the Cold War. To discover if this is so, we start by asking whether the most successful belief systems had any "cold" periods in which they missed a good many of their predictions.

WESTERN PARAMETERS

Table 6.1 presents the interaction units for the Western parameters chronologically, numbered in order of occurrence from W1 to W62. The leading belief system, CCE, makes a total of ten incorrect predictions. Some of these are well-scattered, but from unit W40 to unit W48 (October, 1956, to May, 1960), CCE makes only three correct predictions and six incorrect ones. Other belief systems have more success during this segment of the Cold War, as Table 6.2 indicates.

The most successful belief system for the period W40 – W48 is DEC with 89 percent. DEC, it will be recalled, is the "left wing" or Chinese view of the West. The West, it argues, was not merely expansionist

92

Table 6.1

A Chronological Analysis of Success for Belief Systems
about Western Parameters

INTERACTION UNIT[a]			PREDICTIONS OF WESTERN RESPONSES[b]						
Number	Date[c]	Type	DEC	DEE	ECE	EEC	EEE	CCE	CEE
W1	3/46	(5R/NB)	R	R	R	c	c	R	c
W2	3/46	(1R/B)	c	R	R	c	R	R	R
W3	3/46	(XR/B)	–	–	–	–	–	–	–
W4	7/46	(7R/NB)	R	R	c	c	c	c	c
W5	8/46	(2R/B)	c	–	R	c	–	R	–
W6	10/46	(5R/NB)	R	R	R	c	c	R	c
W7	3/47	(7R/NB)	R	R	c	c	c	c	c
W8	7/47	(5R/NB)	R	R	R	c	c	R	c
W9	9/47	(3R/B)	c	c	R	c	c	R	c
W10	12/47	(3R/B)	c	c	R	c	c	R	c
W11	1/48	(5R/B)	R	R	R	c	c	R	c
W12	3/48	(3R/B)	c	c	R	c	c	R	c
W13	4/48	(3R/B)	c	c	R	c	c	R	c
W14	8/48	(4R/NB)	–	–	R	c	–	R	–
W15	9/48	(3R/NB)	c	R	R	c	R	R	R
W16	4/49	(4R/NB)	–	–	R	c	–	R	–
W17	1/50	(5R/NB)	R	R	R	c	c	R	c
W18	6/50	(5R/NB)	R	R	R	c	c	R	c
W19	9/50	(3R/B)	c	c	R	c	c	R	c
W20	11/50	(2R/NB)	c	R	R	c	R	R	R
W21	12/50	(1R/B)	c	R	R	c	R	R	R
W22	4/51	(5C/B)	r	r	r	C	C	r	C
W23	6/51	(7C/NB)	r	r	C	C	C	C	C
W24	11/51	(6C/NB)	r	r	–	C	C	–	C
W25	5/52	(5R/NB)	R	R	R	c	c	R	c
W26	2/53	(5R/NB)	R	R	R	c	c	R	c
W27	4/53	(7C/NB)	r	r	C	C	C	C	C
W28	6/53	(7C/NB)	r	r	C	C	C	C	C
W29	7/54	(8C/X)	r	r	–	–	–	C	C
W30	7/54	(5C/NB)	r	r	r	C	C	r	C
W31	7/54	(9C/NB)	r	r	r	r	r	C	C
W32	10/54	(5R/NB)	R	R	R	c	c	R	c
W33	1/55	(5R/NB)	R	R	R	c	c	R	c
W34	2/55	(4R/B)	–	–	R	c	c	R	c
W35	4/55	(6C/NB)	r	r	–	c	c	–	c

Table 6.1 – continued

INTERACTION UNIT[a]			PREDICTIONS OF WESTERN RESPONSES[b]						
Number	Date[c]	Type	DEC	DEE	ECE	EEC	EEE	CCE	CEE
W36	5/55	(7C/NB)	r	r	C	C	C	C	C
W37	9/55	(7C/NB)	r	r	C	C	C	C	C
W38	10/56	(5R/NB)	R	R	R	c	c	R	c
W39	10/56	(5R/NB)	R	R	R	c	c	R	c
W40	10/56	(5C/NB)	r	r	r	C	C	r	C
W41	11/56	(1C/B)	C	r	r	C	r	r	r
W42	7/58	(5R/NB)	R	R	R	c	c	R	c
W43	7/58	(1C/B)	C	r	r	C	r	r	r
W44	9/58	(7R/NB)	R	R	c	c	c	c	c
W45	9/58	(7R/NB)	R	R	c	c	c	c	c
W46	9/59	(5R/NB)	R	R	R	c	c	R	c
W47	5/60	(5R/NB)	R	R	R	c	c	R	c
W48	5/60	(1C/X)	C	r	r	C	r	r	r
W49	7/60	(1R/NB)	c	R	R	c	R	R	R
W50	8/60	(4R/B)	–	–	R	c	c	R	c
W51	11/60	(3R/NB)	c	R	R	c	R	R	R
W52	1/61	(4R/NB)	–	–	R	c	–	R	–
W53	3/61	(5R/NB)	R	R	R	c	c	R	c
W54	4/61	(6R/NB)	R	R	–	c	c	–	c
W55	5/61	(5R/B)	R	R	R	c	c	R	c
W56	7/61	(5R/NB)	R	R	R	c	c	R	c
W57	8/61	(1R/B)	c	R	R	c	R	R	R
W58	5/62	(5R/NB)	R	R	R	c	c	R	c
W59	10/62	(4R/NB)	–	–	R	c	–	R	–
W60	10/62	(9C/B)	r	r	r	r	r	C	C
W61	6/63	(6C/NB)	r	r	–	C	C	–	C
W62	7/63	(8C/NB)	r	r	–	–	–	C	C

[a]A capsule description of the type of interaction unit is included here. The first figure specifies the adversary pattern, ranging from "1" for extremely belligerent through "9" for extremely accommodative. An "X" indicates an inconsistent pattern. This pattern description is followed by a letter indicating a refractory (R) or conciliatory (C) response. Finally, "NB" denotes a responder-nonbelligerent period, "B" a responder-belligerent period, and "X" a responder-inconsistent period. The units are numbered chronologically.

[b]A prediction in a capital letter (e.g., R) is a correct prediction, a prediction in a lowercase letter is incorrect, and a dash (–) indicates a pass or no prediction.

[c]The date indicated is the month and year of the major Western action ending the period.

Table 6.2

Success Rates for Belief Systems about Western Parameters
for "Cold" Period for Leading Belief System (CCE)

W40 TO W48
(October, 1956, to May, 1960)

Belief system	Number of predictions	Number of correct predictions	Success rate	ALL OTHER		
				Number of predictions	Number of correct predictions	Success rate
CCE	9	3	33%	48	44	92%
ECE	9	3	33	46	40	87
DEE	9	5	56	45	26	58
DEC	9	8	89	46	19	41
CEE	9	1	11	47	21	45
EEE	9	1	11	45	17	38
EEC	9	4	44	50	10	20

but destructionist, yielding when pressured and exploiting any sign of receptivity or laxity by the Soviet side. Furthermore, the West recognized the consolidationist nature of its Soviet adversary. It is rather difficult to imagine that all three Western parameters could suddenly change and then swing back in such Jekyll and Hyde fashion. Therefore, we will more closely examine this period for some other plausible explanation of the apparent switch.

The period in question runs from the Suez crisis in late October, 1956, to the U-2 episode in May, 1960, an interval of about three and a half years. There has rarely been greater disarray in Western policy than during the two crises that mark the boundaries of this interval. The Suez crisis was characterized by a sharp division in the Western coalition when the United States opposed the Anglo-French intervention. Two major conciliatory actions are missed by CCE during this crisis — the United States pledge of nonintervention in Suez and the joint agreement by the United Kingdom, France, and Israel to withdraw. The U-2 incident was also characterized by disarray, caused on this occasion by the clumsiness of the United States rather than disagreement among the Western allies. This crisis produces another error.

The reader has every right to be wary of efforts to excuse errors by ad hoc explanations. An advocate of even the most unsuccessful belief system could find some plausible explanation for its failures on a case-by-case basis. However, we must decide whether the observed departure from the usual success rate for CCE represents an error produced by something other than the parameters, or whether it represents a genuine change in parameter values. To argue the latter means to accept two extremely sharp discontinuities in Western parameters — one at the beginning and one at the end of the period. Furthermore, the switch to Mr. Hyde, if it was real, did not correspond to the accession of a harsh anti-Communist such as Joseph McCarthy or John Foster Dulles. Rather it occurred much later, in a period encompassing the Spirit of Camp David and the Khrushchev visit to the United States.

In sum, given the implausibility of a genuine parameter change and given the indication of unusual disarray in Western policy during several of the errors for CCE, we are not inclined to accept the occurrence of parameter changes. We believe that the Western parameters can best be described as CCE for the entire eighteen-year period under study.

SOVIET PARAMETERS

The question of parameter changes must be raised anew for the Soviet coalition, and here the answer is more complicated. We start by examining the interaction units for Soviet parameters in chronological order as presented in Table 6.3. Although the most successful belief system, CCE, makes twelve errors in prediction, these are well scattered throughout the Cold War. In fact, CCE never misses more than two predictions in a row.

There are, however, two periods worth examining more closely: from unit S1 to unit S7 (January to November, 1946), CCE manages only three successful predictions out of seven; from unit S38 to unit S60 (October, 1956, to October, 1962), CCE does well (69 percent correct), but DEC does even better (78 percent correct). Table 6.4 presents the complete figures for these two segments of the Cold War and for the balance.

In the early Cold War (S1 to S7), no belief system does exceptionally well: a coin-flipper would equal or surpass the best of them more than one-third of the time. This period, covering most of 1946, is characterized by varied responses to Western behavior. Extremely belligerent Western patterns result in both conciliatory and refractory responses,[1] and balanced Western patterns produce varied responses as well. One interpretation of this period is that the Soviet parameters were not yet firm.

There is another factor, however, that might help to explain the erratic pattern in this period. "The American air force," Neal reminds us, "controlled the skies. The American navy controlled the seas. . . . And the United States, and it alone, possessed the atom bomb" (1960, p. 151). The United States was rapidly demobilizing, of course, but the Soviet army was still reeling from the losses of World War II and hardly in a position to risk too sharp a confrontation with a former ally that happened to be sole possessor of the atomic bomb.

The implication of this strategic situation for our analysis may not be immediately clear. Our analysis, as we pointed out in Chapter Four (pp. 63–65), assumes a rough strategic parity between the two sides. In general, we believe that a strong case can be made for this assumption, but the case is weakest for the year 1946. For that time, it might be argued that the combination of the American atomic monopoly and overall military strength plus Soviet war wounds created a strategic inferiority for the Soviet coalition.

Such a strategic inferiority means that, even though a coalition perceives its adversary's belligerent behavior as aggressive, it will not always resist because it sometimes cannot resist. The belief system CCE predicts that extremely belligerent Western behavior will pro-

---

[1] Incidentally, this accounts for the fact that none of the belief systems show outstanding success in predicting Soviet responses to belligerent Western patterns. See Table 5.6 (p. 83).

Table 6.3

A Chronological Analysis of Success for Belief Systems about Soviet Parameters

	INTERACTION UNIT[a]		PREDICTIONS OF SOVIET RESPONSES[b]						
Number	*Date*[c]	*Type*	*DEC*	*DEE*	*ECE*	*EEC*	*EEE*	*CCE*	*CEE*
S1	3/46	(4R/NB)	–	–	R	c	–	r	–
S2	3/46	(1C/B)	C	r	r	C	r	r	r
S3	3/46	(1R/NB)	c	R	R	c	R	R	R
S4	4/46	(1C/B)	C	r	r	C	r	r	r
S5	8/46	(5R/NB)	R	R	R	c	c	R	c
S6	8/46	(1C/B)	C	r	r	C	r	r	r
S7	10/46	(5C/NB)	r	r	r	C	C	r	C
S8	9/47	(4R/NB)	–	–	R	c	–	R	–
S9	10/47	(4R/NB)	–	–	R	c	–	R	–
S10	10/47	(4R/NB)	–	–	R	c	–	R	–
S11	2/48	(4R/NB)	–	–	R	c	–	R	–
S12	4/48	(1R/B)	c	R	R	c	R	R	R
S13	6/48	(4R/NB)	–	–	R	c	–	R	–
S14	8/48	(4R/NB)	–	–	R	c	–	R	–
S15	9/48	(6R/NB)	R	R	–	c	c	–	c
S16	2/49	(4R/NB)	–	–	R	c	–	R	–
S17	4/49	(4C/NB)	–	–	r	C	–	r	–
S18	5/49	(6R/NB)	R	R	–	c	c	–	c
S19	6/50	(4R/NB)	–	–	R	c	–	R	–
S20	10/50	(2R/B)	c	–	R	c	–	R	–
S21	11/50	(4R/B)	–	–	R	c	c	R	c
S22	6/51	(6C/NB)	r	r	–	C	C	–	C
S23	7/51	(9C/NB)	r	r	r	r	r	C	C
S24	8/51	(XR/NB)	–	–	–	–	–	–	–
S25	11/51	(6C/NB)	r	r	–	C	C	–	C
S26	5/52	(5R/NB)	R	R	R	c	c	R	c
S27	3/53	(4C/NB)	–	–	r	C	–	r	–
S28	6/53	(6C/NB)	r	r	–	C	C	–	C
S29	6/53	(XR/NB)	–	–	–	–	–	–	–
S30	7/53	(5C/NB)	r	r	r	C	C	r	C
S31	7/53	(9C/NB)	r	r	r	r	r	C	C
S32	3/54	(6R/NB)	R	R	–	c	c	–	c
S33	7/54	(7C/NB)	r	r	C	C	C	C	C
S34	5/55	(7C/NB)	r	r	C	C	C	C	C
S35	5/55	(6C/NB)	r	r	–	C	C	–	C
S36	7/55	(7C/NB)	r	r	C	C	C	C	C

Table 6.3 — continued

INTERACTION UNIT[a]			PREDICTIONS OF SOVIET RESPONSES[b]						
Number	*Date*[c]	*Type*	*DEC*	*DEE*	*ECE*	*EEC*	*EEE*	*CCE*	*CEE*
S37	9/55	(7C/NB)	r	r	C	C	C	C	C
S38	10/56	(6R/NB)	R	R	—	c	c	—	c
S39	11/56	(1R/B)	c	R	R	c	R	R	R
S40	10/57	(5R/NB)	R	R	R	c	c	R	c
S41	6/58	(6R/NB)	R	R	—	c	c	—	c
S42	7/58	(3R/B)	c	c	R	c	c	R	c
S43	7/58	(XC/B)	—	—	—	—	—	—	—
S44	8/58	(7R/NB)	R	R	c	c	c	c	c
S45	9/58	(3C/B)	C	C	r	C	C	r	C
S46	11/58	(5R/NB)	R	R	R	c	c	R	c
S47	5/60	(6R/NB)	R	R	—	c	c	—	c
S48	5/60	(XR/B)	—	—	—	—	—	—	—
S49	6/60	(4R/B)	—	—	R	c	c	R	c
S50	7/60	(5R/B)	R	R	R	c	c	R	c
S51	9/60	(3R/B)	c	c	R	c	c	R	c
S52	2/61	(6R/NB)	R	R	—	c	c	—	c
S53	4/61	(4C/NB)	—	—	r	C	—	r	—
S54	8/61	(4R/NB)	—	—	R	c	—	R	—
S55	8/61	(2R/B)	c	—	R	c	—	R	—
S56	10/61	(5R/B)	R	R	R	c	c	R	c
S57	7/62	(6R/NB)	R	R	—	c	c	—	c
S58	10/62	(5R/NB)	R	R	R	c	c	R	c
S59	10/62	(1C/B)	C	r	r	C	r	r	r
S60	10/62	(1C/B)	C	r	r	C	r	r	r
S61	11/62	(XC/NB)	—	—	—	—	—	—	—
S62	7/63	(7C/NB)	r	r	C	C	C	C	C
S63	11/63	(6C/NB)	r	r	—	C	C	—	C

[a]*A capsule description of the interaction unit is included here. The first figure specifies the adversary pattern, ranging from "1" for extremely belligerent through "9" for extremely accommodative. An "X" indicates an inconsistent pattern. This pattern description is followed by a letter indicating a refractory (R) or conciliatory (C) response. Finally, "NB" denotes a responder-nonbelligerent period, "B" a responder-belligerent period, and "X" a responder-inconsistent period. The units are numbered chronologically.*

[b]*A prediction in a capital letter (e.g., R) is a correct prediction, a prediction in a lowercase letter is incorrect, and a dash (—) indicates a pass or no prediction.*

[c]*The date indicated is the month and year of the major Soviet action ending the period.*

Table 6.4

Success Rates for Belief Systems about Soviet Parameters
for Selected Segments of the Cold War

Belief system	S1 TO S7 (January, 1946, to October, 1946)			S38 TO S60 (October, 1956, to October, 1962)			ALL OTHER		
	Number of predictions	Number of correct predictions	Success rate	Number of predictions	Number of correct predictions	Success rate	Number of predictions	Number of correct predictions	Success rate
CCE	7	3	43%	16	11	69%	22	19	86%
ECE	7	3	43	16	11	69	22	17	77
DEC	6	4	67	18	14	78	19	4	21
DEE	6	2	33	17	13	76	18	5	28
CEE	6	2	33	18	2	11	19	14	74
EEE	6	2	33	18	2	11	19	12	63
EEC	7	4	57	21	4	19	30	13	43

duce a refractory Soviet response. That is, a coalition that believes its adversary is expansionist will resist what it perceives to be its adversary's aggressive behavior. It is precisely this prediction that produces three of the four errors that CCE makes during the segment S1 to S7. Three times the Soviet coalition responds to extreme Western belligerence with a major concession, a pattern which occurs after 1946 only twice — both times during the Cuban missile crisis of 1962.

The errors for CCE, then, are exactly those that one would expect to occur if a normally CCE coalition were temporarily unable to resist what it believed to be aggressive behavior.[2] Once the Soviet coalition recovered sufficiently from the war to acquire the capability to resist, a rough strategic parity was established. Indeed, after 1946 CCE enjoys a very high rate of successful prediction. Thus, we interpret the erratic patterns in S1 to S7 as the result of temporary and short-lived Soviet strategic inferiority. Soviet behavior, under these conditions, is consistent with what we would expect from a CCE coalition and there is little or no reason to postulate a different set of parameter values.

The period S38 to S60 is, unfortunately, more complicated and difficult to interpret. It runs from the almost simultaneous Suez and Hungarian interventions in October–November, 1956, to the Cuban missile crisis in October, 1962. The two generally strongest belief systems, CCE and ECE, make a respectable showing with 69 percent each, so there is hardly cause for rejecting them. But two others, DEC and DEE, do even better with 78 percent and 76 percent respectively. And to make matters more perplexing, this second pair is sharply different in spirit and in predictions from the first pair.

How is it that such opposing belief systems can both do well in the same segment of the Cold War? Table 6.5 breaks this segment down by pattern of Western behavior and we can begin to see what is occurring. DEC and CCE make opposite predictions for belligerent and accommodative patterns but both, for different reasons, predict a refractory response (or pass) on balanced patterns. On the belligerent and accommodative patterns where they disagree, there is a standoff, each getting four right and four wrong. On balanced patterns where they agree, the Soviet coalition was refractory on all occasions except one during this period. Thus, both DEC and CCE are able to maintain a high success rate. DEE is similar to DEC in its predictions, and ECE is identical to CCE; thus, these two belief systems also obtain high success rates.

[2] We make no judgment here that Western belligerence was in fact aggressive during 1946. Our results suggest that it stemmed from the belief that Soviet goals were expansionist and the assumption that the Soviets recognized the West as consolidationist.

Table 6.5

Success Rates in Segment S38 to S60 by Type of Western Pattern

Belief system	BELLIGERENT PATTERNS			BALANCED PATTERNS			ACCOMMODATIVE PATTERNS		
	Number of predictions	Number of correct predictions	Success rate	Number of predictions	Number of correct predictions	Success rate	Number of predictions	Number of correct predictions	Success rate
DEC	7	3	43%	10	10	100%	1	1	—[a]
DEE	6	2	33	10	10	100	1	1	—
CCE	7	4	57	8	7	88	1	0	—
ECE	7	4	57	8	7	88	1	0	—
EEC	7	3	43	13	1	8	1	0	—
CEE	6	2	33	11	0	0	1	0	—
EEE	6	2	33	11	0	0	1	0	—

[a]*Too few cases for meaningful percentages.*

A closer look at Table 6.5 indicates that much of the impasse stems from the failure of any belief system to perform well on the belligerent patterns. This, in turn, results from the fact that Soviet responses to such patterns were rather inconsistent — four times they were refractory and three times conciliatory. It is tempting to try to explain away either the refractory or conciliatory responses on an ad hoc basis, but this proves very difficult. The conciliatory actions include two dramatic concessions during the Cuban missile crisis (S59 and S60) and the cessation of Chinese shelling of the offshore island of Quemoy following a show of force by the United States (S45). The refractory actions include threats of military intervention in Suez (S39) and Lebanon (S42) following military actions by the West, and the resumption of atmospheric testing in the midst of the Berlin Wall crisis (S55). Evidently, Soviet responses to Western belligerence were genuinely vacillating and ambivalent during this period, much as they were during the first year of the Cold War. In this case, however, the vacillation cannot be attributed to strategic inferiority, and we must look elsewhere for an explanation.

Another noteworthy feature of Soviet behavior during this period was a propensity to be refractory in the face of relatively accommodative Western patterns. The West was genuinely accommodative only once, but it was balanced flexible on five other occasions. In all six cases, the Soviet response was refractory. (During other parts of the Cold War, such patterns led to a refractory response less than one-fourth of the time.) Two of these refractory responses relate to the Hungarian uprising and can perhaps be understood in terms of the overriding importance to the Soviet Union of maintaining its coalition intact, irrespective of Western action. The others, however, have a rather heady, militant quality: a sudden massive shelling of Quemoy by China (S44), a threat of unilateral military intervention in the Congo (S52), and a major military build-up in Cuba leading to the placement of missiles (S57). Evidently, the Soviet coalition was more willing than usual to behave militantly in the absence of immediate Western provocation.

In general, then, Soviet behavior shows a paradoxical mixture of vacillation and militancy. No belief system can successfully capture the vacillating side, but DEC and DEE can best capture the militant side because both share the assumption of destructionist goals. Unfortunately, these two belief systems represent a radical departure from the parameter values that best explain Soviet behavior during the rest of the Cold War. We are reluctant to accept such a discontinuity unless our data indicate it quite clearly. In this case, they certainly do not: CCE and ECE trail by a scant nine percentage points in overall performance.

Our inclination, then, is to try and understand Soviet behavior within a CCE or ECE framework. We will argue that a special set of factors combined during this period to produce a Soviet policy that was at once heady and uneasy. The heady side did not produce a change to destructionist goals, but it did lead to certain refractory excursions during periods of Western accommodation. The uneasy side did not produce a more benign view of Western goals, but it did lead to certain tactical retreats in the face of Western belligerence.

Consider first the heady side of the Soviet mood. By the summer of 1957, Khrushchev had fully consolidated his power by removing the last of his major political opponents (the so-called anti-party group) from positions of influence. For the first time in four years the leadership of the coalition was stable and unambiguous. In October of that same year, the Soviet Union launched its first Sputnik and demonstrated conclusively that it had developed intercontinental ballistic missiles capable of delivering nuclear warheads. With the Soviet Union riding a crest of scientific and military achievements and with Khrushchev firmly in control at home, Soviet leaders probably felt that things were going quite well. Optimism was reflected in boasts such as "We will bury [outlive] you," and "Your grandchildren will live under Communism."

But there was another uneasy side to the Soviet mood. First, there were strains in Eastern Europe dramatized by the Soviet intervention in Hungary. Second, there were small but ominous signs of the emerging Sino-Soviet discord — indeed, by 1962 China was at war with India and the Soviet Union was giving military aid to the Indians. The Communist alliance was in trouble. With resentful and rebellious partners in Europe and with an uncertain ally in Asia, Soviet leaders undoubtedly felt some malaise about the security of their position, in spite of Sputniks circling the globe.

This combination of apparent success and insecurity might have been sufficient to give Soviet foreign policy a certain element of bravado. But this element was greatly magnified by developments in the Third World. The sudden upsurge of nationalist and anticolonial movements presented the Soviet Union with a new combination of opportunity and danger. Many such movements claimed fealty to the socialist brotherhood and looked to the Soviet Union for protection in the face of Western opposition and power. The Soviet Union could not ignore these pleas for help nor could it ignore the easy access to increased prestige and power that they offered. Yet, for the Soviet Union to lend its support and accept the windfall carried with it the danger

of commitments beyond the effective reach of Soviet power and threatened to embroil it in costly and risky conflicts.

A weaker Soviet Union might have resisted the temptation to make
such commitments, responding as Stalin did when he refused to help
the Greek Communists during the civil war following World War II.
But Khrushchev claimed, "We have now stockpiled so many rockets,
so many atomic and hydrogen warheads, that, if we were attacked, we
could wipe from the face of the earth all our probable opponents"
(*Pravda*, November 15, 1959). Could such a country refuse to support
a beleaguered ally, even if this ally might be more self-appointed than
sought after? Evidently not. This portion of the Cold War is rife with
instances of Soviet refractory actions aimed at helping such allies in
Latin America, Southeast Asia, the Middle East, and even Africa. Nor
did these actions always come in response to Western provocation;
sometimes they followed periods when the West had been relatively
accommodative.

The aid that the Soviet Union gave to the Third World entangled it,
sometimes exposing it to unanticipated dangers. Cuba is a case in
point. It must have been gratifying to find an enthusiastic ally within
Latin America and only a few miles from the coast of the United
States. But Castro was not an unmixed blessing. In committing itself
to the support of the new Cuban government, the Soviet Union opened
the door to involvement in conflicts at inconvenient and disadvan-
tageous times and places to defend interests quite peripheral to its own
security. The missile crisis of 1962 seemed to reflect this Soviet ambivalence.

The Soviet Union, we are suggesting, succumbed to the temptation
to make commitments it could not easily honor. As a consequence, it
sometimes found itself in dangerous situations where resistance to
Western belligerence seemed foolhardy. The result was a certain
vacillation: it resisted Western belligerence most of the time by responding in a refractory fashion, but it also made major concessions on
a number of occasions where the stakes seemed disproportionate to the
potential costs. In addition to its concessions during the Cuban missile
crisis, it also agreed to a cease-fire in Laos following another United
States show of strength. (These cases account for three of the five
errors made by CCE and ECE for this segment of the Cold War.)

Note that we are not arguing that the Soviet Union *interpreted*
Western belligerence differently in these instances. It continued to see
the West as aggressive but responded in a conciliatory fashion despite
this interpretation. It simply felt that discretion was the better part of
valor in areas that were of peripheral importance to Soviet security. It
is as if Soviet leaders told themselves, "Yes, the Americans have ag-

gressive designs in Indochina and Cuba but we cannot afford to be the policemen for the world. We have our own problems managing what we now control and must resist Western expansion where it touches us more directly. We feel sorry for our friends in Cuba and Laos but they must come to terms with Western power as best they can. They are not worth risking millions of Soviet lives." From the Soviet standpoint, these concessions were a kind of appeasement — an unhappy decision to allow Western aggression to succeed while the Soviet Union undertook a necessary retrenchment from commitments that were more stumbled into than deliberately sought.

What, then, can be said about the Soviet parameters during this period? We maintain that the Soviet coalition continued to perceive the West as expansionist and to believe that it was seen as consolidationist. As for its goals, we are less certain. We have already rejected as implausible the suggestion that its goals suddenly became destructionist. Possibly, they remained consolidationist, but this would imply that the Soviets made no effort to seek and create opportunities for expansion in the Third World, merely allowing themselves to be sucked into unwise commitments. Such a wholly passive role is also implausible. In fact, the "arrogance of power" position, ECE, seems most in keeping with the spirit of this period. As Zimmerman puts it, "In the Khrushchev period, hubris . . . was the watchword of Soviet perspectives on the international system" (1969, p. 136). The Soviets, in this view, had expansionist designs and played an active role in promoting and exploiting their opportunities. The fact that they found would-be allies and supporters among the Third World nations made it easier for Soviet leaders to convince themselves that Western opposition was aggression rather than resistance provoked by fears of Soviet expansion.

CONCLUSION

Except for the period just discussed, we are led to conclude that the parameters of the Cold War remained fairly stable throughout — CCE for both coalitions. On the Western side, CCE is surpassed by other belief systems in only one segment (1956–1960), and this seems due more to confusion and disarray within the coalition than to any change in goals or in perception of the adversary.

On the Soviet side, there are two segments in which CCE is surpassed by other belief systems: 1946 and 1956–1962. Its failure during the opening months of the Cold War can be attributed to the dubious status of one of our underlying assumptions: rough parity in the strategic capabilities of the two coalitions. If, as seems quite reasonable, the Soviet Union felt at a strategic disadvantage during this period, its erratic reaction to Western belligerence can easily be squared with CCE parameters.

The segment between 1956 and 1962 presents greater problems despite the fact that CCE has a very respectable success rate. Much of this chapter has been devoted to examining the combination of headiness and uneasiness that underlay Soviet policy in this period. Our conclusion is that the Soviet coalition continued to see the West as expansionist and continued to believe the West perceived it as consolidationist. It is possible that its goals remained consolidationist, but in some ways it seems more reasonable to argue that they shifted in an expansionist direction.

Chapter Seven

PHASES OF THE COLD WAR

THE BASIC FINDINGS AND THEIR IMPLICATIONS

The distinctive method developed in this book has been the strategy of testing belief systems. We have now pursued this strategy to its conclusion. The preceding two chapters provided relatively clear answers to the questions we posed. While we can perform further analyses on our data (and will do so in a later portion of this chapter), it should be clear that such analyses go beyond the basic framework that has guided us this far. Before laying this framework aside, we pause to assess where it has taken us.

The effort to separate description from interpretation has been at the core of our research strategy. We began by developing a coding scheme that permitted us to describe the Cold War as an interaction — a sequence of interdependent actions generated by the Soviet and Western coalitions from 1946 to 1963. We then turned to the issue of interpretation. Both from the logic of an interaction framework and from a review of the literature, we saw that differing assumptions about the nature of the coalitions lay at the root of rival explanations of the Cold War. These differing assumptions were summarized in the form of competing belief systems which we then sought to test systematically.

If one accepts the logic and conventions of our testing strategy, what finally emerges from our analysis is a general portrait of the Cold War protagonists. Specifically, we find that their overall interaction can best be understood if we assume that both coalitions had consolidationist goals, that both believed their goals were accurately perceived by the other, and that both actually misperceived the other's goals as expansionist.[1]

---

[1] The sole exception to this generalization is the 1956–1962 period where, as noted in Chapter Six, Soviet goals may well have been expansionist.

This finding comprises our basic contribution to the study of the Cold War. It is a general statement, not an interpretive running account of the entire Cold War. We have not set for ourselves the objective of a complete history. Our method aims only at a general portrait of the protagonists in the Cold War or in any dyadic conflict to which it might be applied.

This disclaimer should not be mistaken for an apology. The type of statements yielded by our research framework have profound implications for more fine-grained analyses of a conflict. To say that the Cold War was fought by adversaries with particular long-range goals and particular misperceptions of one another is to say a great deal. It places basic constraints on the possible interpretations of virtually any event. For example, one cannot explain the Berlin blockade or the onset of the Korean War by pointing to Soviet expansionist or destructionist goals — unless, of course, one can demonstrate that our own findings are invalid.

More generally, if one accepts our emergent portraits of the Cold War protagonists, it follows that certain historical analyses are, a priori, more likely to be accurate than others. To the extent that a historian's assumptions about the two coalitions coincide with our own findings, his interpretations of specific Cold War events are likely to be more accurate. D. F. Fleming's history (1961), for example, would seem to meet this criterion. This is not to say that we necessarily agree with every detail of his analysis. The mere fact that his underlying assumptions about the protagonists appear sound does not guarantee accurate interpretations of specific events, but it does increase the likelihood that he will come close to the mark.

Apart from providing guidelines for evaluating past historical analyses, our findings reveal a number of important areas for future research. One such area concerns the phenomenon of mutual misperception. The propensity of each coalition to misperceive the other as expansionist while failing to realize that the other was doing the same evidently played a major part in sustaining the Cold War conflict. It seems important, then, to improve our understanding of the general conditions that create and foster such mutual misperception. A certain amount of research has been done in this area (Bronfenbrenner, 1961; Oskamp, 1963; Jecker, 1964; Eckhardt and White, 1967), but most of it has been concerned with documenting the existence of a "mirror-image in Soviet-American relations" rather than with explaining it. The few explanations offered tend to be psychological in nature, pointing to such mechanisms as projection and denial.

A more structural approach seems appropriate. This might focus, for example, on how the position of decision-maker may make one especially susceptible to certain kinds of misconceptions about the adversary. Furthermore, misperceptions may be functional for important groups within a society: no imputation of insincerity is necessary to observe that myths or mistaken beliefs may be strongly supported and defended by those who derive benefits from their continued currency. We emphasize this because it is easy to assume that one should strive to understand stable misperceptions through an analysis of psychological processes. But the key to misperceptions that lasted over such a sustained period and were so widely shared can best be sought by looking for the institutional factors that helped to sustain them.

Some version of mutual misperception is likely to be present in almost any international conflict.[2] But many other questions, specific to the Cold War, remain beyond those that can be answered by such misperceptions. In the remainder of this chapter, we intend to pursue one such issue — a problem that can be studied fruitfully using the data already at our disposal. At the same time, we hope to illustrate the ways in which our basic findings on goals and perceptions provide important constraints and guidelines. The question we propose to investigate is this: Can the overall Cold War interaction be subdivided into distinct phases; and if so, what explanations can be offered for the nature and timing of these phases? Pursuing this question will afford us an opportunity to review and interpret some of the major events of the Cold War. In effect, our answer will constitute a chronological outline of the conflict — an outline that could be expanded into a detailed historical analysis.

IDENTIFYING AND DESCRIBING THE PHASES

All the belief systems tested in this book predict varying combinations of coalition behavior and adversary response. The fact that one belief system (CCE) fared consistently well does not preclude the possibility that different types of interaction units were characteristic of different segments of the Cold War. If we find this to be true, then we can think of these segments as phases, and the points of change as historical watersheds.

Tables 7.1 and 7.2 present chronological summaries of the Cold War interaction. The first shows all interaction units ended by a major Soviet action, and the second shows all interaction units ended by a major Western action. Both tables indicate that there were phases and summarize their nature and timing. It is fortunate that both tables partition the Cold War into essentially the same segments because

[2] This theme runs through the work of the Stanford group on World War I. See, for example, Holsti, North, and Brody (1968) and Zinnes (1968).

Table 7.1

Interaction Units with the Soviet Coalition as Responder, Ordered Chronologically 1946-1963

UNIT NUMBER[a]

Western pattern	S001–S007	S008–S021	S022–S037	S038–S060	S061–S063
Extremely belligerent	C R C C	R		R C C	
Quite belligerent				R	
Fairly belligerent		R			
Balanced firm	R	R R R R R R R C R R	C	R C R C R	
Balanced	R C		R C	R R R R	
Balanced flexible		R R	C C C R C	R R R R	C
Fairly accommodative			C C C C	R	C
Quite accommodative			C C		
Extremely accommodative					
Inconsistent			R R	C R	C
	Phase I January, 1946, to October, 1946	Phase II November, 1946, to November, 1950	Phase III December, 1950, to September, 1956	Phase IV October, 1956, to October, 1962	Phase V November, 1962, to November, 1963

Key: R = refractory Soviet response.
C = conciliatory Soviet response.

[a]*Read down as S01, S02. . . . , S63.*

Table 7.2

Interaction Units with the Western Coalition as Responder, Ordered Chronologically 1946-1963

UNIT NUMBER[a]

Soviet pattern	W01–W07 (Phase I)	W08–W22 (Phase II)	W23–W37 (Phase III)	W38–W45 (Phase IVa)	W46–W59 (Phase IVb)	W60–W62 (Phase V)
Extremely belligerent	R	R		C C	, C R R	
Quite belligerent	R	R				
Fairly belligerent		R R R R R	R		R R R R	
Balanced firm		R R R				
Balanced	R	R R R	C R R	R R C R	R R R R R	C
Balanced flexible			C		R	
Fairly accommodative	R R		C C C	R R		C
Quite accommodative			C C			
Extremely accommodative			C C			C
Inconsistent	R					

	Phase I	Phase II	Phase III	Phase IVa	Phase IVb	Phase V
	January, 1946, to March, 1947	April, 1947, to December, 1950	January, 1951, to September, 1956	October, 1956, to September, 1958	October, 1958, to October, 1962	November, 1962, to November, 1963

Key: R = refractory Western response.
      C = conciliatory Western response.

[a] Read down as W01, W02 . . . , W62.

112

this permits us to talk of phases of the Cold War rather than phases of Soviet and Western policy.

The first, short phase runs from the beginning of the Cold War to the announcement of the Truman Doctrine in March, 1947. This phase is characterized by relatively belligerent Western behavior and varied or erratic Soviet behavior. While the West was uniformly refractory in its major actions and had no pattern below balanced, the Soviet coalition had a mixture of conciliatory and refractory responses and patterns ranging from fairly accommodative to extremely belligerent.

The second phase begins in 1947 and lasts until the beginning of the stalemate in Korea following the full-scale Chinese entry into the war. It is characterized by relatively belligerent behavior and refractory responses by both coalitions.

The Korean stalemate begins the third phase, which ends with the almost simultaneous interventions in Suez and Hungary in October and November, 1956. It is characterized by relatively accommodative behavior and an unusually high percentage of conciliatory responses by both sides.

The fourth phase begins with Suez-Hungary and ends with the Cuban missile crisis in October, 1962. We do not consider Phase IVa a genuine phase of the Cold War for the reasons discussed in detail in Chapter Six (see p. 96). Still, Phase IV as a whole is more complicated than Phase II, which it resembles. Both sides tended to respond in a refractory fashion to a range of patterns; however, the Soviet coalition also responded to Western belligerence in a conciliatory fashion on a number of occasions.

The final phase runs from the Cuban missile crisis to the end of our analysis in November, 1963. The few interaction units here, like those of the third phase, reflect mutual accommodation.

Our analysis, then, identifies four watersheds in the eighteen years of the Cold War. On the whole, these are not surprising. But it is surprising that no watersheds occurred at various other times when we might have expected them — the Berlin blockade in 1948, the first Soviet atomic bomb in 1949, the outbreak of the Korean War in 1950, the death of Stalin and the accession of John Foster Dulles in 1953, the U-2 episode in 1960, or the transfer of power to the Kennedy administration in 1961. Among the many possibilities for watersheds, our analysis has singled out four that are neither more nor less obvious than the others.

EXPLAINING THE PHASES

Having identified five somewhat distinct phases in the Cold War, we will now examine why they occurred and what caused the transition from one to another. The key to explaining the phases does not lie in parameter changes. We have already explored this possibility at length in Chapter Six and concluded that probably none took place.[3] Indeed, one of the most impressive characteristics of CCE, the leading belief system for both coalitions, is its success in making correct predictions across so many different phases of the Cold War. Both Phase II and Phase III, for example, are precisely what CCE would expect — refractory responses to belligerence and conciliatory responses to accommodation, respectively. This, then, illustrates the importance of our earlier findings in providing guidelines for attacking the present problem. However we choose to explain the phases and transitions, we cannot contradict those earlier findings. Basically, this means we must assume the phases were generated by two CCE coalitions.

Phase I: The Capability Gap

This phase of the Cold War is characterized by a series of vacillating Soviet responses in the face of prevailing Western belligerence. In March, 1946, a Soviet troop movement toward Teheran brought a sharp Western reaction. The Soviet Union at first stood its ground, issuing a volley of countercharges and refusing to allow the matter to be brought before the newly founded United Nations. Then, in a surprise conciliatory speech, Stalin praised the United Nations and affirmed that the Soviet Union had no aggressive intentions in Iran. When the West insisted on bringing the issue before the Security Council, the Soviet Union first tried to block the issue from the agenda and then boycotted the sessions. Shortly thereafter, however, it agreed to evacuate its troops from Iran.

Toward the latter half of 1946 the vacillation in Soviet policy was still apparent. In August, Yugoslavia shot down two American planes in ten days and then, faced with a Western ultimatum, suddenly apologized and released all surviving United States airmen. Through late 1946 and early 1947 the West, apparently convinced of Soviet expansionist intentions, persisted in its hard line. It sought to curb the Soviet veto in the Security Council and responded to the Greek Civil War with the Truman Doctrine. The beginning of Phase II is marked by more stable and sharper Soviet responses to Western belligerence.

We argue that the vacillation in Soviet policy that characterizes Phase I can be attributed to a strategic inferiority. There are a number of good strategic histories of the Cold War with extensive discussions

---

[3] The one possible exception is a change in Soviet goals to expansionist during Phase IV. This is not suggested by our data but neither is it precluded. Furthermore, while our interpretation of this period does not logically imply that Soviet goals shifted, a change to expansionist goals is very compatible with the spirit of our interpretation.

of the capabilities of the two sides.[4] Quester (1971) divides the Cold War into five phases based on the strategic position of the two sides: (1) the United States atomic monopoly, 1945–1949; (2) the monopoly eliminated, 1949–1953; (3) the new look, 1953–1957; (4) the missile gap, 1957–1961; and (5) the Kennedy administration, 1961–1963. By and large, this partitioning of the Cold War cuts across, rather than coincides with, our phases. It suggests that usually changes in capabilities do not account for the shifts we have identified. However, capabilities do seem relevant to understanding the transition from Phase I to Phase II.

When Phase I ended in the early months of 1947, the American atomic monopoly was still intact, but other strategic changes were occurring. Though the United States was rapidly demobilizing, the process had only begun by 1946. The American navy and air force remained extremely powerful, and American naval units were still deployed in the Mediterranean during the Spring of 1946. Furthermore, and perhaps most important, the Soviet Union was still reeling from its war wounds and the gigantic problems of recovery. These factors, along with the American atomic monopoly, may have led Stalin to believe that he must give ground to perceived Western encroachments — sometimes resisting, sometimes retreating — until the strategic situation allowed him to resist more consistently and forcefully. It would appear that by early 1947 the combination of Soviet recovery and Western demobilization had reached a point where he felt prepared to do this. The transition from Phase I to Phase II, then, is marked by a change in capabilities so that the Soviet Union now felt able to defend its interests consistently whenever it believed them to be threatened by the West.

Phase II: Mutual Belligerence

In 1947, the Cold War settled into a phase of marked, mutual hostility. Each side became increasingly convinced of the other's aggressive designs as bellicose exchanges took place over the Greek Civil War, the Truman Doctrine, the Marshall Plan, the Czechoslovakian coup, the joint administration of Germany, and the Berlin blockade. In 1949 the blockade was lifted, but the theater of conflict rapidly shifted to the Far East. By late 1950, the West was involved in a land war against North Korea and China, and the Soviet Union was providing heavy military aid to the Communist side.

It is not entirely clear why such a steady escalation culminating in

[4] See, for example, Bloomfield et al. (1966), Horelick and Rush (1966), Quester (1971), and Wolfe (1964).

open warfare should suddenly give way to a phase of mutual accommodation. Part of the answer seems to lie in the fact that consolidationist coalitions will respond to accommodation with accommodation. Thus, a single, dramatic accommodative act may be sufficient to reverse a belligerent cycle. But why should either coalition engage in such an action? Evidently, because of the escalation itself. The dynamics we have in mind involve a march to the brink of total war culminating in a critical event that makes one coalition decide to back away. The decision to back away need not arise from any insight into the process that brought the antagonists to a breaking point. Rather, it may merely reflect a new assessment that events are getting out of hand and that the matter at issue is not worth the likely cost of continuing to press one's position.

This explanation seems to fit the transition from Phase II to Phase III with the United States initiating the disengagement. The turning point in this mutually belligerent phase came shortly after the full-scale Chinese intervention in the Korean War. In December of 1950, President Truman proclaimed a state of national emergency and asked for steps toward a full war basis. By the early spring of 1951, the Chinese offensive had been halted and the outlines of a military stalemate were appearing. With his commander in Korea and political opponents at home calling for a wider war that would allow the bombing of mainland China, Truman was faced with a difficult decision. He chose, with the support of General Bradley and the Joint Chiefs of Staff, to recall General MacArthur and to emphasize the more limited nature of United States goals in Korea. The unification of Korea by military means was put aside and the interaction process reversed direction, beginning a phase of mutual accommodation.

Notice that we do not postulate that any parameter change was caused by these events. We are not contending that Truman understood how American belligerence contributed to the dynamics of the Cold War interaction during this phase. It is perfectly consistent with our explanation that the West continued to perceive the other side's belligerence as aggressive and its own as defensive. The West moderated its goals in Korea, we are arguing, not because it suddenly realized that its adversary needed reassurance but because the interpretation of its adversary's behavior had become, for the moment, irrelevant. The West became self-oriented rather than adversary-oriented, weighing the real interests involved against the likely cost of continuing.

Phase III: Wary Accommodation

With the recall of MacArthur, the two adversaries began a period of wary accommodation. Truce negotiations began in Korea, and though painfully slow at the outset, they eventually began to yield results: a preliminary truce agreement, an exchange of sick and wounded prisoners, a breakthrough in the deadlock over POW repatriation, and finally an armistice in July of 1953. The following year brought further agreements between the coalitions: a treaty gave Austria its independence, and the Geneva accords brought a temporary peace to Indochina. In the summer of 1955, a summit conference convened in Geneva and carried on its work in an atmosphere of unusual friendliness that came to be called the "Spirit of Geneva."

Interestingly enough, this accommodative phase was unaffected by leadership changes in both camps. Stalin's death and the advent of the Eisenhower administration both occurred in early 1953. These events fall right in the middle of Phase III but produce no discernible differences in the characteristic interaction pattern.[5]

Despite the mutual accommodation that characterized this phase, each coalition continued to see the other as expansionist and, hence, as untrustworthy. This gave the detente a fragile quality. Indeed, by late 1956 the "Spirit of Geneva" was dissipating and a series of events were conspiring to return the interaction to a more belligerent phase. Change in leadership may be relevant here since the transition occurs near the end of the Soviet "interregnum" following the death of Stalin. After some years of jockeying for leadership, Khrushchev consolidated his position shortly after the beginning of Phase IV (clearly by S40 at least). We have already suggested in Chapter Six how this may have contributed to the "heady" quality of Soviet behavior during the next phase.

But entrenchment of leadership was only one of many events that were occurring at the end of Phase III. In the Soviet sphere, control over Eastern Europe was threatened. Hungary and Poland and perhaps others seemed in danger of following the earlier Yugoslavian path or worse. On the Western side, the nationalization of the Suez Canal by an increasingly anti-Western regime in Egypt threatened to accelerate the deterioration of Western influence in the Middle East. The phase of mutual accommodation was too fragile to withstand such shocks.

Phase IV: Entangling Alliances

The Cold War interaction was global but its geographical focus changed from time to time. The hot spot of Soviet-Western conflict was, from time to time, Europe, Asia, Africa, the Middle East, or Latin America. Each of the phases of the Cold War has, to some degree, a characteristic theater of conflict.

In Table 7.3, we classify major Soviet and Western actions by the

[5] The shift from Eisenhower to Kennedy, also in the middle of a phase (IV), did not produce discontinuity either.

Table 7.3

Geographical Area of Major Soviet and Western Actions during Different Phases of the Cold War

SOVIET ACTIONS

Theater	PHASE I		PHASE II		PHASE III		PHASE IV		PHASE V	
	Number of responses	%	Number of responses	%	Number of responses	%	Number of responses	%	Number of responses	%
General[a]	1	14	3	21	0	0	5	22	2	—b
Europe	3	43	8	57	3	19	4	17	0	—
Asia	0	0	3	21	13	81	5	22	0	—
Middle East, Africa, and Latin America	3	43	0	0	0	0	9	39	1	—
Total	7	100	14	100	16	100	23	100	3	—

WESTERN ACTIONS

Theater	PHASE I		PHASE II		PHASE III		PHASE IV		PHASE V	
	Number of responses	%	Number of responses	%	Number of responses	%	Number of responses	%	Number of responses	%
General[a]	2	29	2	14	0	0	2	9	2	—
Europe	3	43	8	57	4	25	4	18	0	—
Asia	0	0	4	29	12	75	5	23	0	—
Middle East, Africa, and Latin America	2	29	0	0	0	0	11	50	1	—
Total	7	100	14	100	16	100	22	100	3	—

[a]This category includes actions that have no specific geographical locus, e.g., "Soviet Union accuses U.S. of seeking war in vitriolic condemnation of U.S. Policy" (S8).
[b]N is too small to compute meaningful percentages.

geographical area or theater in which they occurred. During the first two phases, Europe was the major theater of conflict, with about half of each coalition's major responses occurring there. This percentage dropped sharply during Phase III when Asia (primarily Korea) became the modal theater. The theater shifted again in Phase IV, this time to the developing world: the Middle East, Africa, and Latin America. Phase V is too brief to be characterized by a dominant theater.

The shift in theater seems especially relevant to understanding the Cold War interaction in Phase IV. As long as Europe and Korea were the focal points of Soviet-Western interaction, the terrain had a certain stability. The aims of each coalition might be thwarted or threatened by the actions of the adversary but they were only occasionally threatened by events beyond the control of either coalition.

When the locus of conflict became the former colonial areas, the coalitions frequently found themselves the captive of forces beyond the reach of their power. This lack of control over events was frequently overlooked by the adversary. Thus, a coalition was treated as responsible when situations accrued to its benefit, even though it had done little to bring them about.

Still, the Soviet coalition, riding the euphoria of its scientific and military achievements, showed considerable willingness to exploit its windfalls. It engaged in a more active diplomacy and aid program than in the past; and in shifting its attitude toward greater sympathy with non-Communist, anti-Western governments, it found quite a few in that category who sought some degree of friendship and support.

The Soviet Union during this phase seemed not yet to have come to terms with the limits of its power. Its relationships with governments and would-be governments in the Third World were quite different from its earlier relationships with Eastern European governments under the guns of the Red Army. Its influence with allies in the Middle East, Africa, and Latin America stopped far short of complete control.

When such allies became involved in conflicts with the West, the Soviet Union found itself in a dilemma. It could become a full party to the conflict, offering a variety of support to its ally, but to do this was to risk a confrontation with the West that might threaten its vital interests for the sake of quite peripheral ones. On the other hand, it could allow the West to encroach on its friend, thus calling into question the value of Soviet friendship. The result of such ambivalence was a certain amount of inconsistency, reflected in both conciliatory and refractory responses to Western belligerence.[6]

[6] This inconsistent period in Soviet policy is discussed at length at the end of Chapter Six and we shall not repeat that discussion here.

While the rising tide of nationalism in the Third World was a dangerous temptation to the Soviet coalition, it was a direct threat to the West, especially to England and France. This contributed to a period of internal confusion and inconsistency in Western policy. The Anglo-French invasion of Suez in 1956 split the coalition, and United States opposition contributed to a retreat in the face of Soviet belligerence. Two years later, the United States landed Marines in the Middle East in an effort to bolster a pro-Western regime. In May of 1960, an ill-timed U-2 overflight of the Soviet Union led to the collapse of the pending Summit Conference in Paris. Again Western policy was inconsistent. At first, the United States sought to justify its overflight; then, in the face of Soviet anger, it canceled the entire U-2 program.

However, from the collapse of the Paris Summit Conference to the Cuban missile crisis of October, 1962, there was a period of virtually unrelieved mutual tension and hostility. The confrontation over Cuba provided the impetus for a Soviet retrenchment and a return to the pattern of mutual accommodation. Whereas at the end of Phase II the United States backed off, this time the Soviet Union stepped back from the brink to break the cycle of mutual belligerence.

Phase V: Detente

Our analysis ends with November, 1963. There are only a few interaction units after the Cuban missile crisis but they resemble the mutual accommodation of Phase III. This earlier phase was a fragile one and it gave way to Phase IV, a period of renewed hostility and tension. How is it that the detente of Phase V has apparently survived to this writing? How stable is it? Can we expect a return to a new phase of mutual hostility? We speculate on these questions in the next section.

CONCLUSION

We make no claim that the preceding interpretation of the Cold War is more "scientific" than that of a historian or political scientist using more traditional methods. Our method of generating the interpretation is different, however, and has both advantages and disadvantages. The disadvantages include the many simplifying assumptions necessary to carry out the analysis. We lose the richness of detail and much of the color of Soviet-Western interaction. The actors do not come alive in our abstract account, and the dramatic, human decisions and confrontations that marked this conflict are lost in the manipulation of numbers.

But there are important advantages as well. Our method of analysis is quite general — capable of being applied to almost any conflict in which the protagonists are sometimes refractory and sometimes conciliatory.[7] Further, this method is "objective" in the sense that anyone using our coding procedures should be able to recreate the data tables from which we work. But most important, our procedures put more constraint on interpretation than historians and political scientists normally experience: we must deal with what our data show. There are, to be sure, some degrees of freedom, and no single interpretation is dictated by our results. The data do not entirely speak for themselves, but they have some voice of their own — some independence and resistance to interpretations that we might wish to impose. We do not enjoy the luxury of selecting the facts that fit our thesis while blurring or ignoring those that embarrass it.

This greater constraint is an advantage because it increases the probability of surprise and discovery. We might have argued, for example, that both the Berlin blockade of 1948 and the Cuban missile crisis of 1962 were historical watersheds in the Cold War interaction. No doubt we could have made a case for both of these by the usual methods of historical analysis. But our analysis of interaction units clearly indicates that one of these events was a watershed and one was not.

Our interpretation, then, must deal with the intractable numbers in our various tables. Perhaps there are other interpretations consistent with these numbers but there surely are many that are not. The one we have argued grew out of an attempt to make sense of our results — it did not precede them.

But what of Soviet-Western relations after 1963? Here we can make no claim to being guided and constrained by our data, but we have some speculations that grow out of our analysis. Once before in the Cold War, the two adversaries found themselves in a period of mutual accommodation, but this proved unstable and gave way to renewed hostility and tension. The question we pose is this: Are the same instabilities still present in Soviet-Western relations or does the present interaction contain some new source of stability?

If both coalitions have consolidationist goals, a mutually accommodative phase *could* continue indefinitely. However, as long as each perceives the other as expansionist, and each fails to recognize the other's erroneous perception, such a phase will be inherently unstable. The first sign of belligerence, whatever its source, can be sufficient to

---

[7] All that is required to study such a conflict is a description based on our coding procedures. If our argument in Chapter Four is correct in concluding that the seven belief systems used here are the only logically meaningful ones, then both the belief systems and their predictions would remain unchanged when applying our procedure to another conflict.

reverse the cycle. Under these conditions, a third party with an interest in increasing Soviet-Western tension for its own ends can quite easily upset a detente by building on the existing suspicions of one side or the other. Or, with suspicions running high, the detente may be accidentally upset by events which threaten one coalition with a loss of influence. Even a remote connection between the adversary and the threatening events may be enough to convince a coalition that its adversary is merely being more subtle and indirect in its aggression.

It is entirely possible that the wary accommodation of Phase III broke down because Soviet goals became somewhat more expansionist. We do not intend to deny this possibility. But it is important to realize that no such assumption is *necessary* to explain the breakdown of mutual accommodation among coalitions that perceive each other as expansionist. The instability is inherent in the situation, and many events can precipitate the breakdown of such a fragile detente.

Since 1963, the Soviet-Western detente has undergone a number of severe tests. It has survived the massive bombing of a Communist country by the United States; Soviet military aid to a country at war with the United States; an Arab-Israeli war in which the Soviet Union supported Arab ambitions and the United States supported Israeli military actions; and the Soviet intervention in Czechoslovakia. Some of these events bear a striking resemblance to those that upset the detente of Phase III.[8]

The ability to withstand such shocks suggests that the current detente is much more stable. And this, in turn, suggests a parameter change. Notice that if *either* side corrects its perception of the adversary's goals and recognizes it as consolidationist, the detente will be much more stable. If both do, the stability is virtually complete. When this occurs, each side's refractory action will be interpreted by the other as limited and defensively oriented, rather than as possible preludes to renewed aggression.

President Kennedy's speech at American University in June, 1963, was probably the first indication that a heretofore minority view of the Soviet Union as consolidationist was beginning to get some tentative, cautious sympathy in official circles. "It is sad," said the President, "to read these Soviet statements [about Western expansionist aims] — to realize the extent of the gulf between us. But it is also a warning — a

---

[8] In addition, it is worth noting that since 1964 the United States seems to have been going through an "arrogance of power" phase similar to the one the Soviets went through in the fourth phase of the Cold War. It is not hard to find similar evidence of headiness and uneasiness leading to overcommitment. Yet the detente is even surviving the provocations associated with this period of American foreign policy.

warning to the American people not to fall into the same trap as the Soviets, not to see only a distorted and desperate view of the other side. . . . Among the many traits the peoples of our two countries have in common, none is stronger than our mutual abhorrence of war. . . . We are both caught up in a vicious and dangerous cycle with suspicion on one side breeding suspicion on the other, and new weapons begetting counter weapons." One should not exaggerate the thrust of this speech — it reverts to official orthodoxy a number of times — but it suggests a new beginning in Western perceptions of the Soviet Union. Perhaps the best indication of change on the part of both coalitions is the restraint that each side has exercised in challenging actions that surely would have been regarded as highly provocative at the height of the Cold War.

If each side is moving toward a perception of the other as consolidationist, then the Soviet-Western detente will continue. In spite of disagreements from time to time, there will be no return to the tense interaction surrounding the Berlin blockade or the Cuban missile crisis. The danger of nuclear war remains, but it has receded substantially since 1962.

Some observers see a new danger in the Soviet-Western detente that replaces the old one of nuclear war. If each side is circumspect in challenging the actions of its former adversary, each is also relatively freer in using its power over third parties. If the West is unhappy about developments in the Dominican Republic, it will more readily impose its will when it is confident that this will not bring it into serious conflict with the Soviet Union. If the Soviet Union is unhappy about the evolution of Czechoslovakian politics, it is freer to impose its will when it knows that it need not fear a Western response. The Cold War conflict offered a certain protection to the weak — albeit a frequently perfidious and erratic one purchased at the continual risk of a nuclear war.

There is some truth in this new danger. But the "weak" sometimes turn out to have surprising resourcefulness in resisting the will of the powerful; and the powerful sometimes find limits imposed by the disenchantment and revulsion of their own citizens. Ultimately, these are safer constraints than those provided by a hostile interaction among mutually suspicious countries armed with nuclear weapons.

Methodological Appendices

The following section contains three appendices which, taken together, give a detailed exposition and justification of the methodology used in this study. Appendix A gives the complete rules for coding refractory and conciliatory actions, for combining these actions into an overall score for a time period, and for defining the boundaries of a time period. Appendix B addresses the many issues raised by the use of the New York Times *as the primary data source. Finally, Appendix C describes the rules by which we translate a set of parameter values into a set of interpretations of an adversary's behavior. Combined with the decision model presented in Chapter Four, this appendix completes the explanation of how predictions are derived from belief systems.*

Appendix A

Measuring the Interaction Unit

The basic unit of our analysis is the *interaction unit*. Each unit is made up of two components: a major action by one coalition; and a pattern of actions by its adversary in the immediately preceding time period. The major action is coded as either refractory or conciliatory. The adversary's preceding pattern is assigned an overall score on a continuous scale (the belligerent/accommodative scale). For the purposes of analysis, this continuous scale is subdivided into nine discrete categories that range from extremely belligerent to extremely accommodative. A completely coded interaction unit, then, contains a description of the responding coalition's major action (e.g., refractory), and a description of the adversary's preceding pattern of behavior (e.g., extremely belligerent). The construction of such interaction units involves three central methodological problems:

1. How does one identify and measure single refractory and conciliatory actions?
2. How does one combine a series of these actions, taken over a given time period, into an overall score on the belligerent/accommodative scale?
3. How does one define the boundaries of a time period — that is, how does one determine which actions should be included in the overall score?

IDENTIFYING AND MEASURING REFRACTORY AND CONCILIATORY ACTIONS

The basic data source for this study is the daily *New York Times*. We will defer until Appendix B all discussion of the validity of this source for our purposes. For the moment, we will address ourselves to how we used the *New York Times* to develop a daily score of concilia-

127

tory and refractory action for each coalition during the period from January 1, 1946, to November 22, 1963.

The coding process involved several steps. First, a research assistant examined the front page of the *New York Times* for every day during the period covered and prepared a brief summary of each article that pertained to interaction between the Soviet and Western coalitions. Each of the authors then independently coded these summaries and reconciled all disagreements after discussion. A third person, an undergraduate research assistant, coded selected periods to provide a further check on reliability.

The coding rules assign to each article a *magnitude score* based on the size of the *New York Times* headline introducing the story. This does not require any judgment on the part of the coder: it is based strictly on mechanical criteria to be discussed below. The coder is required to make only two judgments about each article:

1. Does it report tactically contingent conciliatory or refractory actions by one or both coalitions; or are the reported actions neutral? In other words, should the story be included in the tabulation or not?
2. If included, how should its total magnitude score be allocated between the two coalitions and between their refractory and conciliatory columns?

Most of this appendix will be devoted to a discussion of the rules that guide a coder in making these two decisions. First, however, we take up the issue of magnitude scores.

The Magnitude Score

Our magnitudes are determined by the *Benny Profane Method*. Benny Profane, the hero of Thomas Pynchon's novel, *V*, was not much interested in foreign policy: "Profane's newspaper reading was in fact confined to glancing at the front page of the *New York Times*. If there was no banner headline on that paper, then the world was in good enough shape." We take the Benny Profane Method, add to it the usual arcana of the social scientist, and use it to measure the importance of refractory and conciliatory actions.

The total magnitude score of an article is determined by a combination of position on the front page and size of the headline that introduces the story. An article beginning in the upper third of the front page receives a weight of 3, an article appearing in the middle third receives a 2, and an article in the bottom third receives a 1. This weight is then multiplied by the number of columns over which the headline extends to get the final magnitude score.[1] To be included in the study, an article has to have a magnitude of at least 3. This means that, as a minimum, an article needs a one-column headline at the top of the front page (a score of 3) or a two-column headline in the middle of the front page (a score of 4).

There is one exception to this method of calculating magnitude. An eight-column headline at the top of the page is given a score of 36, rather than 24, to reflect the fact that the physical dimensions of the paper place an artificial upper limit on the magnitude of major articles.

Sometimes multiple stories emanate from the same headline. For example, a five-column headline at the top may feed two different articles, either related or unrelated to each other. In such a case, the magnitude of a story is its proportional share of the headline magnitude plus an additional score of 1 for each column of its *sub*headline. Thus, for example, if two articles emanating from the same five-column headline have one- and two-column subheadlines, they receive scores of 8.5 (i.e., $1\frac{5}{2} + 1$) and 9.5 (i.e., $1\frac{5}{2} + 2$) respectively. For convenience, we always round up so that these stories actually receive magnitudes of 9 and 10 respectively.

Coder Decisions

We start by considering the simplest case: an article which reports a single, unilateral action. The coder must make only one decision on such an article: Does it report an action by either coalition that affected disagreements between them (either increasing or decreasing them)? In most cases, the determination is quite clear, but there are a number of ambiguous situations that must be considered.

TACTICAL CONTINGENCY. Only the tactically contingent actions of a coalition, i.e., those actions for which the decision calculus includes what the other side has done or might do as one important element, are eligible to be coded as refractory or conciliatory. Thus, when the nature *or timing* of an action is essentially independent of the adversary's behavior, the action is excluded. For example, most actions relating to the development and testing of new weapons are excluded since their timing is assumed to be governed primarily by the pace of research. The explosion of an atomic bomb, the development of a missile-carrying submarine, or the cancellation of a manned bomber program would all be excluded despite the broadly contingent nature of the overall defense program of which they are a part. Reciprocal and negotiated arms agreements would, of course, be included, as would any major arms mobilization or major shift in defense policy.

---

[1] This measure, incidentally, correlates better than .90 with column inches.

Such shifts must, however, be contingent on the behavior of the other side to some important degree and not simply a function of domestic political and economic considerations, or of technological developments that involved changes in defense hardware without reference to what the adversary was doing.

Speeches by high government officials that are domestically-oriented and largely ceremonial in nature are another example of actions that are excluded because they fail to meet the criterion of tactical contingency. Thus, a State of the Union message containing ritual Cold War phrases to the effect that American policy was helping to "protect the free world from Communist tyranny" would be excluded, as would a Soviet ceremonial speech reaffirming the necessity of combating "capitalist imperialism around the world."

Apart from cases of weapon development and ceremonial speeches, there are no simple rules for determining whether an action is tactically contingent. The coder must use his best judgment. In each case he must ask himself; "was the decision to take this action based to an important degree on a consideration of what the other side had done or might do, or was it instead based essentially on other considerations unrelated to the adversary's behavior?" In cases of doubt, a coder is encouraged to err in the direction of inclusion.

OFFICIAL SPOKESMEN. To be included, the action reported must be that of a national actor. A national actor is one who acts on behalf of the nation rather than as a member of a subgroup or by himself. For example, an off-duty American soldier who attacks an East German policeman is not considered a national actor although the incident may subsequently lead to relevant actions by national actors (for example, official protests or demands for release of the soldier).

A more ambiguous situation arises when certain high officials, for example, the chairman of the Atomic Energy Commission or of the Senate Foreign Relations Committee, make policy declarations that affect disagreements. Except when such individuals are clearly speaking as critics of the government and publicly disassociate themselves from official policy (or are publicly repudiated by higher officials), they are regarded as speaking for the government. Therefore, in the absence of clear disassociation from official policy, they are treated as national actors. The same rule has even greater application to the less autonomous Soviet situation.

ACTIONS, WORDS, AND SPIRITS. From time to time the Cold War was visited by "spirits," most notably the Spirit of Geneva and the Spirit of Camp David. The contribution of such spirits to the resolution of conflict is a matter of some dispute among observers of the Cold War.

How does our code deal with such spirits? More generally, how do we deal with such matters as summit conferences and friendly visits of high officials?

To answer these questions we must refer back to our distinction between *disintegrative forces* and *integrative bonds* (Chapter One, pp. 11–12). To review, disintegrative forces reflect the level of conflict in a relationship, and vary as a direct function of the number and intensity of outstanding disagreements. On the other hand, integrative bonds reflect the capacity of a relationship to withstand conflict, and vary as a direct function of the number and strength of existing joint mechanisms for handling disagreement and pursuing common goals. Each is logically independent of the other. Establishing a new joint mechanism (e.g., exploratory talks during a war) does not necessarily reduce the level of conflict; and reducing the level of conflict (e.g., a unilateral bombing halt) does not necessarily create or strengthen joint mechanisms. To be sure, changes in one *may* lead to changes in the other, but this is an empirical question and not a matter of definition.

This distinction between disintegrative forces and integrative bonds is especially important in avoiding confusions about *conciliatory* actions. In this study, the term "conciliatory" refers only to actions that reduce outstanding disagreements. It is not meant to be a catch-all that encompasses all manner of cooperative activity between the coalitions. Much of this activity affects only integrative bonds while leaving outstanding disagreements unchanged.

Summit conferences (or visits by an adversary head of state) have their major impact on integrative ties. They create a joint forum in which representatives of the coalitions can try to resolve outstanding differences. But merely getting together does not constitute a concrete step toward such a resolution. Therefore, all articles reporting merely that a summit conference (or a visit) was in progress, or was about to take place, are excluded from our analysis. On the other hand, any article indicating that such a meeting was resolving disagreements is coded as conciliatory; and any article reporting that such a meeting was producing further disagreements is coded as refractory.

This treatment of summit conferences and visits does not ally us with those skeptics who view them as meaningless exercises. The issue for us is the more technical one of whether these actions affect disintegrative forces or integrative bonds. To illustrate this further, an article reporting "Khrushchev declares his exclusion from Disneyland removes possibility of Berlin settlement" would be included, but an article reporting "Khrushchev praises pigs on Iowa farm visit" would not. Visits and cultural exchanges, meetings that result in a "healthy airing of views," and agreements on platitudes (e.g., that it is better to negotiate than to fight over differences), may all affect integrative bonds; however, they are excluded as long as they do not affect outstanding disagreements as well.

We make one exception to the exclusion of articles dealing with integrative bonds. The manipulation of such ties is used sometimes to increase or dramatize outstanding disagreement. For example, the cancellation of the Paris Summit Conference following the U-2 incident was a refractory action even though the Conference itself would probably have had its main effect on integrative bonds. The cancellation, given the circumstances in which it occurred, did not simply remove an integrative bond. It was carried out in a manner and context that enhanced disagreement between the Soviet Union and the United States. Similarly, the severing of diplomatic or trade relations in the context of a crisis is coded as a refractory action, although the simple expiration of a three-year trade pact in a noncrisis context would not be included.

We do not, in any of the above remarks, intend to imply a distinction between actions and mere words. We regard such a distinction as untenable. The importance of an action is not an intrinsic property but merely a reflection of how much one or the other party wishes to make of it. If a coalition chooses to ignore or to play down some unilateral move by its adversary, then the action does not significantly increase disagreements even if the act in question clearly had hostile intent. By the same token, a verbal barrage or a renewed assertion of a position may sharply affect the saliency of a disagreement. For example, while Soviet and Western differences concerning Berlin were chronic during the period of study, a new speech by a Soviet official strongly attacking the Western presence in Berlin would be coded as a refractory act for having made the chronic disagreement more salient.

REACTIONS VS. COUNTERACTIONS. A major event is often followed by a spate of related stories. The construction of the Berlin Wall, for example, might lead to an article such as, "West denounces Berlin Wall as act of barbarity — Claims propaganda victory." Should this article be coded as a refractory Western action?

To handle such problems, we distinguish between a *reaction* and a *counteraction*. A reaction is any expression of opinion about an action of the other side that occurs on the same day as the original action or on a consecutive day, providing that it does not include any *new* action by the reacting side. A counteraction, which may occur either right away or later, goes beyond merely stating feelings about the original action and implies, promises, or threatens some new action in response.

Reactions are coded as part of the magnitude of the original action. Thus, in the example of the building of the Berlin Wall and the Western comment on this action, both stories would be counted as part of the original action. The magnitude of this Soviet action is the combined total of the scores of all articles reporting the action and reactions.

The reaction and counteraction categories are, of course, mutually exclusive. Any time an article reports events that are considered counteractions, it is not counted as a reaction regardless of any expression of feeling that is also included. The fact that a counteraction may be very much a response to some immediately preceding action by the other side does not alter its coding. The critical element in using the reaction category is the absence of any behavioral component in the response of the reacting side. Counteractions might follow later.

CONTINUING PROGRAMS. Single actions that are part of a continuing refractory program are considered neutral rather than refractory.[2] For example, each American participation in a Korean battle would not be coded as refractory, nor would each new American overflight of Cuba in a continuing U-2 Program. However, the initial commitment to the program and any reassertion of this commitment (i.e., an expression to continue or accelerate it) would be coded as refractory. Under these rules, the 1960 U-2 incident is handled as follows: since the flight itself was part of a continuing refractory program of U-2 missions and the shooting down of the plane was part of a continuing refractory program of downing any airplanes that violate Soviet airspace, these actions themselves are neutral. However, many other actions in this incident are included: Soviet threats to bomb bases from which U-2 planes originate; the denunciation of the United States for its provocations; the Western recommitment to the program and justification of its continuance; and the subsequent cancellation of these flights by the West.

Spy programs and arrests are handled in a similar manner. Both sides are assumed to have continuing espionage and counter-espionage programs. The arrest of an individual spy or the collection of secret information by such spies is not coded as a refractory action. However, counteractions that grow from such instances enter as refractory actions.

Since the initiation of a continuing program counts but actions that

[2] We have some retrospective doubt about this decision. A case might be made for including some regular contribution for such continuing refractory activity. However, as far as we can tell, this would not have made any significant difference in this study.

are part of the program are treated as neutral, how does one know when the initiation ends and the body of the program begins? The rule of thumb we use here is that an action becomes part of a continuing program when the decisions involved are no longer made or approved by the head of the state involved but by whoever is responsible for the day-to-day operations of the program. For example, United States actions at the beginning of the Korean war are counted as long as they were directed by President Truman. Once they became simply military tactical decisions, they are no longer counted. Battles are excluded but decisions to bomb new territory or to shift the nature or extent of United States commitment in some way, such as by crossing the 38th parallel, are included.

INSURRECTIONS. A related problem concerns insurrections and riots. Should they be considered strictly internal or a part of Soviet-Western interaction? In a conflict between a coalition and some insurgents, actions taken by the adversary coalition would be included. Thus, if the United States had supplied arms or other aid to East Berlin rioters, this Western action would be coded as refractory and included. The more difficult question is whether to treat the actions of the insurgent group itself as part of the Cold War interaction.

Treating the conflict between a coalition and a group of insurgents as part of Soviet-Western interaction is equivalent to treating the insurgents as part of the adversary coalition. The rules that apply here are those that govern temporary membership in a coalition (see Chapter One, pp. 8–9). The insurgents are a neutral "group" in conflict with one coalition. Two criteria determine whether this group can be considered a temporary member of the adversary coalition. First, the adversary coalition must identify itself with the cause of the insurgents, giving them at least verbal support. Second, the insurgents must seek and accept the support offered. The order of initiation does not matter. By these criteria, the Hungarian insurgents against Soviet control in 1956 are treated as temporary members of the Western coalition, after they invited and accepted recognition and support from the West. On the other hand, the actions of the East Berlin rioters in 1953 fail to qualify because the rioters never received formal support and recognition from the West.

CHARGES. A particularly difficult set of articles to code are those involving charges by one side of refractory actions by the other side — for example, charges that opponents are warmongers, are bent on world conquest, are using germ warfare, or have bombed an area in violation of a truce agreement. To help in handling these articles, we distinguish three kinds of charges.

1. *Charges that are subsequently verified.* In many cases, charges that are initially denied or ignored are tacitly verified by later actions that acknowledge their validity. An example is a Soviet denial of charges that its troops were at particular locations in Iran, followed a few days later by a pledge to remove these troops by a certain date.

2. *Charges that are potentially verifiable but are never proven or disproven.* Examples are charges that the United States employed germ warfare in Korea or that the Soviet Union aided the rebellion in Greece.

3. *Charges that are not subject to verification because of their vagueness and use of interpretive language.* Charges that focus on the bad motives of the other side or which, in other ways, interpret actions rather than contest facts are always considered unverifiable. An example is the Soviet charge that the West was wrecking the four-power rule of Germany by its actions. The existence of given actions is not in dispute here, but the notion that these actions were leading to the wrecking of four-power rule in Germany is an unverifiable interpretation not shared by the other side. Even clearer examples are charges that the Soviet Union never honors its treaty commitments or that the United States government is run by imperialist war-mongers and neofascists.

Charges of the first type are counted as refractory actions *by the side that is charged.* Charges of the last type are counted as refractory actions *by the side that does the charging.* As for the second type, we resist the temptation to use our own beliefs about such things as the germ-warfare charge as the basis for classification. Instead, we simply exclude such stories in which both sides maintain their position indefinitely.

Denial of charges is counted as neutral unless accompanied by some counterattack on the side making the charge. On the other hand, admission of the truth of a charge combined with effort at justification (as, for example, the United States did in the U-2 incident of 1960) is coded as a refractory action.

COMPOUND ARTICLES. Up to now we have considered the handling of articles reporting a single action by one coalition. Many articles, however, either explicitly or implicitly report several actions simultaneously, e.g., actions by different sides or both refractory and conciliatory actions by the same side. Before such a *compound* article can be coded, it must be divided into "parcels" corresponding to its several components. Each such parcel contains the actions of one coalition in one direction.[3] All actions by the same coalition in the same direction

---

[3] The "direction" of an action refers to whether it is conciliatory or refractory.

are included in the same parcel. Hence, a compound article can be divided at most into four parcels: one corresponding to the actions of each coalition in each direction.

For coding purposes, each parcel is treated as if it were a separate article. It is assigned a magnitude equal to its proportionate share of the total magnitude of the article from which it derives. Thus, if an original compound article were divided into n parcels, each parcel would receive $1/n$th of the original magnitude. To be included in our data, a parcel must meet the usual minimum magnitude requirement (i.e., its magnitude must be ≥ 3 after being rounded up to the nearest integer).

There are several types of compound articles. The least problematic is one that refers to only one party, but reports both conciliatory and refractory actions. There are two parcels in such an article — one conciliatory and one refractory. An example would be "Russians release American fliers; denounce U.S. for deliberately provocative acts."

A more complicated type of compound article is one that reports actions by both sides either implicitly or explicitly. We distinguish three kinds of compound articles of this type.

1. *Explicit joint actions.* The article reports actions that are the result of direct coordination between the two coalitions. The clearest example is the negotiated settlement of a disagreement. Other examples would include reports of progress or stalemate in a negotiation and reports of bitter or useful exchanges.

2. *Implicit joint actions.* The article reports the actions of only one coalition, but these actions clearly imply activity by the other coalition as well. Included here are those actions that take place in the context of a continuing negotiation — i.e., in a setting where there are regularly scheduled meetings between the two coalitions aimed at seeking a coordinated solution to some disagreement. Any action in a continuing negotiation that is conditional on the other party's *negotiating* behavior is treated as an implicit joint action.

The actions included here are typically those implying either deadlock or progress; for example, denunciations of the other side's position, justifications of one's own position, or praise and encouragement for the other side's conduct. Most actions that occur in the context of a United Nations debate are of this type, including, for example, vetoes or walkouts. A Soviet veto of a Western-backed proposal implies the existence of a Western effort to have its proposal adopted. We thus avoid the selective emphasis of the *New York Times* in such jointly controlled situations.

Not every action that occurs in the context of a continuing negotiation is considered joint. Policy shifts by one side — whether away from or toward the adversary's position — are considered unilateral actions. But mere reiteration of a former position, implying that neither side has moved, is treated as joint action.

The United Nations is sometimes used as a forum for unilateral action. To distinguish between an action that is unilateral and one that is implicitly joint, we use a rule of relevance. If the action is relevant to a particular issue under discussion at the time, then it is considered part of the continuing negotiation and is coded as an implicit joint action. If, on the other hand, it is not relevant to the issue being debated, then it is treated as a unilateral action for which the UN merely serves as a convenient forum.

Explicit joint actions and implicit joint actions are coded in identical fashion. Articles reporting either type are divided into two parcels, one of which is assigned to each coalition. The distinction is made to alert the coder to the existence of implicit jointness even where only one side's actions are emphasized.

3. *Parallel actions.* The article reports unilateral actions taken separately by each coalition. These articles are also parceled but, unlike joint actions, it is possible here for the two parcels to be different in direction. Such articles might, for example, report Soviet conciliatory and Western refractory behavior in the same story — as in the article, "Russians promise early withdrawal of troops from Iran; U.S. to press case in UN."

By combining one or more of the above types of articles, it is possible to get even more complicated compounds. These are handled by simple extensions of the above rules. For example, the article, "Russians lift rail blockade but threaten drastic measures if West proceeds with currency reform; West remains adamant," would be treated as three parcels of parallel action: a Soviet conciliatory parcel, a Soviet refractory one, and a Western refractory one.

AN EXCEPTION TO PARCELING. Parceling an article greatly reduces the magnitude that each coalition receives. Ordinarily this seems justified since the joint participation may make the story bigger. In this reasoning, the individual parcels might, by editorial decision, have been separated into two articles of half magnitude, but they are combined because of relatedness of content. This reasoning seems unsatisfactory for those negotiations that end in the successful resolution of some disagreement. The joint nature of the agreement is so intrinsic that it seems to underestimate the magnitude to split it between the two sides.

For this reason, we make one exception to the parceling rule for compound stories. For those articles that report explicit, substantive agreements on some outstanding difference, each coalition receives the full magnitude of the article. For example, a three-column headline at the top of the page reporting "French and Reds in accord on armistice supervision; Geneva plan includes veto" is scored as a nine-point conciliatory action for each side instead of being parceled into two articles with magnitudes of 4.5 each.

Only specific agreements that remove differences are included in the above exception. Reports of progress or of fruitful exchanges are parceled as indicated above. Similarly, agreement on procedure (places to meet, dates, and agenda) is parceled in the normal manner as is any other agreement on a matter that is not contested in the negotiation.

PROPOSALS. A final coding problem involves the handling of proposals. We distinguish four kinds.

1. *Ambiguous proposal.* This refers to a proposal that is neither a clear hardening nor a loosening of a coalition's previous position. The adversary does not immediately react but indicates that it will take the proposal under consideration.

An ambiguous proposal is coded as a neutral act by the proposer. If it is subsequently rejected by the adversary, the rejection is coded as joint refractory action (one side made an unacceptable proposal and the other refused to accept it). If it is subsequently accepted by the adversary, the acceptance is coded as a joint conciliatory action (one side made an acceptable proposal and the other agreed to accept it).

2. *Request for concession.* This refers to a proposal in which the adversary is asked to make a concession. It differs from a demand proposal discussed below in that no refractory actions are implied if the proposal is rejected and often conciliatory actions are implied if the proposal is accepted.

A request for concession is coded as a neutral act by the proposer. If it is subsequently rejected by the adversary, the rejection is coded as joint refractory. (The two sides simply underlined their previous disagreement.) If it is subsequently accepted, it is coded as a conciliatory action for the coalition that accepted the proposal.

3. *Demand proposal.* This refers to a proposal in which the adversary is asked to make a concession. However, it differs from a request for a concession in that refractory actions are threatened or implied if the proposal is not accepted.

A demand proposal is coded as a refractory action for the side that made the proposal. If it is subsequently rejected by the adversary, the rejection is coded as a joint refractory action. If the demand proposal is subsequently accepted, the acceptance is coded as a conciliatory action for the side that accepted the proposal.

4. *Conciliatory proposal.* This refers to a proposal that includes concessions or shifts toward the adversary's position although it might contain requests for concessions as well. A conciliatory proposal is coded as a conciliatory action for the side that makes the proposal. If it is rejected outright, the rejection is coded as a refractory action by the rejecting side. If it is not accepted but met by a counterproposal, the counterproposal is coded according to the above rules on proposals. If the conciliatory proposal is accepted, it is coded as an explicit *joint* conciliatory action.

A Summary by Months

These then are the coding rules that yield a daily refractory and conciliatory score for each coalition for some 6,574 days of the Cold War. Since these scores may be of use to other investigators for a variety of purposes, they are summarized by month for each coalition in Appendix D. In addition to the raw score for each month, a standard score is provided. This standard score expresses each monthly score in standard deviations above or below the mean monthly score for that coalition during the 216 months from 1946 to 1963.

Major Actions

Articles reporting major actions are coded in the same manner as any other article. They differ only in their magnitude score. A major action by a coalition is one that receives a score of 12 on a single day or a combined score of 15 on two successive days (including at least one single-day score of 9). Typically, a major action is one that captures at least a four-column front-page headline.

An action that is a straightforward extension or follow-up of a previous major action does not constitute a *separate* major action even though it may meet our magnitude criteria. For example, if the Soviet Union agreed to Korean truce talks on Monday and China agreed to such talks on Thursday and both actions were reported by eight-column headlines, the second action is considered an extension of the first. This means it is coded normally, but it is not treated as the major action for a separate interaction unit.

Two major actions that do not meet our magnitude criteria are included by the use of a "closure" convention. This convention states that if an action that ended a crisis qualifies by the magnitude criteria, then the action that began the crisis qualifies automatically. This convention enables us to include two highly significant actions that would

otherwise fail to qualify: the start of the Berlin blockade and the beginning of Soviet military build-up and missile enplacement in Cuba.
For special reasons, neither would qualify by using the headline criteria. The 1948 Berlin blockade began so gradually and erratically that
no sufficiently dramatic single action ever took place. The 1962 em-
placement of missiles in Cuba was carried out secretly and was not
discovered by the West (or its press) for some weeks.

A complete list of major Soviet and Western actions is included in
Appendix E. As it turns out, there are 63 major Soviet actions and 62
major Western actions.

The Dating of Actions

Ordinarily, an action is given the same date as the issue of the *New
York Times* that reported it. Since a newspaper typically reports the
preceding day's events, this procedure simply introduces a constant
one-day lag in all our data. (Such a constant lag in no way affects our
analyses.) On rare occasions, however, there may be a much longer
delay in reporting because of secrecy surrounding a certain action.
Even in such a case, the reporting date is generally acceptable for our
purposes because it can be considered, in most cases, as equivalent to
the date on which the action was discovered by the other side. Recall
that in our analytical framework, the actions of one coalition are
treated as inputs that influence the other coalition's major actions.
Clearly, an action becomes an input to the other coalition, not when it
is performed, but when it is discovered.

The dating of major actions, however, is more complicated. Such
actions play a dual role as input and response. When they are treated
as part of the adversary's previous actions to which a coalition is
responding, they are dated from the time of discovery just like any
other action. However, when they are treated as a response, the time
of performance becomes the relevant date.

Should the time of performance be dated from the moment when the
decision was made to perform the action or from the time the decision
began to be implemented? The latter date is the one used here. Time
of decision is inappropriate for both practical and theoretical reasons:
it is difficult to obtain accurate information on exactly when a decision
was made; but more important, use of this criterion might exclude
relevant actions by the adversary. Decisions can still be changed anytime before they are actually implemented. They are often made
tentatively, or conditionally, pending some final signal to proceed. This
means that the adversary's actions can still influence a decision. The
point of no return is reached only after implementation begins.

Time of discovery is not appropriate when we are considering an action as response. To use it can lead to the inclusion of irrelevant actions by the adversary. Specifically, it would make eligible for inclusion as inputs those adversary actions that occur *after* the responding coalition has already passed the point of no return in its response.

Since it is usually very difficult to keep a major action secret, the time of discovery almost always corresponds with the time of implementation. A discrepancy between these two dates occurs only once in our study, and in this case, we use two separate dates for the action. This one exception is the Soviet military build-up leading to placing missiles in Cuba. As a response to Western action, it is dated in July when the military build-up began. As an input to a major Western response, it is dated in October when United States aerial reconnaissance established the fact that ground-to-ground missiles were being deployed.

Coding Reliability

There are various ways to estimate reliability. The most stringent method is to ask whether two independent coders agree exactly on whether or not each article should be included or excluded and, if included, on how its magnitude should be allocated. Using such reliability checks for selected time periods, we were able to obtain exact agreement slightly better than 80 percent of the time.[4] Even joint coding experience did not raise reliability much above this figure since an irreducible number of borderline judgments or ambiguous articles remained. Intercoder, product-moment correlations over daily scores were generally .8 or above.

These figures are respectable but they substantially *underestimate* the reliability of the data in the aggregated form in which it is ultimately used. The reliability of a monthly total, for example, is considerably higher. There are three major reasons for this. First, many coding errors are offsetting and cancel each other out when daily scores are aggregated. Second, coders tend to make fewer errors on major or high magnitude actions, perhaps because the impact of such actions on disagreements is clearer and they are more fully reported. These major actions make a large contribution to a monthly total. Finally, the sheer number of articles to code varies greatly from month to month and is highly related to the final magnitude score for the month. Thus, in a quiet month, the coders might disagree on 5 of 25 articles and still arrive at agreement on a low score for each coalition;

---

[4] These checks included comparing the authors' codes with each other and each, in turn, with a third coder, usually an undergraduate research assistant.

in an active month with 100 articles, they might disagree on 20 and still arrive at agreement on high scores for both sides. Thus, their monthly scores would reflect high agreement in spite of disagreement on 20 percent of the individual articles coded.

These considerations explain why we obtain much higher coder agreement when monthly scores are compared. *The correlation between independent coders on this more relevant measure of reliability is approximately .95.* Thus, while it would be unwise to place too much reliance on any given daily score (unless it is a major action), scores aggregated over a month or a time period are quite reliable. The validity of such scores is, of course, another question, one that we address in Appendix B.

CHARACTERIZING SEQUENCES OF ACTIONS

Thus far we have elaborated on the procedures for identifying and scoring single actions. These procedures enable us to measure one component of an interaction unit (the responding coalition's major action), and they generate the raw scores needed to assess the remaining component (the adversary's preceding pattern of behavior). The adversary's behavior consists of an array of actions, each of which has a refractory or conciliatory score attached to it. Our problem, then, is one of translating this multitude of scores into a parsimonious and usable single score that does justice to the entire array.

The adversary's sequence of actions covers a time period that may vary in length from one month to upwards of a year. We begin by dividing the time period into calendar months. For each month, we compute a total refractory score for the coalition by simply summing the scores of all its refractory actions.[5] Eventually, we want to weight these monthly scores, sum them, and arrive at an average refractory score for the entire time period. However, the first problem that confronts us is that of partial months. Since time periods can begin or end in the middle of a calendar month, we are likely to find partial months at the beginning and/or end of any given time period. The scores of such partial months are adjusted according to the following rules.

1. If the number of days in such a month is less than 15, the month is not given independent status. Rather, these days are treated as part of the adjacent month. For example, if a time period ended on April 7, the refractory score for the first seven days in April would be added to the March total and March would be con-

[5] For simplicity, the procedure is here stated in terms of refractory scores. An exactly parallel set of operations is carried out on conciliatory scores as well.

sidered a 38-day "month." Such extra-length months then have their scores adjusted downward to correspond to a standard month of 30.5 days. (The formula used to accomplish this will be described below.)

2. Any partial month of 15 or more days is treated as a separate month and its score is adjusted upward to correspond to a standard month of 30.5 days.

3. Any partial or extra-length month whose length is between 28 and 33 days is considered sufficiently similar to a standard month to make further adjustment unnecessary.

4. Months over 33 or under 28 days in length are adjusted by using the following formula:

$$R' = R/D \times 30.5,$$

where R' is the adjusted refractory score for the month, R is the unadjusted refractory score, and D is the number of days in the irregular-length month. This formula simply takes the average daily score of an irregular month and multiplies it by the number of days in a standard month.

To illustrate the above formula, imagine that a refractory score of 40 in March is followed by an additional score of 10 during the first seven days of April. This makes March an irregular 38-day month with a total refractory score of 50. Applying the formula to adjust this score gives us:

$$R' = 50/38 \times 30.5 = 40.13.$$

Having adjusted the scores of irregular months, each monthly score in the time period is converted to a standard score (R^s). This is accomplished by means of the following formula:

$$R^s = \frac{R' - \overline{R}}{\sigma_R},$$

where R' is the adjusted monthly score, $\overline{R}$ is the coalition's mean monthly score for the entire Cold War (1946–1963), and σ_R is the standard deviation of these monthly scores.[6] This formula takes a coalition's monthly score and expresses it as a positive or negative deviation from its own mean.

This conversion to standard scores serves two purposes. First, it permits us to measure each coalition's behavior relative to its own base-

---

[6] Appendix D contains the mean and standard deviation of each coalition's monthly refractory scores and monthly conciliatory scores.

line. This avoids the necessity of assuming that our data source is equally sensitive to the behavior of both coalitions. If a coalition obtains a high standard score in a given month, this simply means that it was more refractory than usual *relative to its own average*. No attempt is made to assess how refractory one coalition is by comparing it with the other. In addition, conversion to standard scores translates the refractory and conciliatory components of a coalition's behavior into the same unit of measurement (i.e., into units of standard deviation). This permits us to combine these components into a single score by subtracting each month's standard conciliatory score from its standard refractory score.

Having standardized the refractory scores for each month, a weighted average of these scores is then calculated. The score of the month closest in time to the period-ending action is given a weight of 10, the score of the next closest month a weight of 9, the score of the next closest month a weight of 8, and so on until the last ten months in the period have been weighted. Any earlier months are given zero weight and, hence, contribute nothing to the weighted average. The computational formula used to obtain the weighted average ($\hat{R}$) is as follows:

$$\hat{R} = \frac{\displaystyle\sum_{i=1}^{i=n} (11 - i) \times R_i^s}{W},$$

where R_i^s is the standard score of the ith most recent month in the time period, n (≤ 10) is the total number of months in the period, and W is the sum of the weights used.[7] Since this formula is designed to give greater weight to more recent months, an accelerating pattern of monthly scores will yield a higher $\hat{R}$ score than a decelerating pattern. In other words, a time period characterized by a closing refractory burst is considered more refractory than one characterized by an opening refractory burst. This reflects an assumption that the salience, or perceived magnitude, of an action recedes somewhat with the passage of time and, hence, that the responding coalition will give greater weight to the more recent actions of its adversary.

[7] W can be calculated from the equation:

$$W = \frac{21n - n^2}{2},$$

where, again, n is the total number of months in the time period (or $n = 10$ for time periods containing more than ten months).

Having similarly calculated a weighted average of standard monthly conciliatory scores $(\hat{C})$, we subtract this weighted average from the weighted average of refractory scores to obtain a final figure for the coalition, called a "belligerence/accommodative score" (b/a):

$$b/a = \hat{R} - \hat{C}.$$

Such scores have a theoretical range from $-\infty$ to $+\infty$ with high scores being associated with belligerent patterns, low scores with accommodative patterns, and zero-order scores with balanced patterns.

These b/a scores are calculated *both* for the responding coalition in the time period prior to its major action, *and* for the adversary coalition in the same period. When the score is used to characterize the adversary's behavior, it is translated into one of nine verbal categories according to the rules shown in Table A.1. On the other hand, when the score is used to characterize the responding coalition's behavior, it is translated into one of two verbal categories according to the rules shown in Table A.2. (The latter two categories represent a simple, logical collapsing of the original nine.)

Before attempting to justify the rules shown in Table A.1, we will illustrate the procedures outlined above by applying them to Western behavior in the time period ended by the first major Soviet action. This time period runs from January 1 to March 12, 1946, and consists of two months: an ordinary month in January, and an irregular, 40-day month running from February 1 to March 12. The unadjusted Western refractory scores for these two months are 16 and 78, respectively; the unadjusted conciliatory scores are 5 and 6. In each case, the second score must be adjusted downward to correspond to a 30.5-day month.

Table A.1
Converting an Adversary's *b/a* Scores into Verbal Categories

Period score on b/a scale	Verbal category
+3.00 or greater	Extremely belligerent
+2.00 to < +3.00	Quite belligerent
+1.00 to < +2.00	Fairly belligerent
> + .33 to < +1.00	Balanced firm
− .33 to + .33	Balanced
> − 1.00 to < − .33	Balanced flexible
> − 2.00 to − 1.00	Fairly accommodative
> − 3.00 to − 2.00	Quite accommodative
− 3.00 or less	Extremely accommodative

Table A.2
Converting a Responding Coalition's *b/a* Scores
into Verbal Categories

Period score on b/a *scale*	Verbal category
+1.00 or greater	Responder-belligerent
< +1.00	Responder-nonbelligerent

When this adjustment is made, the scores become 16 and 59.48 for refractory, and 5 and 4.58 for conciliatory. All scores are then standardized. When this is done they became −.61 and +.71 for refractory, and −.23 and −.26 for conciliatory.

February scores are weighted by 10, January scores by 9, and the products are summed and divided by 19. The resulting weighted monthly averages are +.087 for refractory and −.247 for conciliatory. In other words, in this period, the West was very slightly above average in refractory behavior and below average in conciliatory behavior. These weighted averages combine into a *b/a* score of +.334 and Table A.1 tells us that this is just barely high enough to qualify as a balanced firm pattern.

Why is the *b/a* scale subdivided into categories in the manner shown in Table A.1 rather than in some other manner? Although certain logical considerations are involved, the division is to some degree arbitrary. That is, it reflects one reasonable way of translating the continuous *b/a* scale into a required discrete scale.

The following considerations entered into the construction of Table A.1. First, we could deduce that nine categories were required to draw out the relevant distinctions among the various belief systems being tested (see Chapter Four). Second, it is clear that the zero-point of the *b/a* scale represents the most balanced possible pattern; hence, we coordinated the middle (or balanced) category to this zero-point. Third, since the *b/a* scale is theoretically symmetric about its zero-point, we felt that the category boundaries should also be symmetric about this point (i.e., if +2 were made the boundary between "fairly belligerent" and "quite belligerent," then −2 should be made the boundary between "fairly accommodative" and "quite accommodative").

These considerations reduced our task to one of drawing four category boundaries. At this point, however, the logical constraints became weaker. We did have some a priori notions about the relative belligerence of certain specific periods: a period containing the Cuban missile crisis or the outbreak of the Korean War would have to be classified as extremely belligerent. Beyond this, we wanted a reasonable distribution of cases across the various categories (although we realized that a preponderance of time periods should fall in the balanced categories simply because these reflect "average" behavior).

Based on such additional considerations, we arrived at the boundaries shown in Table A.1. The round numbers in this chart reflect the fact that we are not particularly committed to specific boundary values. *Since most belief systems make identical predictions over a range of consecutive categories, we do not believe that our overall results could be altered by changing the boundaries somewhat.*

In the end, our category boundaries led to the following distribution of the 125 interaction units studied: 12 percent extremely belligerent, 3 percent quite belligerent, 8 percent fairly belligerent, 17 percent balanced firm, 25 percent balanced, 14 percent balanced flexible, 12 percent fairly accommodative, 2 percent quite accommodative, and 3 percent extremely accommodative.

An additional 5 percent of the interaction units were classified as "inconsistent." In terms of their b/a scores, such cases might be classified in the balanced categories. They are not so classified because they contain strong and roughly equal components of *both* refractory and conciliatory behavior. In short, they represent contradictory and confusing patterns of behavior rather than balanced ones. All belief systems are allowed to "pass" on such patterns rather than having to make a prediction. A pattern is classified as inconsistent if, and only if, it meets both of the following requirements.

1. Both its weighted conciliatory score $(\hat{C})$ and its weighted refractory score $(\hat{R})$ are larger than 1.
2. Its b/a score is between -3 and $+3$.

In other words, inconsistency requires that both the refractory and conciliatory components of the coalition's behavior be relatively extreme, and that neither clearly dominates the other.

When b/a scores are used to characterize the behavior of the responding coalition, inconsistent patterns are once again singled out by the above rules. Here, however, only those belief systems making different predictions for belligerent and nonbelligerent patterns are allowed to pass. Only 3 percent of the responder patterns are classified as inconsistent.

This concludes our discussion of the rules for translating sequences of single actions into overall scores for a time period. Appendix F lists the b/a scores and verbal categorizations for each of the 125 interaction units used in this study. Table A.3 shows the frequency of the different patterns for each coalition.

THE BOUNDARIES OF TIME PERIODS

A final and important methodological problem concerns the length of a time period. There are consequences of using either too long or too short a period. If we used too long a period, we would introduce a great deal of "noise" — information that is irrelevant to the response being predicted. This is a conservative error, blurring or obscuring patterns rather than revealing false ones. If the period is too short, action relevant to the response may be excluded, and the remaining actions might then have relatively little effect on the response. Again this is a conservative error, obscuring results rather than creating them. Nevertheless, we want to avoid such conservative errors as much as possible lest we find ourselves in the end with *no consistent relationship* between the behavior of one coalition during a time period and the response of its adversary at the end.

The end of a time period presents no special problem. We wish to include those actions of the adversary that occur anytime up to the implementation of a major action by the responder.[8] The beginning of a time period is also marked by a major action of the responding coalition. Usually, this is its immediately preceding major action — the one that ended the previous time period. Our object is to set the beginning boundary in such a way that the adversary's behavior *within the time period* will have as much tactical unity as possible. (This permits us to characterize the behavior more meaningfully in terms of a single belligerent/accommodative score.) Thus, we avoid any major inputs from the other coalition that might substantially alter the adversary's pattern of behavior in the middle of a time period. Major actions by the responding coalition would constitute one such input, and it is for this reason that we generally run time periods from one major action of the responding coalition to the next.[9]

Unfortunately, it is not always possible to adhere to this convention without harming other requirements. A time period must be at least long enough to include adversary actions that occur during the

[8] Similarly, in measuring responder-belligerence or responder-nonbelligerence, we include actions up to but not including the major action that ends the period.

[9] For this same reason, when major actions are used to mark the beginning of a period, they are dated by time of discovery rather than time of implementation. The time of discovery is the point at which the major action becomes a relevant input to the adversary. We do not want such a point to fall in the middle of a time period.

Table A.3
Frequency of Belligerent/Accommodative Patterns for Each Coalition

	Responder-belligerent periods	Responder-nonbelligerent periods	Total
Western patterns (in periods ended by major Soviet actions)			
Extremely belligerent	6	2[a]	8
Quite belligerent	2	0	2
Fairly belligerent	3	0	3
Balanced firm	2	13	15
Balanced	2	7	9
Balanced flexible	0	13	13
Fairly accommodative	0	6	6
Quite accommodative	0	0	0
Extremely accommodative	0	2	2
Inconsistent	2	3	5
Total	17	46[b]	63
Soviet patterns (in periods ended by major Western actions)			
Extremely belligerent	5	2[a]	7
Quite belligerent	1	1	2
Fairly belligerent	5	2	7
Balanced firm	2	4	6
Balanced	3	19	22
Balanced flexible	0	4	4
Fairly accommodative	0	9	9
Quite accommodative	0	2[a]	2
Extremely accommodative	1	1	2
Inconsistent	1	0	1
Total	18	44[c]	62

[a]*One of these occurs in a responder-inconsistent rather than in a responder-nonbelligerent period.*
[b]*This total includes one responder-inconsistent period.*
[c]*This total includes two responder-inconsistent periods.*

planning stages of the major response. But if major actions occur hard upon each other, the brief period between them may not include these relevant adversary actions. We run too much danger in such situations of excluding the bulk of the adversary's most influential actions.[10] The following two exceptions to the general convention are designed to avoid this dilemma.

1. If the planning and implementation of the period-ending action could not have been carried out in the time after the previous major action, we proceed backward in time to the next most recent major action until a logically sufficient time period is obtained.
2. If, among the three preceding major actions, there is one that is part of the same crisis as the period-ending action, then the most recent *related* major action marks the beginning of the time period.

There is a final exception very much in the same spirit. Occasionally events occur that, while not refractory or conciliatory, provide the same kind of major input for the adversary. Stalin's death or the testing of the first Soviet atomic bomb in August, 1949, are examples of such inputs for the West. For the purposes of defining the beginning of a time period, such events (meeting our magnitude criterion for major actions) are treated as major actions. Thus, Stalin's death would mark the beginning of a new time period.

To summarize these rules on the boundaries of time periods:

1. A time period generally runs from one major action of the responding coalition to the next (with the exceptions noted above).
2. All adversary actions that fall between these two major actions are included in determining its belligerent/accommodative score.
3. All actions of the responding coalition, including the major action that begins the period but excluding the period-ending action, are included in determining whether the period is one of responder-belligerence or responder-nonbelligerence.

Since the major action at the beginning makes a large contribution to the total, especially in short periods, responder-belligerent periods are typically those begun by a major refractory action. Conversely, a period begun by a major conciliatory action would require a sus-

[10] Note that the opposite danger — having too long a time period that includes too many irrelevant adversary actions — is partially handled by the weighting procedure described in the preceding section. Actions more than ten months distant from the period-ending action are not used to characterize the adversary's behavior.

tained series of minor refractory actions to qualify as a responder-belligerent period.

SUMMARY

We have indicated how specific articles are coded for refractory and conciliatory actions and how such actions are given magnitude scores and allocated to the two coalitions. We have shown how major actions are operationalized and how individual actions are combined to yield an overall belligerent/accommodative score for a whole time period. Finally, we have explained how the boundaries of a time period are determined. This completes our discussion of measurement. However, we have left open one fundamental issue: the validity of our data source, the *New York Times*. Appendix B is devoted entirely to this question.

Appendix B

The *New York Times* as a Data Source

Our primary source of data in this study is the daily *New York Times*. On the face of it, this might seem a shaky base on which to build conclusions about the Cold War and its protagonists, but it is our contention that the *New York Times* is an excellent data source which meets all of our essential requirements. We hope, in this appendix, to convince those who may be skeptical about such a source.

Review, for a moment, the process which the coder goes through in using the *New York Times*. First, he must decide whether any given article reports conciliatory or refractory actions by either or both sides. Once he has made this decision on relevance and direction of effect, the size of the headline and its placement on the front page of the *New York Times* tell him the magnitude of the effect. Finally he must decide to allocate this magnitude to the Soviet or Western coalition or to divide it among them according to the complete set of rules described in Appendix A.

A number of quite plausible arguments can be made *against* using the *New York Times* as a data source. These arguments take three basic forms: (1) that the degree of prominence which the *New York Times* gives events does not reflect their true impact on Soviet-Western relations; that, instead, prominence is largely determined by idiosyncratic factors peculiar to the editor; (2) that the immersion of the *New York Times* editor and staff in the events being reported makes them unable to view such events in proper perspective; and (3) that even if events are given the proper amount of prominence, the reporting of them is so selective and biased that a person coding conciliatory and refractory Western and Soviet actions will be seriously misled. We now take up each of these arguments in detail.

THE IDIOSYNCRATIC ARGUMENT

This argument may be stated as follows: You claim to be studying Soviet-American relations but what you are really studying is the behavior of the *New York Times* editor. The composition of a daily newspaper is a hit-or-miss affair at best. Even one editor might make different decisions on what should be the lead story on a given day, depending on many things. He may have a momentary interest or be temporarily irritated with the reporter who wrote the story. He may be blinded to the importance of one event and greatly overrate the importance of another. He is so wrapped up in the pressures of the moment that he can take no perspective on events and his judgments of news value are subject to daily or even hourly variation.

When we bring in the problem of more than one editor, the variability is compounded. One man may have one set of news values, the next man a different one. One may be interested in local news and give international events smaller space than another. In short, coding the *New York Times* tells us something about the momentary news judgments of its editors but it tells us little of significance about the importance of events for Soviet-Western disagreement.

Basically, this argument may be broken down into two subarguments. First, it suggests that there is no consensus about the magnitude of events. The size of the headline reflects little of what is going on out in the world, i.e., little of the stimulus properties of the event, but it reflects much of what is going on in the hurly-burly of the newspaper office and in the heads of those who are putting the paper together. If this is so, then when we compare different newspapers, we should find little agreement among them on the magnitude given to different events. But if we find there is much consensus and that different newspapers give the same relative magnitudes to a set of events, then it is clear that they share some common definition of what is newsworthy.

Second, it is possible to find that there is a considerable consensus among newspapers, but that the *New York Times* is peculiar. Perhaps its editors do not share the typical definition of what is newsworthy. If this is so, some other newspaper or pool of newspapers would be necessary to reflect this consensus. However, if we find that there is high agreement among newspapers on the magnitude that they give to different events and that the *New York Times* is highly correlated with this consensus, then we must dismiss the arguments made above. It will then be clear that the *New York Times* editors do far more than reflect a personal and idiosyncratic judgment and that we are on safe grounds in interpreting their judgment as a reflection of a view widely shared *at the time* on the relative importance of different events.

Note that this first argument calls into question only the prominence that the *New York Times* gives to events; our analysis need compare only the *total* magnitude that different newspapers give to events. The question of whether this total magnitude can be accurately parceled by a coder into various types of Soviet and Western behavior can be postponed until we consider the bias argument. Two kinds of comparison will be used to answer the present argument. First, we will compare a group of newspapers on the relative magnitude they give events dealing with Soviet-Western conflict during two one-month sample time periods. Second, we will compare a group of newspapers on the similarity of their lead articles on Soviet-Western conflict during four ten-day sample time periods.

Comparison by Events

For the first comparison, June, 1953, and April, 1958, were used as sample time periods. The seven papers compared included the *Chicago Daily Tribune,* the *Christian Science Monitor,* the *London Times,* the *Manchester Guardian,* the *New York Herald Tribune,* and *Pravda* and *Izvestia* (in combination, using the *Current Digest of the Soviet Press*). For April, 1958, the two British papers were not available.

There are some problems involved in obtaining a comparable magnitude measure for papers using widely different formats. Essentially, we used either the Benny Profane Method described in Appendix A or a measure based on column inches. The justification for using one or the other method for a given newspaper and the details of application are described in an addendum to this appendix.

In forming a pool of events for comparison, we started with a collation of all articles in all papers which reported conciliatory or refractory actions. It is not easy to define a unit-event since differences in format and in the time of publication may lead one paper to combine in a single article events which are dealt with in separate articles by another paper. To handle this problem, events were subdivided into three crude categories.

1. Continuing diplomatic exchanges or other continuing processes. Newspapers tune in and out on continuing events such as negotiations, sometimes reporting several days' events in one story when things are quiet. The Korean truce negotiations are an example; UN debate lasting over several days would be another. When a newspaper contains several articles about such continuous proceedings, we sum these into a single magnitude score so that the whole proceedings are treated as a single event.

2. Focal points in continuing proceedings. The continuing stories covered in the first category are sometimes punctuated by actions which create discontinuities. Such focal points are treated as additional events in their own right. Examples are a break-off of talks

or a threatened break-off, an agreement which moves the talks ahead to other matters, or a dramatic new offer.

3. Single and completed events. Many events are not part of a continuous flow but represent discrete points. The announcement by the Soviet Union that it would stop nuclear testing and the removal by the Soviet Union of a long-standing demand on Turkish territory are examples.

From the original collection of articles from *all* newspapers, it was possible to identify 19 relevant events for June, 1953, and 17 for April, 1958. No newspaper included all 36 events, but as Table B.1 indicates, the *New York Times* came closest with 35 of 36, trailed closely by the *New York Herald Tribune*.

The *New York Times,* then, is apparently unsurpassed in completeness. But to explore the idiosyncratic argument, we must ask if, in reporting these events, it tends to give them the same relative magnitudes as do other newspapers. How, in fact, does each paper compare with the others in the relative prominence it gives events? Each newspaper has a magnitude score based on the number of column inches or the size of the headlines allotted to a given event. These scores provide a rank ordering for each newspaper of the total pool of events. Table B.2 shows the rank order correlations (Rho) between each pair of newspapers for June, 1953 (above the diagonal) and for April, 1958 (below the diagonal).

The correlations are uniformly positive and generally quite high. For June, 1953, no correlation is below .5 and many are .8 or higher. The correlations are generally lower for April, 1958, but still remain positive and moderately high. June, 1953, was characterized by a number of dramatic events including a prisoner-of-war agreement (remov-

Table B.1

Completeness of Seven Daily Newspapers

	Total events	Included events	Percentage
New York Times	36	35	97
New York Herald Tribune	36	33	92
Chicago Daily Tribune	36	29	81
Manchester Guardian	19[a]	15	79
London Times	19[a]	14	74
Christian Science Monitor	36	25	69
Pravda-Izvestia	36	18	50

[a]*Not coded for April, 1958.*

Table B.2

Intercorrelations of Seven Newspapers' Rankings
of International Events in Two Sample Periods

JUNE, 1953 (n=19 EVENTS)

	New York Times	New York Herald Tribune	Chicago Daily Tribune	Christian Science Monitor	Pravda-Izvestia	London Times	Manchester Guardian
New York Times		.96	.69	.80	.79	.80	.62
New York Herald Tribune	.56		.74	.73	.88	.73	.55
Chicago Daily Tribune	.63	.57		.53	.80	.75	.52
Christian Science Monitor	.37	.38	.71		.59	.80	.77
Pravda-Izvestia	.66	.38	.54	.08		.70	.55
London Times	a	a	a	a	a		.61
Manchester Guardian	a	a	a	a	a	a	

APRIL, 1958 (n=17 EVENTS)

ªNo comparison made for this period.

ing the last major obstacle to a Korean truce), and Syngman Rhee's efforts to prevent the truce by unilaterally releasing prisoners of war. There was considerable consensus among all papers on the importance of such events. On the other hand, April, 1958, was rather uneventful.[1] Faced with a fuller range of events from minor to major, the newspapers are in greater agreement than in the less eventful month when they must distinguish among a narrower range of ordinary events. If this explanation accounts for the different correlations in the two sample periods, the figures for June, 1953, are likely to be a more accurate estimate of agreement among newspapers. This month comes closer to reflecting the full range of magnitudes of Cold War events.

The coefficient of concordance, a measure of overall agreement among the newspapers, is .72 for June, 1953, and .55 for April, 1958. Clearly, there were some widely shared standards on importance when *Pravda-Izvestia* correlated .80 with the *Chicago Daily Tribune* and .88 with the staunchly Republican *New York Herald Tribune*.

Over and above this high general agreement among newspapers, the *New York Times* in particular does extremely well. We can answer the question of how well individual newspapers reflect the consensus by comparing each paper's own rank ordering of the events with their average rank based on the whole pool. Table B.3 makes this comparison for each period. The *New York Times* emerges as the best overall reflector of this consensus. For June, 1953, it has a remarkable .99 correlation with the average rank, dropping to a more modest .82 correlation for April, 1958. This means that a magnitude measure based on a pool of these seven newspapers would yield results which are almost exactly the same as one would get from the *New York Times* alone.

The seven newspapers are all similar but some are more similar than others. In other words, although the newspapers tend to cluster, they still differ slightly along certain dimensions which might affect our analysis. For example, if the prominence that events receive is related to an ideological dimension, a Western oriented paper such as the *New York Times* would give us one end of this dimension. The overall high intercorrelations preclude large discrepancies, but using a newspaper at one end of a critical dimension would lead to small but consistent discrepancies with papers at the other end.

---

[1] The five newspapers coded for both months carried about half the total number of articles on Soviet-Western conflict in the later period. For June, 1953, 158 articles were distributed over 19 events. For April, 1958, only 81 articles were distributed over 17 events. This much smaller number of articles for almost the same number of events documents the fact that some of the events in the first period were major ones.

Table B.3

Correlation of Individual Newspaper Ranking of Events
with Consensus Ranking in Two Sample Periods

	June, 1953	April, 1958
New York Times	.99	.82
New York Herald Tribune	.90	.74
London Times	.88	—
Christian Science Monitor	.86	.67
Manchester Guardian	.85	—
Chicago Daily Tribune	.78	.90
Pravda-Izvestia	.77	.68
Number of events ranked	19	17

To check this possibility, we performed a non-metric factor (proximity) analysis on the correlation matrix for the two sample months.[2] For both months, a single factor or dimension accounts for the variance among newspapers. Table B.4 shows the rank order of the newspapers on this dimension. Nothing as obvious or disturbing as an ideological dimension can explain the results. For June, 1953, *Pravda-Izvestia* and the *Chicago Daily Tribune* are adjacent while the *Manchester Guardian* falls at the opposite extreme. The April, 1958, proximity analysis is less determinant, being based on only five newspapers, but it yields similar results.

What is this dimension? An examination of the events creating the major discrepancies between newspapers at opposite ends suggests an answer. Newspapers at the *Pravda-Izvestia* end seem to do less anticipatory reporting, tending to wait until an event has occurred before giving it full treatment. Papers at the other end are more likely to anticipate, covering events which may lead to major stories even though not much has happened at the time they are reported. The coverage in this latter group seems more continual, with less of a tendency to tune in and out on events that run several days or weeks.

The newspapers differ, then, on a factor concerning style of news

---

[2] The newspapers in each matrix can be permuted in such a manner that the correlation coefficients decrease systematically away from the diagonal and from bottom to top. The existence of such a simplex matrix indicates that the rank order of distance relations embodied therein can be accounted for in one dimension. For each set of data, the rank order of newspapers on this factor or dimension is precisely their order in the simplex matrix. See Louis Guttman (1959).

Table B.4

Ordering of Newspapers on Dimension Accounting
for Major Differences

June, 1953	April, 1958
Chicago Daily Tribune	
Pravda-Izvestia	Pravda-Izvestia
New York Herald Tribune	New York Times
New York Times	Chicago Daily Tribune
London Times	New York Herald Tribune
Christian Science Monitor	Christian Science Monitor
Manchester Guardian	

coverage and not on one which seems likely to affect our results. But even if this factor is important, the *New York Times* is so centrally located on it that its effect is neutralized anyway.

Comparison by Lead Articles

For those who remain unconvinced by the above analysis that the *New York Times* reflects a consensus on the importance of events, we offer an additional piece of evidence. Four ten-day sample periods were coded for a set of nine papers. These nine included all seven of the papers used in the previous analysis (except the *Christian Science Monitor*) plus *Le Monde*, the *Neue Zurcher Zeitung*, and the *Arbeiter Zeitung*. Two of the time periods were chosen because they contained major events: May 11–20, 1955, which included the signing of the Austrian State Treaty, and May 1–10, 1960, which included the U-2 incident. The other two periods, January 1–10, 1952, and November 11–20, 1958, were picked randomly.

For each day in these four periods, the lead article on Soviet-Western relations was recorded for each of the nine newspapers. Table B.5 indicates the extent to which each paper's lead article reported events featured by a plurality of the other papers that day. The *New York Times*, it turns out, is most representative, featuring the consensus choice 75 percent of the time.

THE TIME-BOUND ARGUMENT

It seems overwhelmingly clear that the prominence that an article receives in the *New York Times* is more than a reflection of the personal judgment of the editor of the day. In fact, it reflects with considerable accuracy the prominence that such a story gets in newspapers around the world. But this is simply a reflection of how events

Table B.5
Agreement of Lead Article in a Given Newspaper
with Lead Article Featured by Plurality of Other Newspapers

	Percentage agreement	Number of days in sample
New York Times	75	40
Manchester Guardian	72	20[a]
Chicago Daily Tribune	70	40
New York Herald Tribune	68	40
London Times	58	40
Neue Zurcher Zeitung	56	20[a]
Arbeiter Zeitung	50	20[a]
Pravda-Izvestia	38	40
Le Monde	33	20[a]

[a]Paper not available for 1958 and 1960 sample periods.

appear *at the time they occur*. Any newspaper, it might be argued, is so caught up in day-to-day actions that it fails to give proper perspective. The significance of many an important event is not appreciated until much later. Other events are given world wide coverage but appear trivial in the light of history. The *New York Times*, this argument concludes, may well reflect the views of the day accurately, but it remains time-bound and thus misses the true significance of events.

In answering this argument, we readily grant that the *New York Times* reflects the view of importance prevalent *at the time* and that this is not necessarily the same view of events that prevails today or will prevail fifty years hence. It can be argued, though, that the view at the time is more valid for our purposes than one colored by hindsight. It is easy to blur the impact of an event with the consequences that did or did not occur subsequently. A crisis settled is likely to appear less of a crisis, a threat unfulfilled to appear merely a bluff, and an agreement retracted to appear an illusion. But these subsequent results do not really show that the view at the time was incorrect. For example, the shelling of Quemoy and Matsu by the Chinese may have sharply raised tension at the time because it was viewed as a possible prelude to an invasion of Taiwan. No invasion attempt materialized either because none was ever planned or because the response to the shelling led to some change in plans. If we knew then what we know now — that an invasion attempt was not going to take place — then the action would have been less important in increasing disagreement; but, not knowing this, it *did* in fact raise disagreements. The headlines of the day reflect this accurately.

Nevertheless, it is interesting to ask whether those actions that are singled out as major ones by their headline size in the *New York Times* include those that we consider significant ones today and exclude those that are considered relatively trivial. To explore this question, we asked a group of ten specialists in international conflict to rate the importance of a series of events. Three of the raters were from the Bendix Systems Division of the Bendix Corporation, and four were from the Political Science Department and three were from the Center for Research on Conflict Resolution at the University of Michigan.

Two sets of twenty-four cards were prepared, one containing brief descriptions of events receiving a one- or two-column headline at the top of the front page of the *New York Times* (minor events) and one containing descriptions of events receiving a four-column or larger headline (major events). Each set of twenty-four cards was further subdivided into sets of twelve, one containing events increasing disagreements (refractory actions) and the other containing events decreasing disagreements (conciliatory actions). For control purposes, all of the articles referred to Soviet coalition actions rather than Western actions.

Respondents were given two separate sets of twenty-four cards, one containing major and minor conciliatory Soviet actions and the other containing major and minor refractory Soviet actions. The cards were arranged chronologically within each set and the respondents were asked to sort the cards into three sets of eight cards: (1) those describing actions that slightly increased (decreased) disagreements; (2) those describing actions that moderately increased (decreased) disagreements; and (3) those that greatly increased (decreased) disagreements. They were then asked to subdivide the middle or "moderate" pile further into high moderate and low moderate groups.

The experts' average rating on events was compared with the *New York Times* classification into major and minor events.[3] The experts

---

[3] Each action could be classified by each expert in one of four ways: *slight, low moderate, high moderate,* and *great* decrease/increase in disagreement. These categories were assigned numerical values of 2, 5, 7, and 10 respectively, the smaller distance between 5 and 7 reflecting the relative similarity of the two moderate categories which comprise the middle third. For each event, the experts' judgments were averaged over all ten raters and if the final value was above 6.0, this was classified as a major event by expert-rating. Those 6.0 or under were classified as minor events. These expert ratings were then compared to the *New York Times* classification of major and minor actions.

and the *Times* agree on 75 percent of the forty-eight events. Of the twelve disagreements, seven are on borderline cases in which the experts either have little consensus among themselves or tend to put the actions in the moderate or middle category. There are, however, five genuine disagreements and it is instructive to examine them.

Only one expert of ten thought that a statement by Stalin in March, 1946, had any significant effect on removing disagreements. In it, the Soviet Premier affirmed his faith in the United Nations as a "serious instrument" for preserving peace. This statement came in the midst of a serious crisis in which the United States was pressing for UN action on Soviet troop movements in Iran, at a time when Cold War positions had not hardened and the Soviet attitude toward the United Nations was unclear. The *New York Times* gave the statement a four-column headline.

Similarly, only one expert in ten thought that a pledge by Tito to refrain from further shooting down of planes that flew over Yugoslav territory greatly decreased disagreements. But this pledge came after the second Yugoslavian downing of an American plane in ten days had led to a serious and intense international incident. The five-column *New York Times* headline reflected the ending of this crisis.

Just as the plane incident and the Stalin interview no longer seem to stand out against a twenty-year backdrop of similar statements and incidents, a speech by Andrei Vishinsky in September, 1947, no longer appears in bold relief. The unexpected diatribe drew an eight-column banner headline in the *New York Times* which described the speech as "an amazing address" that "excoriated every phase of United States foreign policy." Other diatribes have followed from both sides but, at that time, Vishinsky's speech represented a sharp new tone in Soviet foreign policy.

On two occasions, the experts judged events to be important that the *New York Times* treated rather casually. They generally agreed that a story reporting the killing of sixty-eight American prisoners of war in Korea was a relatively important event, but the *New York Times* gave it only two columns. Surprisingly, a reported attack on the island of Quemoy a month after the start of the Korean war also received little attention in the *New York Times* despite Nationalist Chinese claims that the Communist Chinese were amassing an invasion fleet for an attack on Taiwan. The experts, on the other hand, were in high agreement on the relative importance of this action.

In sum, there is generally high agreement between the ratings of experts on the importance of events today and the headline size they received in the *New York Times* when they first occurred. While some discrepancies do exist, several of them seem to reflect the difficulties of remembering the context of events occurring ten to twenty years ago rather than the use of different standards in gauging importance.

THE BIAS ARGUMENT

Thus far, our validity checks can give us considerable confidence in the ability of the *New York Times* to reflect accurately the relative impact that different events have on Soviet-Western disagreement. The coder, however, must go beyond merely regarding the magnitude of a given event. He must allocate responsibility for this event to one, the other, or both sides. Isn't he, therefore, dependent on which aspects of an event the *New York Times* chooses to emphasize? Doesn't this dependence undermine the whole study?

To put the argument baldly, the *New York Times* is a virtual house organ of the United States government. It is a restive one, to be sure, capable of frequently embarrassing the government, and it publishes many things that the government would rather not have public. But it views the Cold War through Western eyes. Its editors and reporters reflect the assumptions of United States policy-makers not because of any sanctions that the government might administer but because they are part of the same milieu. In short, to use the *New York Times* as a source of data is to view the world from the corner of one of the major combatants with all the attendant distortions of judgment.

To answer this argument, we must first underline just what demands are being made on this data source. First of all, the major way in which the *New York Times* is likely to differ from a neutralist or Communist newspaper is in the interpretation it gives events. Actions that are presented as defensive by one side are likely to be viewed as aggressive by the other. *But we make no use of such distinctions in coding events.* On June 25, 1950, six North Korean infantry divisions marched across the 38th parallel into South Korea. For the coder, it makes no difference whether this was an improvised response to South Korean provocations or a fully premeditated act of aggression. Such differences lead us into the realm of explanation and interpretation. All the coder pays attention to is the fact that North Korean divisions crossed the 38th parallel into South Korea, and that this event increased disagreement between the Communist and Western coalitions.

This study is also unaffected by differential sensitivity to different categories of events. The *New York Times,* of course, is more attuned to the policy statements of Western officials. It is also likely, although we cannot demonstrate this, that it tends to underplay Western conciliatory actions. But such biases, if they exist, do not affect the analysis. We do not attempt to make statements that compare Soviet refractory actions during any given period with Western refractory actions, nor do we make statements that compare Soviet refractory actions with Soviet conciliatory actions. Each category of action has its *own* baseline. To illustrate, the statement that Western refractory action was high during a given period does not mean that the West was more refractory than the Soviet coalition, or that it was more refractory than it was conciliatory. It simply means that if we compare Western refractory action during the period in question with the average amount of Western refractory action, we find that there was considerably more of such action than average. In sum, we assume only that the *New York Times* bias between categories remains *constant*, not that it is nonexistent.

There are some biases that can be disturbing. Any bias, for example, that cuts across the four major categories of Soviet refractory, Western refractory, Soviet conciliatory, and Western conciliatory actions, can affect the analysis. If the *New York Times* is much more sensitive to European events than to Asian events, this could affect the analysis, but only if there were sharp differences in the refractory or conciliatory nature of Soviet or Western policy in those areas.

It is also possible that in the reporting of a single event, the selection of certain aspects might make a joint action appear unilateral. The code is designed to avoid such possibilities as much as possible by using such concepts as "implicit joint actions." Thus, if the *New York Times* reports a scathing attack on the Western position by the Soviet delegate to a disarmament conference, such an article would be coded as a joint refractory action and the magnitude distributed between the two blocs, even though the Western contribution to the interaction situation is not emphasized in the article.

Despite these precautions, it is still possible that the *New York Times* contains biases that distort the coding. It is necessary, then, to compare the *New York Times* with other newspapers by major categories. It is not enough to find that the total magnitude given events is highly correlated with other sources. We need to know, for example, if the high periods of Western refractory action in the *New York Times* are also the high periods for such action in other newspapers.

Twelve months were chosen at random and coded from the *Times of India* (Bombay) and from the *Manchester Guardian.* In this analysis, the coder followed the coding rules described in Appendix A. In accordance with these rules, he assigned the magnitude of any relevant article (measured in column inches) to one or more of the four categories of action: Soviet refractory, Soviet conciliatory, Western refractory, and Western conciliatory. Each paper was coded by two independent coders. The intercoder reliability ranged from .90 to .98

for the various categories of action. All discrepancies were discussed by the two coders and reconciled.

For each category of action, the *New York Times* monthly score was correlated with the monthly scores from the *Times of India* and the *Manchester Guardian.* As Table B.6 indicates, the correlations are very high, particularly between the *New York Times* and the *Times of India,* ranging from .73 to .90.

The major discrepancy between the papers is due to the *Guardian*'s reporting of events in Suez in the two sample months of August, 1956, and November, 1956. The *Guardian* gave more coverage than the other papers to the London conference over Suez in August, 1956. Deadlocks developed between Egypt, supported by the Soviet Union, and Great Britain, and these were emphasized at the conference. By giving the conference a lot of attention, the *Guardian* produced a

Table B.6

Correlations among Monthly Scores of Three Newspapers for Soviet and Western Conciliatory and Refractory Action[a] (*N* = 12 months)

| | REFRACTORY SCORES | | |
| | Western action | | |
	New York Times	Times of India	Manchester Guardian
Soviet action			
New York Times		.89	.80
Times of India	.73		.78
Manchester Guardian	.43	.68	

| | CONCILIATORY SCORES | | |
| | Western action | | |
	New York Times	Times of India	Manchester Guardian
Soviet action			
New York Times		.90	.85
Times of India	.78		.95
Manchester Guardian	.80	.89	

[a]*Figures in this table are product moment correlations. Those above the diagonals pertain to Western action; those below the diagonals pertain to Soviet action.*

somewhat higher score for Soviet and Western refractory action in that month than did the *New York Times* or *Times of India*. In November, 1956, the *Guardian* gave considerably less play to Soviet threats to intervene with "volunteers" in Suez, and for this month, the Soviet refractory score was somewhat lower for the *Guardian* than for the other two papers. But these discrepancies should not obscure the overall high agreement among the three papers.

That the *New York Times* has biases, like any other observer, we would not challenge. That these biases affect our results, we do challenge. Had we used the *Times of India* to code Western and Soviet refractory and conciliatory behavior, we would get substantially the same results as using the *New York Times*. The code, and the use we make of it, has apparently neutralized biases in such a way that they can have little effect on our results.

CONCLUSION

The *New York Times*, we submit, is a very satisfactory data source for the purposes of this study. It is broad and inclusive in its coverage, and it is calibrated enough to enable us to measure gradations. There is substantial consensus about the importance of events among newspapers around the world and the *New York Times* reflects this consensus very well. On whatever dimension underlies those differences that do exist among newspapers, the *New York Times* is central. The importance that it assigned events when they occurred is not greatly different from that which experts would assign these events today. And where discrepancies exist, there is no evidence that the time-boundedness of the *New York Times* is responsible. Events that stood out in bold relief at the time have become less easy to distinguish from the background of similar, subsequent events. Finally, it seems possible to minimize the biases of the *New York Times* in a variety of ways — by ignoring its interpretations of events, by using coding procedures that reduce the effects of selective reporting, and by using analysis methods that do not assume it is equally sensitive to both coalitions and to both categories of behavior.

ADDENDUM: MAKING COMPARISONS AMONG NEWSPAPERS WITH DIFFERENT FORMATS

In comparing the *New York Times* with other newspapers around the world, certain problems arise from the many differences in format. The *New York Times* carries news of foreign affairs throughout the paper rather than devoting a separate section to such news. Furthermore, its headline format is variable, reflecting an editorial judgment about the absolute importance of an event. The lead story may carry as little as a one-column headline or as much as an eight-column banner headline. Thus, headline size and position in the *New York Times* clearly reflects an editorial judgment about importance.

These same characteristics are generally true of the *New York Herald Tribune* and the *Christian Science Monitor*. However, the *Chicago Daily Tribune* uses a daily eight-column headline for the lead story. While its headlines may distinguish among the relative importance of events in any given day, they give us no measure of the relative importance of lead articles of different days. However, even lead articles differ in column inches and for the *Chicago Tribune* this appears to be a more suitable measure for comparing the magnitude of events over a thirty-day period.

The *Manchester Guardian* presents a similar problem for the periods studied. With rare exceptions, the format is a constant one in terms of headline make-up with the lead story introduced by a one-or two-column title. The *Guardian* does not use headlines in the American sense but descriptive, topical titles — for example, "Korean Prisoner of War Exchange," rather than "UN and Reds Exchange POW's in Korea." The *London Times* also uses a constant format with the relevant stories grouped in a section on "Imperial and Foreign News." For both of these papers, column inches are a suitable measure of magnitude.

For *Pravda* and *Izvestia*, the use of the *Current Digest of the Soviet Press* precluded a magnitude measure based on headline size. However, the *Current Digest* lists the number of words appearing in a given article, and this number is easily enough converted into column inches using an estimate of 35 words per column inch.

With the exception of *Pravda* and *Izvestia*, a distinction was made between articles appearing on the first page of foreign news and on the back pages. For the *London Times*, the first page of foreign news was not page one but, for our purposes, was treated as such. All relevant articles on the lead page received a magnitude score (1) equal to their column inches if they used a "constant-headline" format; or (2) by headline size using the Benny Profane Method described in Appendix A if they used a "variable-headline" format. Articles not originating on the lead page received a constant score of five column inches regardless of their length or a headline weight of one regardless of their headline size.

There is a very high correlation between magnitude scores obtained by the Benny Profane Method and by the column inches method for the *New York Times*, the *Christian Science Monitor*, and the *New York Herald Tribune*. For June, 1953, the two scoring methods correlate .96, .96, and .94, respectively. For April, 1958, these correlations drop somewhat to .72, .96, and .70, respectively.

The editorial page was ignored for all papers except *Pravda* and *Izvestia*. News articles in the American press are governed by different norms than those attending editorials. While violations in practice may occur, the distinction is a meaningful one in the United States. In the Soviet conception, the press is a self-conscious and explicit instrument for achieving societal goals and the distinction between editorials and news makes little sense in this regard. It is possible, however, to distinguish editorials dealing with events of the preceding seven days and those dealing with events more general or more distant in time. Only the latter are excluded from the coding for *Pravda* and *Izvestia*.

Appendix C

The Decision Model and the Derivation
of Predictions: A Systematic Statement

Our decision model has two parts. The first part links a coalition's parameter values to an interpretation of the adversary's previous behavior. The second part links these interpretations to a specific response. As we saw in Chapter Four, the first part is the more critical — once interpretations have been derived, the predicted response follows fairly automatically. In fact, we have already shown in Table 4.2 (p. 64) the exact connection between each possible interpretation of an adversary's behavior and the resultant response. This appendix, then, need concern itself only with the issue of deriving interpretations from the parameter values.

The reasoning used to accomplish this is always the same: certain parameter values can be used to eliminate certain interpretations. Thus, a coalition's parameter values place a series of *restrictions* on the possible meanings of its adversary's behavior. This reasoning was used in Chapter Four to derive interpretations for belligerent and accommodative behavior. Before tackling the thornier problem of balanced behavior, we will review these derivations in a more compact, systematic fashion.

INTERPRETING THE ADVERSARY'S
BELLIGERENT BEHAVIOR

Here a coalition must determine whether its adversary is being *aggressive* or *resistant*. The value of the coalition's second and third parameters (reflected image and perception of the adversary's goals) can be used to eliminate one or the other interpretation.[1]

1.1. Restriction placed by the coalition's reflected image:

[1] The second and third parameters can never take on the value of destructionist; for a review of the reasoning, see p. 28.

    a. If consolidationist, eliminate resistant. The adversary cannot be resisting if it believes it is dealing with a consolidationist. Consolidationists pose no threat and, hence, the adversary's belligerence must be aggressive.

    b. If expansionist, neither interpretation can be eliminated.

1.2. Restriction placed by the coalition's perception of its adversary's goals:

    a. If consolidationist, eliminate aggressive. Since a consolidationist is not aggressive, the adversary's belligerence must be resistant in intent.

    b. If expansionist, neither interpretation can be eliminated.

The only case not covered by the above restrictions is the coalition whose second and third parameters are *both* expansionist (i.e., –EE).[2] Here, the interpretation depends on the coalition's *own* recent behavior. The following restriction applies only to –EE coalitions.

1.3 Restriction placed by the coalition's recent behavior:

    a. If nonbelligerent, eliminate resistant. The responding coalition has not been engaging in threatening actions and, hence, the adversary's belligerence must be aggressive.

    b. If belligerent, the interpretation depends on the extent of the adversary's belligerence. If the adversary is only fairly belligerent, eliminate aggressive; given the context of responder-belligerence, the adversary's behavior must be interpreted as resistant. If the adversary is extremely belligerent, eliminate resistant; despite the context, the adversary is being too belligerent for mere resistance and its behavior must be interpreted as aggressive. If the adversary is in between, or quite belligerent, no interpretation is possible and futher cues must be awaited.

INTERPRETING THE ADVERSARY'S ACCOMMODATIVE BEHAVIOR

The basic question a coalition must ask here is whether its adversary is being *receptive* or *lax*. These alternatives are two sides of the same coin, and hence the answer to the question will be more a matter of preference than logic. A lax adversary can be exploited; a receptive adversary can be approached and bargained with. The preference of a coalition depends on its goals.

---

[2] A "–" in the position of a parameter indicates that the parameter is not relevant to the discussion.

2.1. Restriction placed by the coalition's goals:
   a. If destructionist, eliminate receptive. A destructionist coali-
      tion is interested in exploitation rather than mutual accom-
      modation, and hence it will always view accommodative
      behavior as lax rather than receptive.
   b. If consolidationist, eliminate lax. A consolidationist coalition
      is interested in mutual accommodation rather than exploita-
      tion, and hence it will always view accommodative behavior
      as receptive rather than lax.

A coalition with expansionist goals (E– –) is interested both in mutual
accommodation and in exploitation. Here, the interpretation hinges on
the coalition's own recent behavior. The following restriction applies
only to E– – coalitions.

2.2 Restriction placed by the coalition's recent behavior;
   a. If belligerent, eliminate receptive. Given the context of
      responder-belligerence, the adversary's accommodative be-
      havior is a sign of laxity.
   b. If nonbelligerent, the interpretation depends on the extent of
      the adversary's accommodativeness. If the adversary is only
      fairly accommodative, eliminate lax; given the absence of re-
      sponder-belligerence, the adversary cannot be considered lax
      and must be treated as receptive. If the adversary is extremely
      accommodative, eliminate receptive; despite the context, this
      is sufficiently accommodative to be considered lax. If the
      adversary is in between, or quite accommodative, no interpre-
      tation is possible and further cues must be awaited.

INTERPRETING THE ADVERSARY'S
BALANCED BEHAVIOR

Before taking up the interpretation of balanced behavior, a word needs
to be said about the distinction between balanced patterns and inconsistent patterns. In general, balanced patterns contain roughly equal
components of refractory and conciliatory behavior. But we wish to
exclude from the balanced category those adversary patterns that
contain *very large* components of both. Such *inconsistent* patterns are
simply confusing and do not lend themselves to interpretation. Unlike
balanced patterns where the refractory and conciliatory components
blend into some overall policy thrust, inconsistent patterns have clash-
ing components — as if the adversary were in temporary disarray about
its direction. We do not attempt to derive predictions for inconsistent

patterns, and they are not included under the definition of balanced behavior.[3]

Since balanced behavior has both refractory and conciliatory components with neither clearly predominating, the problem of interpretation becomes especially difficult. Because the adversary's behavior contains a distinct refractory component, a coalition might view it as aggressive or resistant; because it contains a distinct conciliatory component, a coalition might view it as receptive or lax. In short, balanced behavior is in-between behavior and, as such, lends itself to all the interpretations that can be applied to the more extreme categories of behavior. Here, then, a coalition's parameter values must enable it to distinguish among four possible meanings: *aggressive, resistant, lax,* and *receptive.*[4]

A number of the restrictions used earlier to eliminate interpretations of belligerent and accommodative behavior can be applied to balanced behavior as well. In particular, restrictions 1.1, 1.2, and 2.1 are relevant. If a coalition's parameter values permit it to exclude *unconditionally* a certain interpretation of belligerent or accommodative behavior, then this interpretation can be excluded for balanced behavior as well.[5] To these three restrictions we add a fourth.

3.1. Restriction placed by the coalition's interpretation of belligerent and accommodative behavior:
   a. If any belligerent pattern is interpreted as resistant, then no balanced pattern can be interpreted as aggressive. Since belligerent behavior is more threatening than balanced behavior, a coalition that rejects the possibility of aggression at the belligerent level will surely reject it at the balanced level.
   b. If any accommodative pattern is interpreted as receptive, then no balanced pattern can be interpreted as lax. Since balanced behavior is firmer than accommodative behavior, a coalition that rejects the possibility of laxity at the accommodative level will surely reject it at the balanced level.

[3] As might be expected, such patterns are empirically rare: altogether they occur in less than 5 percent of the interaction units observed in this study. See Appendix A for the operational definition of an inconsistent pattern.

[4] Actually, there is one further possibility: the coalition may simply decide the behavior is ambiguous and uninterpretable. This is a viable alternative and will be discussed below.

[5] Restrictions 1.3 and 2.2 (using the responder's own recent behavior) cannot be applied because they are not unconditional. Their logic hinges critically on the extent of the adversary's belligerence or accommodativeness; hence their conclusions will not be valid for balanced behavior.

APPLYING THE RESTRICTIONS

These six restrictions take us pretty far toward a set of interpretations for the seven belief systems, but unfortunately not all the way. Tables C.1 and C.2 apply the restrictions and allow us to see where there is still need for further specification. The problematic cells contain a question mark. Clearly, there is still ambiguity in interpreting an adversary's balanced behavior, and we still need some additional conventions before we can arrive at a final set of interpretations.

The problem of further specifying the interpretation of balanced behavior is essentially one of drawing boundary lines. As may be seen from Tables C.1 and C.2, a coalition's interpretation of belligerent behavior tends to extend downward into the zone of balanced behavior, while its interpretation of accommodative behavior tends to extend upward. Somewhere in the balanced zone these interpretations must meet. The pattern at which they meet is a *boundary pattern*. A boundary pattern will appear ambiguous and uninterpretable to the coalition (although patterns above and below it will have a clear interpretation). For example, if a coalition views accommodative behavior as lax and belligerent behavior as resistant, there must inevitably be some gray area where the adversary's behavior is not clearly one or the other. Our final problem, then, is one of specifying the boundary pattern that corresponds to this gray area for each belief system. This process is necessarily somewhat arbitrary: the more compelling logical constraints implicit in the parameter values have already been used to carry us this far.

BOUNDARY CONVENTIONS

1. The boundary between aggressive and resistant. This problem arises *only* in responder-nonbelligerent periods for belief systems of the –EE type. Since a –EE coalition believes it is perceived by its adversary as expansionist, we may assume it has a certain tolerance for relatively firm adversary behavior, even in the absence of responder-belligerence. Therefore, we make "balanced firm" the uninterpretable boundary pattern. This means that, in most cases, such a coalition will view its adversary's balanced behavior as resistant rather than aggressive.

2. The boundary between receptive and lax. This problem arises *only* in responder-belligerent periods for belief systems of the E– – type. Since an expansionist coalition is interested in mutual accommodation (i.e., is not committed to making gains through exploitation), we may assume it will hesitate to pass up an opportunity to reach accommodation unless the adversary shows unmistakable signs of laxity.

Table C.1

Belief System Interpretations of Adversary Behavior
in Responder-Belligerent Periods (Applying First Six Restrictions)

BELIEF SYSTEM

Adversary's behavior	DEC	DEE	ECE	EEC	EEE	CCE	CEE
Extremely belligerent	Resistant	Aggressive	Aggressive	Resistant	Aggressive	Aggressive	Aggressive
Quite belligerent	Resistant	Uninterpretable	Aggressive	Resistant	Uninterpretable	Aggressive	Uninterpretable
Fairly belligerent	Resistant	Resistant	Aggressive	Resistant	Resistant	Aggressive	Resistant
Balanced firm	? { Resistant or lax	? { Resistant or lax	? { Aggressive, receptive, or lax	? { Resistant, receptive, or lax	? { Resistant, receptive, or lax	? { Aggressive or receptive	? { Resistant or receptive
Balanced							
Balanced flexible							
Fairly accommodative	Lax	Lax	Lax	Lax	Lax	Receptive	Receptive
Quite accommodative	Lax	Lax	Lax	Lax	Lax	Receptive	Receptive
Extremely accommodative	Lax	Lax	Lax	Lax	Lax	Receptive	Receptive

Table C.2

Belief System Interpretations of Adversary Behavior
in Responder-Nonbelligerent Periods (Applying First Six Restrictions)

BELIEF SYSTEM

Adversary's behavior	DEC	DEE	ECE	EEC	EEE	CCE	CEE
Extremely belligerent	Resistant	Aggressive	Aggressive	Resistant	Aggressive	Aggressive	Aggressive
Quite belligerent	Resistant	Aggressive	Aggressive	Resistant	Aggressive	Aggressive	Aggressive
Fairly belligerent	Resistant	Aggressive	Aggressive	Resistant	Aggressive	Aggressive	Aggressive
Balanced firm	? { Resistant or lax	? { Aggressive, resistant, or lax	? { Aggressive or receptive	? { Resistant or receptive	? { Aggressive, resistant, or receptive	? { Aggressive or receptive	? { Aggressive, resistant, or receptive
Balanced							
Balanced flexible							
Fairly accommodative	Lax	Lax	Receptive	Receptive	Receptive	Receptive	Receptive
Quite accommodative	Lax	Lax	Uninterpretable	Uninterpretable	Uninterpretable	Receptive	Receptive
Extremely accommodative	Lax	Lax	Lax	Lax	Lax	Receptive	Receptive

Therefore, we make "balanced-flexible" the uninterpretable boundary pattern. This means that, in most cases, such a coalition will treat its adversary's balanced behavior as receptive rather than lax.

3. The boundary between aggressive and receptive. This problem arises *only* for belief systems of the –CE type. Since a –CE coalition believes it is seen as consolidationist and perceives its adversary as expansionist, we may assume it will feel threatened even by balanced adversary behavior. Therefore, we make "balanced flexible" the uninterpretable boundary pattern. This means that, in most cases, such a coalition will view its adversary's balanced behavior as aggressive rather than receptive.

4. The boundary between resistant and lax. This problem arises *only* for coalitions of the type D––. Since a destructionist coalition is committed to making gains by exploiting its adversary, we assume it will seek to avail itself of every reasonable opportunity to do so. Therefore, we make "balanced firm" the uninterpretable boundary pattern. This means that, in most cases, such a coalition will treat its adversary's balanced behavior as lax rather than resistant.

These additional conventions enable us to remove most of the ambiguity in Tables C.1 and C.2 concerning the interpretation of balanced behavior. Tables C.3 and C.4 repeat the previous tables with the greater specification now possible. The boundary between "resistant" and "receptive" still remains unspecified for a number of belief systems but, as we saw in Chapter Four (Table 4.2, p. 64), this boundary is of no consequence since both interpretations imply the same response. Using Tables C.3 and C.4 in conjunction with Table 4.2, we can arrive at the final set of predictions summarized in Table 4.3 (p. 66).

Table C.3

Belief System Interpretations of Adversary Behavior in Responder-Belligerent Periods (Applying All Restrictions and Conventions)

BELIEF SYSTEM

Adversary's behavior	DEC	DEE	ECE	EEC	EEE	CCE	CEE
Extremely belligerent	Resistant	Aggressive	Aggressive	Resistant	Aggressive	Aggressive	Aggressive
Quite belligerent	Resistant	Uninterpretable	Aggressive	Resistant	Uninterpretable	Aggressive	Uninterpretable
Fairly belligerent	Resistant	Resistant	Aggressive	Resistant	Resistant	Aggressive	Resistant
Balanced firm	Uninterpretable	Uninterpretable	Aggressive	Resistant or receptive ?	Resistant or receptive ?	Aggressive	Resistant or receptive ?
Balanced flexible	Lax	Lax	Uninterpretable	Uninterpretable	Uninterpretable	Uninterpretable	Resistant or receptive ?
Fairly accommodative	Lax	Lax	Lax	Lax	Lax	Receptive	Receptive
Quite accommodative	Lax	Lax	Lax	Lax	Lax	Receptive	Receptive
Extremely accommodative	Lax	Lax	Lax	Lax	Lax	Receptive	Receptive

Table C.4
Belief System Interpretations of Adversary Behavior in Responder-Nonbelligerent Periods (Applying All Restrictions and Conventions)

BELIEF SYSTEM

Adversary's behavior	DEC	DEE	ECE	EEC	EEE	CCE	CEE
Extremely belligerent	Resistant	Aggressive	Aggressive	Resistant	Aggressive	Aggressive	Aggressive
Quite belligerent	Resistant	Aggressive	Aggressive	Resistant	Aggressive	Aggressive	Aggressive
Fairly belligerent	Resistant	Aggressive	Aggressive	Resistant	Aggressive	Aggressive	Aggressive
Balanced firm	Uninterpretable	Uninterpretable	Aggressive	? { Resistant or receptive	Uninterpretable	Aggressive	Uninterpretable
Balanced	Lax	Lax	Aggressive		? { Resistant or receptive	Aggressive	? { Resistant or receptive
Balanced flexible	Lax	Lax	Uninterpretable			Uninterpretable	
Fairly accommodative	Lax	Lax	Receptive	Receptive	Receptive	Receptive	Receptive
Quite accommodative	Lax	Lax	Uninterpretable	Uninterpretable	Uninterpretable	Receptive	Receptive
Extremely accommodative	Lax	Lax	Lax	Lax	Lax	Receptive	Receptive

Data Appendices

Appendix D

Monthly Refractory and Conciliatory Scores for the Soviet and Western Coalitions, January, 1946, to December, 1963

This appendix contains the raw data of this study; from this data, the interaction units used in the analysis were constructed. The summary below aggregates the scores by months for convenience and economy but daily scores are available on request.

Two scores are provided for each measure — a raw score and a standard score. The raw scores are simply the sum of the magnitudes of daily scores during the month in question. These raw scores have certain disadvantages. First, they have little intrinsic meaning and are, therefore, difficult to interpret by themselves. Second, they are not comparable between coalitions or between refractory and conciliatory scores. For example, in June, 1946, the Soviet coalition had a raw score of 27 on refractory behavior while the Western coalition had a score of 33 on this measure. This should not be interpreted to mean that the Western coalition was higher in refractory behavior than the Soviet coalition was during June, 1946, because we cannot assume that the *New York Times* is equally sensitive to Western and Soviet behavior.

These disadvantages are removed by the use of the standard scores provided next to the raw scores. The standard scores express each measure in relation to its own average. Specifically,

$$R_i^s = \frac{R_i - \overline{R}}{\sigma_R},$$

where R_i is the raw refractory score for a coalition for the ith month, $\overline{R}$ is the mean monthly refractory score for this coalition over all months, and σ_R is the standard deviation of its monthly refractory scores from the grand mean. A standard score of $-.98$, for example, indicates that, during this month, the coalition was almost one standard deviation under its normal refractory score.

181

Standard scores can be interpreted more easily than the raw scores. They tell us immediately whether a given level of refractory or conciliatory behavior is above or below average for a given coalition. Furthermore, they provide some basis for comparison since we can say whether one coalition was being more refractory than usual while the other was being less so. Thus, in June, 1946, the Western coalition was slightly less refractory than its average while the Soviet coalition was slightly more refractory than its average. Finally, we can more meaningfully combine the refractory and conciliatory scores for a coalition into a single score.

For some purposes, a single combined score for a coalition may be more useful than separate refractory and conciliatory scores. We have provided this in the form of the refractory standard score minus the conciliatory standard score. A combined score of zero means average or offsetting scores, a high positive value means high belligerence, and a high negative value means high accommodativeness.

Key:

R = raw monthly refractory score
R^s = standard refractory score
C = raw monthly conciliatory score
C^s = standard conciliatory score

1946	WESTERN						SOVIET					
	Combined	Refractory		Conciliatory			Combined	Refractory		Conciliatory		
	$R^s - C^s$	R	R^s	C	C^s		$R^s - C^s$	R	R^s	C	C^s	
January	-.373	16	-.603	5	-.230		-.378	6	-.686	5	-.308	
February	+.060	33	-.088	6	-.148		+.328	20	-.115	3	-.443	
March	+3.74	138	+3.10	0	-.641		+3.97	162	+5.68	35	+1.71	
April	-1.57	44	+.246	30	+1.82		-3.63	42	+.782	75	+4.41	
May	-.213	24	-.361	6	-.148		-.671	17	-.237	16	+.434	
June	-.350	33	-.088	11	+.262		-.466	27	+.170	19	+.636	
July	-.128	43	+.216	12	+.344		-.152	38	+.619	21	+.771	
August	+1.56	96	+1.82	11	+.262		-1.22	88	+2.66	31	+1.44	
September	-.432	33	-.088	12	+.344		+1.67	48	+1.03	0	-.645	
October	+1.74	72	+1.10	0	-.641		-.103	26	+.130	13	+.231	
November	-.902	31	-.148	17	+.754		-1.96	25	+.089	40	+2.05	
December	-1.40	31	-.148	23	+1.25		-2.11	21	-.062	40	+2.05	
1946 totals		594		133				520		298		

1947	WESTERN					SOVIET				
	Combined	Refractory		Conciliatory		Combined	Refractory		Conciliatory	
	$R^s - C^s$	R	R^s	C	C^s	$R^s - C^s$	R	R^s	C	C^s
January	-.823	12	-.725	9	+.098	-.985	6	-.686	14	+.299
February	+.064	25	-.330	3	-.394	-.914	16	-.278	19	+.636
March	+1.73	99	+1.91	10	+.180	+.143	32	+.374	13	+.231
April	-1.49	44	+.246	29	+1.74	-1.46	24	+.048	32	+1.51
May	+.553	33	-.088	0	-.641	+.367	16	-.278	0	-.645
June	+.792	49	+.398	3	-.394	+1.55	50	+1.11	3	-.443
July	+2.37	93	+1.73	0	-.641	+1.39	41	+.741	0	-.645
August	+.644	36	+.003	0	-.641	+.979	31	+.334	0	-.645
September	+2.46	96	+1.82	0	-.641	+2.40	71	+1.96	3	-.443
October	-.061	29	-.209	6	-.148	+.983	46	+.945	9	-.038
November	+.337	34	-.057	3	-.394	+.981	36	+.538	3	-.443
December	+1.80	85	+1.49	4	-.312	+.058	20	-.115	7	-.173
1947 totals		635		67			389		103	
1948										
January	+1.56	66	+.914	0	-.641	-.472	7	-.645	7	-.173
February	+.579	42	+.185	3	-.394	+3.83	101	+3.19	0	-.645
March	+4.53	164	+3.89	0	-.641	+.411	27	+.170	6	-.241
April	+1.56	66	+.914	0	-.641	-.129	27	+.170	14	+.299
May	+.949	65	+.883	7	-.066	+.221	24	+.048	7	-.173
June	+.644	36	+.003	0	-.641	-.318	24	+.048	15	+.366
July	+1.04	49	+.398	0	-.641	+1.79	51	+1.15	0	-.645

	WESTERN					SOVIET				
	Combined	Refractory		Conciliatory		Combined	Refractory		Conciliatory	
1948 (cont.)	$R^s - C^s$	R	R^s	C	C^s	$R^s - C^s$	R	R^s	C	C^s
August	+.537	46	+.307	5	−.230	+1.13	58	+1.43	14	+.299
September	+.974	81	+1.40	13	+.426	+.700	44	+.864	12	+.164
October	+2.64	102	+2.00	0	−.641	+2.23	70	+1.92	5	−.308
November	+.246	31	−.148	3	−.394	+.532	25	+.089	3	−.443
December	+.402	28	−.239	0	−.641	+.326	15	−.319	0	−.645
1948 totals		776		31			473		83	
1949										
January	−.235	7	−.876	0	−.641	−.286	0	−.931	0	−.645
February	+.189	21	−.452	0	−.641	+.979	31	+.334	0	−.645
March	−.053	13	−.694	0	−.641	−.041	6	−.686	0	−.645
April	+.553	33	−.088	0	−.641	−1.80	9	−.564	28	+1.24
May	−.277	30	−.179	9	+.098	−.350	53	+1.23	33	+1.58
June	−.425	17	−.573	6	−.148	−.241	11	−.482	6	−.241
July	+.189	21	−.452	0	−.641	+.041	8	−.604	0	−.645
August	−.449	0	−1.09	0	−.641	−.286	0	−.931	0	−.645
September	+.007	15	−.634	0	−.641	−.163	3	−.808	0	−.645
October	−.084	12	−.725	0	−.641	+.693	24	+.048	0	−.645
November	+.064	25	−.330	3	−.394	−.403	12	−.441	9	−.038
December	+.098	18	−.543	0	−.641	+.204	12	−.441	0	−.645
1949 totals		212		18			169		76	

	WESTERN					SOVIET				
	Combined	Refractory		Conciliatory		Combined	Refractory		Conciliatory	
1950	$R^s - C^s$	R	R^s	C	C^s	$R^s - C^s$	R	R^s	C	C^s
January	+.094	26	−.300	3	−.394	+.505	21	+.062	3	−.443
February	+1.09	51	+.458	0	−.641	+.081	9	−.564	0	−.645
March	−.175	9	−.816	0	−.641	−.286	0	−.931	0	−.645
April	+.978	47	+.337	0	−.641	+.326	15	−.319	0	−.645
May	+.857	43	+.216	0	−.641	−.163	3	−.808	0	−.645
June	+2.01	81	+1.37	4	−.641	+1.55	45	+.904	0	−.645
July	+2.92	122	+2.61	0	−.312	+.530	20	−.115	0	−.645
August	+2.86	109	+2.22	0	−.641	+1.83	52	+1.19	0	−.645
September	+.770	51	+.458	4	−.312	+.736	30	+.293	3	−.443
October	+2.21	131	+2.88	16	+.672	+1.39	41	+.741	0	−.645
November	+.944	81	+1.37	13	+.426	+4.24	111	+3.60	0	−.645
December	+3.31	124	+2.67	0	−.641	+1.02	32	+.374	0	−.645
1950 totals		875		40			379		6	
1951										
January	+2.35	111	+2.28	7	−.066	+1.06	33	+.415	0	−.645
February	+.250	23	−.391	0	−.641	+.122	10	−.523	0	−.645
March	−.155	34	−.057	9	+.098	−.470	12	−.441	10	+.029
April	−6.31	23	−.391	80	+5.92	−.893	0	−.931	9	−.038
May	−.355	22	−.421	7	−.066	−.286	0	−.931	0	−.645
June	−2.56	25	−.330	35	+2.23	−2.79	8	−.604	42	+2.19
July	−2.83	62	+.792	52	+3.62	−4.72	35	+.497	87	+5.22

| | WESTERN | | | | | SOVIET | | | | |
	Combined $R^s - C^s$	Refractory R	Refractory R^s	Conciliatory C	Conciliatory C^s	Combined $R^s - C^s$	Refractory R	Refractory R^s	Conciliatory C	Conciliatory C^s
1951 (cont.)										
August	+1.67	97	+1.85	10	+.180	+1.73	66	+1.76	10	+.029
September	+1.25	56	+.610	0	-.641	+1.22	37	+.578	0	-.645
October	-.637	10	-.785	6	-.148	-1.04	3	-.808	13	+.231
November	-1.78	21	-.452	24	+1.33	-1.41	12	-.441	24	+.973
December	-.844	14	-.664	10	+.180	-.391	9	-.564	7	-.173
1951 totals		498		240			225		202	
1952										
January	+.614	35	-.027	0	-.641	-.121	9	-.564	3	-.443
February	-.887	18	-.543	12	+.344	-.770	3	-.808	9	-.038
March	-.604	3	-.998	3	-.394	-.323	9	-.564	6	-.241
April	+.038	16	-.603	0	-.641	-.041	6	-.686	0	-.645
May	+.402	28	-.239	0	-.641	+1.51	44	+.864	0	-.645
June	+.402	28	-.239	0	-.641	+.530	20	-.115	0	-.645
July	-.175	9	-.816	0	-.641	+.081	9	-.564	0	-.645
August	-.266	6	-.907	0	-.641	+.081	9	-.564	0	-.645
September	-.240	15	-.634	3	-.394	-.566	8	-.604	9	-.038
October	-.114	11	-.755	0	-.641	-.041	6	-.686	0	-.645
November	-.482	7	-.876	3	-.394	-.041	6	-.686	0	-.645
December	-.266	6	-.907	0	-.641	-.286	0	-.931	0	-.645
1952 totals		182		21			129		27	

1953	WESTERN					SOVIET				
	Combined	Refractory		Conciliatory		Combined	Refractory		Conciliatory	
	$R^s - C^s$	R	R^s	C	C^s	$R^s - C^s$	R	R^s	C	C^s
January	+.311	25	−.330	0	−.641	−.163	3	−.808	0	−.645
February	+1.09	67	+.944	6	−.148	+.328	15	−.319	0	−.645
March	+.553	33	−.088	0	−.641	−1.75	12	−.441	29	+1.31
April	−1.32	28	−.239	21	+1.08	−2.75	14	−.360	45	+2.39
May	−.128	43	+.216	12	+.344	−.820	15	−.319	17	+.501
June	−1.45	67	+.944	37	+2.39	−1.64	23	+.007	34	+1.65
July	−3.77	77	+1.25	69	+5.02	−4.45	17	−.237	72	+4.21
August	−.623	24	−.361	11	+.262	−.224	23	+.007	13	+.231
September	+.151	36	+.003	6	−.148	+.081	9	−.564	0	−.645
October	−.874	13	−.694	10	+.180	+.081	9	−.564	0	−.645
November	−.425	17	−.573	6	−.148	+.124	15	−.319	3	−.443
December	−.820	31	−.148	16	+.672	+.017	19	−.156	7	−.173
1953 totals		461		194			174		220	

1954	WESTERN					SOVIET				
	$R^s - C^s$	R	R^s	C	C^s	$R^s - C^s$	R	R^s	C	C^s
January	−.334	20	−.482	6	−.148	.000	7	−.645	0	−.645
February	−.787	24	−.361	13	+.426	+.081	9	−.564	0	−.645
March	+.761	48	+.367	3	−.394	+.326	15	−.319	0	−.645
April	+.032	51	+.458	13	+.426	+.573	26	+.130	3	−.443
May	−.052	32	−.118	7	−.066	+1.31	44	+.864	3	−.443
June	−.765	22	−.421	12	+.344	−.243	6	−.686	3	−.443
July	−3.36	50	+.428	54	+3.79	−1.86	31	+.334	42	+2.19

| | WESTERN | | | | | SOVIET | | | | |
| | Combined | Refractory | | Conciliatory | | Combined | Refractory | | Conciliatory | |
1954 (cont.)	$R^s - C^s$	R	R^s	C	C^s	$R^s - C^s$	R	R^s	C	C^s
August	-.917	17	-.573	12	+.344	-.163	3	-.808	0	-.645
September	+.610	43	+.216	3	-.394	-.080	10	-.523	3	-.443
October	.000	31	-.148	6	-.148	+.083	14	-.360	3	-.443
November	-.856	19	-.512	12	+.344	+.449	18	-.196	0	-.645
December	-.708	32	-.118	15	+.590	+.124	15	-.319	3	-.443
1954 totals		389		156			198		60	
1955										
January	+.027	40	+.125	9	+.098	-.318	24	+.048	15	+.366
February	+.943	54	+.549	3	-.394	+.045	18	-.196	6	-.241
March	+.273	40	+.125	6	-.148	-.404	7	-.645	6	-.241
April	-2.06	12	-.725	24	+1.33	-.766	13	-.400	15	+.366
May	-1.34	11	-.755	15	+.590	-2.26	11	-.482	36	+1.78
June	-.357	3	-.998	0	-.641	-.092	13	-.400	5	-.308
July	-1.76	16	-.603	22	+1.16	-1.74	22	-.033	35	+1.71
August	-.482	7	-.876	3	-.394	-2.25	3	-.808	31	+1.44
September	-1.65	9	-.816	18	+.836	-1.38	8	-.604	21	+.771
October	-.058	21	-.452	3	-.394	-.444	11	-.482	9	-.038
November	-.118	19	-.512	3	-.394	+.734	25	+.089	0	-.645
December	+.242	39	+.094	6	-.148	+.403	45	+.904	17	+.501
1955 totals		271		112			200		196	

	WESTERN					SOVIET				
	Combined	Refractory		Conciliatory		Combined	Refractory		Conciliatory	
1956	$R^s - C^s$	R	R^s	C	C^s	$R^s - C^s$	R	R^s	C	C^s
January	-.235	7	-.876	0	-.641	+.163	11	-.482	0	-.645
February	-.455	16	-.603	6	-.148	-.041	6	-.686	0	-.645
March	-.668	9	-.816	6	-.148	+.081	9	-.564	0	-.645
April	-1.26	3	-.998	11	+.262	-1.31	3	-.808	17	+.501
May	-.331	12	-.725	3	-.394	-1.04	3	-.808	13	+.231
June	-.696	0	-1.09	3	-.394	-.259	0	-.904	0	-.645
July	-.486	15	-.634	6	-.148	-.365	3	-.808	3	-.443
August	-.357	3	-.998	0	-.641	+.081	9	-.564	0	-.645
September	-.144	10	-.785	0	-.641	-.286	0	-.931	0	-.645
October	+1.23	77	+1.25	8	+.016	+.979	59	+1.48	17	+.501
November	-1.76	146	+3.34	70	+5.10	+3.32	95	+2.94	4	-.376
December	+1.13	52	+.489	0	-.641	-.286	0	-.931	0	-.645
1956 totals		350		113			198		54	
1957										
January	-.235	7	-.876	0	-.641	+.206	17	-.237	3	-.443
February	-.391	10	-.785	3	-.394	-.325	4	-.768	3	-.443
March	-.023	14	-.664	0	-.641	+.081	9	-.564	0	-.645
April	-.209	16	-.603	3	-.394	-.163	3	-.808	0	-.645
May	-.331	12	-.725	3	-.394	-.770	3	-.808	9	-.038
June	+.397	36	+.003	3	-.394	-.078	15	-.319	6	-.241
July	-.577	12	-.725	6	-.148	-.243	6	-.686	3	-.443

	WESTERN					SOVIET				
	Combined	Refractory		Conciliatory		Combined	Refractory		Conciliatory	
1957 (cont.)	$R^s - C^s$	R	R^s	C	C^s	$R^s - C^s$	R	R^s	C	C^s
August	−.175	9	−.816	0	−.641	+.736	30	+.293	3	−.443
September	−.122	27	−.270	6	−.148	−.159	13	−.400	6	−.241
October	−.040	27	−.270	5	−.230	+.275	22	−.033	5	−.308
November	+.189	21	−.452	0	−.641	−.325	4	−.768	3	−.443
December	−1.40	12	−.725	16	+.672	−.121	9	−.564	3	−.443
1957 totals		203		45			135		44	
1958										
January	−.053	13	−.694	0	−.641	−.365	3	−.808	3	−.443
February	−.685	0	−1.09	3	−.394	−.770	3	−.808	9	−.038
March	−.331	12	−.725	3	−.394	−.039	11	−.482	3	−.443
April	−.058	21	−.452	3	−.394	+.534	30	+.293	6	−.241
May	−.534	8	−.846	4	−.312	−.932	4	−.768	12	+.164
June	−.331	12	−.725	3	−.394	+.979	31	+.334	0	−.645
July	+2.00	143	+3.25	23	+1.25	+1.66	89	+2.70	25	+1.04
August	−1.76	46	+.307	33	+2.07	−1.19	24	+.048	28	+1.24
September	+1.67	86	+1.52	6	−.148	−.032	31	+.334	15	+.366
October	−.924	33	−.088	18	+.836	−.577	16	−.278	14	+.299
November	+.242	39	+.094	6	−.148	+.364	54	+1.27	23	+.906
December	+.493	31	−.148	0	−.641	+.247	18	−.196	3	−.443
1958 totals		444		102			314		141	

| | WESTERN | | | | | SOVIET | | | | |
| | Combined | Refractory | | Conciliatory | | Combined | Refractory | | Conciliatory | |
1959	$R^s - C^s$	R	R^s	C	C^s	$R^s - C^s$	R	R^s	C	C^s
January	−.692	19	−.512	10	+.180	+.303	26	+.130	7	−.173
February	+.098	18	−.543	0	−.641	+.248	23	+.007	6	−.241
March	−.536	13	−.694	6	−.148	−.024	21	−.062	9	−.038
April	+.311	25	−.330	0	−.641	−.163	3	−.808	0	−.645
May	+.357	59	+.701	12	+.344	+1.07	53	+1.23	12	+.164
June	+.614	35	−.027	0	−.641	+.326	15	−.319	0	−.645
July	−.175	9	−.816	0	−.641	−.146	15	−.319	7	−.173
August	−.084	12	−.725	0	−.641	−.202	7	−.645	3	−.443
September	−.134	32	−.118	8	+.016	+.112	23	+.007	8	−.105
October	−.200	19	−.512	4	−.312	−.041	6	−.686	0	−.645
November	−.391	10	−.785	3	−.394	−.188	9	−.564	4	−.376
December	−.088	20	−.482	3	−.394	−.365	3	−.808	3	−.443
1959 totals		271		46			204		59	
1960										
January	−1.11	0	−1.09	8	+.016	−.365	3	−.808	3	−.443
February	+.129	19	−.512	0	−.641	+.204	12	−.441	0	−.645
March	−.947	16	−.603	12	+.344	−.163	3	−.808	0	−.645
April	−.482	7	−.876	3	−.394	−.243	6	−.686	3	−.443
May	+.040	108	+2.19	34	+2.15	+4.44	144	+4.94	17	+.501
June	+.371	27	−.270	0	−.641	+.938	30	+.293	0	−.645
July	+1.76	73	+1.12	0	−.641	+2.29	68	+1.84	3	−.443

	WESTERN					SOVIET				
	Combined	Refractory		Conciliatory		Combined	Refractory		Conciliatory	
1960 (cont.)	$R^s - C^s$	R	R^s	C	C^s	$R^s - C^s$	R	R^s	C	C^s
August	+.796	41	+.155	0	-.641	+.652	23	+.007	0	-.645
September	-.144	10	-.785	0	-.641	+2.98	80	+2.33	0	-.645
October	+1.13	52	+.489	0	-.641	+2.00	66	+1.76	6	-.241
November	-.068	17	-.573	0	-.641	-.325	4	-.768	3	-.443
December	-.098	18	-.543	0	-.641	+.449	18	-.196	0	-.645
1960 totals		388		57			457		35	
1961										
January	+1.80	74	+1.16	0	-.641	-.629	23	+.007	19	+.636
February	-.443	11	-.755	4	-.312	+1.18	36	+.538	0	-.645
March	+1.03	57	+.640	3	-.394	+.206	17	-.237	3	-.443
April	+2.06	107	+2.16	9	+.098	-1.21	17	-.237	24	+.973
May	+.003	23	-.391	3	-.394	-.770	3	-.808	9	-.038
June	+.376	38	+.064	4	-.312	+.098	16	-.278	4	-.376
July	+1.46	63	+.822	0	-.641	+.367	16	-.278	0	-.645
August	+1.89	77	+1.25	0	-.641	+3.83	106	+3.39	3	-.443
September	+.485	47	+.337	6	-.148	+1.22	37	+.578	0	-.645
October	-.574	31	-.148	13	+.426	+2.08	68	+1.84	6	-.241
November	-.938	19	-.512	13	+.426	-.007	25	+.089	11	+.096
December	+.220	22	-.421	0	-.641	-.123	4	-.768	0	-.645
1961 totals		569		55			368		79	

1962	WESTERN					SOVIET				
	Combined	Refractory		Conciliatory		Combined	Refractory		Conciliatory	
	$R^s - C^s$	R	R^s	C	C^s	$R^s - C^s$	R	R^s	C	C^s
January	+.306	33	-.088	3	-.394	-.432	3	-.808	4	-.376
February	-.580	20	-.482	9	+.098	-.549	20	-.115	16	+.434
March	+.129	19	-.512	0	-.641	+1.14	35	+.497	0	-.645
April	-.516	14	-.664	6	-.148	-1.20	4	-.768	16	+.436
May	+.002	50	+.428	13	+.426	-.006	30	+.293	14	+.299
June	-1.66	6	-.907	17	+.754	-.797	4	-.768	10	+.029
July	-1.34	3	-.998	12	+.344	+1.19	46	+.945	6	-.241
August	-.391	10	-.785	3	-.394	+.371	26	+.130	6	-.241
September	+1.43	62	+.792	0	-.641	+.616	37	+.578	9	-.038
October	+2.58	197	+4.89	36	+2.31	-4.38	50	+1.11	91	+5.49
November	-1.46	26	-.300	22	+1.16	-3.28	34	+.456	65	+3.74
December	-.182	25	-.330	6	-.148	-1.32	6	-.686	19	+.636
1962 totals		465		127			295		256	
1963										
January	-.513	6	-.907	3	-.394	+.124	15	-.319	3	-.443
February	+.887	44	+.246	0	-.641	-.078	15	-.319	6	-.241
March	-.425	17	-.573	6	-.148	-.674	7	-.645	10	+.029
April	+.069	36	+.003	7	-.066	-.360	18	-.196	12	+.164
May	-.759	6	-.907	6	-.148	-.121	9	-.564	3	-.443
June	-2.75	0	-1.09	28	+1.66	-.119	14	-.360	6	-.241
July	-3.90	24	-.361	51	+3.54	-3.77	4	-.768	54	+3.00

1963 (cont.)	WESTERN						SOVIET					
	Combined	Refractory		Conciliatory			Combined	Refractory		Conciliatory		
	$R^s - C^s$	R	R^s	C	C^s		$R^s - C^s$	R	R^s	C	C^s	
August	-1.10	3	-.998	9	+.098		-.488	0	-.931	3	-.443	
September	-.235	7	-.876	0	-.641		-.286	0	-.931	0	-.645	
October	-1.25	14	-.664	15	+.590		-.564	13	-.400	12	+.164	
November	+.098	18	-.543	0	-.641		-1.08	7	-.645	16	+.434	
December	-.201	19	-.513	4	-.312		-.555	0	-.931	4	-.376	
1963 totals		194		129				102		129		

Totals

	Western	Soviet
$\sum\limits_{i=1}^{216} R_i$	7779	4929
No. of months	216	216
$\bar{R}$	36.01	22.82
σ_R	32.96	24.52
$\sum\limits_{i=1}^{216} C_i$	1686	2068
No. of months	216	216
$\bar{C}$	7.81	9.57
σ_C	12.19	14.83

Appendix E

Major Soviet and Western Actions, 1946-63

SOVIET ACTIONS

Date	Description of action	Classification[a]
S1. March, 1946	Soviet troops march on Teheran	R
S2. March, 1946	Stalin lauds UN in surprise speech	C
S3. March, 1946	Soviet Union boycotts UN over Iranian issue	R
S4. April, 1946	Soviet Union agrees to evacuate Iran	C
S5. August, 1946	Yugoslavia shoots down second U.S. plane	R
S6. August, 1946	Yugoslavia frees fliers and forbids firing on aircraft	C
S7. November, 1946	Soviet Union agrees on Trieste, troop exit, arms inspection	C
S8. September, 1947	Soviet Union accuses U.S. of seeking war in vitriolic condemnation of U.S. policy	R
S9. October, 1947	Soviet Union revives Comintern	R
S10. October, 1947	Soviet Union pledges to ruin Marshall Plan in renewed attack on United States	R
S11. February, 1948	Communists seize power in Czechoslovakia	R
S12. April, 1948	Soviet Union imposes rail blockade in Germany	R
S13. June, 1948	Soviet Union completes Berlin blockade	R
S14. August, 1948	Soviet Union closes consulates in U.S.	R
S15. September, 1948	Soviet Union threatens Berlin airlanes as Berlin talks collapse	R

SOVIET ACTIONS

Date	Description of action	Classification[a]
S16. February, 1949	Soviet Union threatens Norway over NATO membership	R
S17. April, 1949	Soviet Union agrees to lift Berlin blockade	C
S18. May, 1949	Soviet Union renews Berlin pressure with rail tie-up, clashes with U.S. in Berlin talks	R
S19. June, 1950	North Korea invades South Korea	R
S20. October, 1950	Some Chinese units enter Korean war	R
S21. November, 1950	China enters Korean war in full scale	R
S22. June, 1951	Soviet Union and China propose cease-fire in Korea	C
S23. July, 1951	China makes concession on troop exodus in Korea	C
S24. August, 1951	Communists break off Korean truce talks	R
S25. November, 1951	Communists agree to UN proposal on Korean truce line	C
S26. May, 1952	Soviet Union tightens East German border, sets three-mile buffer zone	R
S27. March, 1953	Communists drop forced repatriation demand in Korea	C
S28. June, 1953	Communists agree on prisoner of war terms and truce line	C
S29. June, 1953	Communists halt truce talks over issue of release of prisoners of war by Rhee	R
S30. July, 1953	Communists agree to resume Korean truce talks in spite of Rhee	C
S31. July, 1953	Communists agree to final Korean truce	C
S32. March, 1954	Viet Minh begins major offensive against Dien Bien Phu	R
S33. July, 1954	Viet Minh agrees to settlement in Indochina	C
S34. May, 1955	Soviet Union agrees to Austrian treaty	C
S35. May, 1955	China frees four U.S. airmen	C
S36. July, 1955	China urges U.S. inclusion in peace pact, frees eleven U.S. fliers	C

APPENDIX E

SOVIET ACTIONS

Date	Description of action	Classification[a]
S37. September, 1955	West Germany and Soviet Union establish diplomatic relations, reach accord on prisoners of war	C
S38. October, 1956	Soviet Union intervenes in Hungary	R
S39. November, 1956	Soviet Union threatens military intervention in Suez crises	R
S40. October, 1957	Soviet Union threatens military intervention in Syrian crisis	R
S41. June, 1958	Soviet Union executes Nagy	R
S42. July, 1958	Soviet Union presses attack in UN on U.S. intervention in Lebanon, makes vague threats of military action	R
S43. July, 1958	Soviet Union agrees to summit talk on Mideast crisis, military threat eased	C
S44. August, 1958	China shells Quemoy in record attack	R
S45. September, 1958	China halts shelling of Quemoy, offers talks	C
S46. November, 1958	Soviet Union issues ultimatum on Berlin settlement	R
S47. May, 1960	Soviet Union threatens rocket attack on bases used by U-2 planes	R
S48. May, 1960	Khrushchev denounces Eisenhower over U-2 flights, cancels his trip; summit conference breaks up	R
S49. June, 1960	China suddenly resumes shelling of Quemoy	R
S50. July, 1960	Soviet Union threatens rocket retaliation over Cuba	R
S51. September, 1960	Soviet Union calls for ouster of UN Secretary-General, substitution of troika	R
S52. February, 1961	Soviet Union calls for ouster of UN Secretary-General over Lumumba death, threatens unilateral action in the Congo	R
S53. April, 1961	Soviet Union agrees to Laotian cease fire and talks	C
S54. August, 1961	Soviet Union seals East Berlin border with wall	R
S55. August, 1961	Soviet Union resumes atmospheric testing	R

SOVIET ACTIONS

Date	Description of action	Classification[a]
S56. October, 1961	Soviet Union explodes 50-megaton bomb over U.S. objections	R
S57. July, 1962	Soviet Union begins military build-up in Cuba leading to placement of missiles	R
S58. October, 1962	Chinese troops march on India	R
S59. October, 1962	Soviet ships veer from Cuba rather than confront quarantine	C
S60. October, 1962	Soviet Union agrees to remove missiles from Cuba	C
S61. November, 1962	China calls cease-fire in India; Soviet Union promises removal of bombers in Cuba	C
S62. July, 1963	Soviet Union agrees to limited test-ban treaty	C
S63. November, 1963	Soviet Union releases Professor Barghorn	C

WESTERN ACTIONS

Date	Description of action	Classification[a]
W1. March, 1946	U.S. protests to Soviet Union on Manchuria and Iran as Churchill assails Soviet policy	R
W2. March, 1946	West presses UN showdown on Iran	R
W3. March, 1946	West forces UN action on Iran over Soviet objections and boycott	R
W4. July, 1946	U.S. and U.K. proceed unilaterally toward joint administration of their zones in Germany	R
W5. August, 1946	U.S. gives Yugoslavia 48-hour ultimatum on freeing fliers	R
W6. October, 1946	Churchill, Atlee press demand for revision of UN veto	R
W7. March, 1947	Truman announces plan to aid Greece and Turkey against Communist threat	R
W8. July, 1947	U.S. excludes Poland and Hungary from Marshall Plan aid and emphasizes danger of Western European drift into Soviet sphere	R

APPENDIX E

WESTERN ACTIONS

Date	Description of action	Classification[a]
W9. September, 1947	West presses plans for UN action on Greek Civil War and curb on Soviet veto in UN	R
W10. December, 1947	U.S. announces abandonment of efforts to seek Soviet cooperation in European reconstruction	R
W11. January, 1948	U.K. calls for Western Bloc in Europe as U.S. publicizes papers on Nazi-Soviet plot	R
W12. March, 1948	U.S. announces plan for long term military reorganization and increased expenditure to combat Soviet threat	R
W13. April, 1948	U.S. troops bar Soviet entry to Berlin rail center	R
W14. August, 1948	U.S. expels Soviet consul	R
W15. September, 1948	U.S. presses UN action on Berlin over Soviet objections	R
W16. April, 1949	Twelve Western powers sign NATO pact	R
W17. January, 1950	Truman orders hydrogen bomb built	R
W18. June, 1950	Truman orders U.S. troops into Korea	R
W19. September, 1950	UN forces cross 38th parallel in Korea as MacArthur calls for surrender, UN backs aim of occupation of N. Korea	R
W20. November, 1950	U.S. troops reach Manchurian border in northeast Korea as UN forces launch major offensive in west Korea aimed at ending war by Christmas	R
W21. December, 1950	Truman proclaims a state of national emergency, asks swift steps toward full war basis	R
W22. April, 1951	Truman recalls MacArthur, bars bombing of China and use of Chinese Nationalist troops	C
W23. June, 1951	UN agrees to principle of Korean truce talks, proposes meeting with Communists	C
W24. November, 1951	UN agrees to Korean truce line	C

WESTERN ACTIONS

Date	Description of action	Classification[a]
W25. May, 1952	Western powers sign peace pact with W. Germany, include W. Germans in defense plans	R
W26. February, 1953	U.S. "unleashes" Chinese Nationalists to raid mainland	R
W27. April, 1953	UN agrees to exchange of sick prisoners of war in Korea	C
W28. June, 1953	UN agrees to Korean prisoner-of-war pact	C
W29. July, 1953	UN signs Korean truce	C
W30. July, 1954	France agrees to yield Hanoi and Haiphong as part of Indochina accord, U.S. may consent to French truce proposal	C
W31. July, 1954	France signs Indochina agreement, U.S. accepts pact in principle	C
W32. October, 1954	Western powers sign pact for W. German sovereignty and rearmament	R
W33. January, 1955	Eisenhower granted broad authority for military defense of Formosa (Taiwan)	R
W34. February, 1955	Dulles promises military action to defend Formosa and related positions	R
W35. April, 1955	U.S. agrees to direct talks with China over Formosan crisis without Chinese Nationalists	C
W36. May, 1955	West agrees to Austrian Treaty	C
W37. September, 1955	W. Germany, with U.S. approval, agrees to diplomatic relations, prisoner-of-war accord with Soviet Union	C
W38. October, 1956	U.S. offers economic aid to East European countries breaking with Soviet Union, presses UN action on Hungary	R
W39. October, 1956	U.K., France, and Israel attack Egypt and try to capture Suez Canal	R
W40. October, 1956	U.S. pledges nonintervention in Suez	C

WESTERN ACTIONS

Date	Description of action	Classification[a]
W41. November, 1956	U.K., France and Israel agree to cease-fire, withdrawal from Suez	C
W42. July, 1958	U.S. sends marines into Lebanon	R
W43. July, 1958	U.S. drops opposition to summit meeting over Mideast crisis	C
W44. September, 1958	U.S. announces plans to take military action to defend Quemoy if necessary	R
W45. September, 1958	U.S. convoys supplies to Quemoy garrison, reasserts determination to fight over island if necessary	R
W46. September, 1959	U.S. denounces Soviet Union and China over Laos, presses for UN observers over Soviet opposition	R
W47. May, 1960	U.S. admits U-2 espionage flights, defends right to make them, and implies that they will continue	R
W48. May, 1960	U.S. announces end to U-2 flights	C
W49. July, 1960	U.S. asserts it will not tolerate Soviet interference in Cuba and Latin America	R
W50. August, 1960	OAS passes U.S.-sponsored condemnation of Communist intrusions in Western Hemisphere	R
W51. November, 1960	U.S. sends Navy to Caribbean to defend against alleged Cuban threat to Guatemala and Nicaragua	R
W52. January, 1961	U.S. breaks diplomatic relations with Cuba	R
W53. March, 1961	U.S. warns Soviet Union on Laos, calls special SEATO meeting to plan appropriate steps to deal with threat	R
W54. April, 1961	U.S.-supported invasion of Cuba launched at Bay of Pigs	R
W55. May, 1961	Western powers announce unity on firm stand in Berlin	R
W56. July, 1961	U.S. orders partial mobilization to meet Soviet threat to Berlin and elsewhere	R

WESTERN ACTIONS

Date	Description of action	Classification[a]
W57. August, 1961	U.S. sends troops to Berlin as vice-president reasserts U.S. commitment in speech to Berliners	R
W58. May, 1962	U.S. sends ships and troops to Thailand as Pathet Lao advances in Laos	R
W59. October, 1962	U.S. imposes arms blockade on Cuba to prevent installation of missiles	R
W60. October, 1962	U.S. lifts Cuban blockade, calls temporary halt to air surveillance	C
W61. June, 1963	Kennedy urges end to Cold War style of thinking, U.S. to forego new atomic testing in atmosphere	C
W62. July, 1963	Western powers agree to treaty banning atmospheric nuclear tests	C

[a]*R = refractory; C = conciliatory.*

Appendix F

Belligerent/Accommodative Scores
for 125 Interaction Units, 1946-63

Period ended by major Soviet action	WESTERN BEHAVIOR		SOVIET BEHAVIOR (RESPONDER)	
	b/a^a	Category	b/a	Category
S1.	+.334	Balanced firm	-.080	Nonbelligerent
S2.	+3.339	Extremely belligerent	+10.452	Belligerent
S3.	+5.409	Extremely belligerent	-5.841	Nonbelligerent
S4.	+3.639	Extremely belligerent	+5.442	Belligerent
S5.	-.111	Balanced	-.382	Nonbelligerent
S6.	+6.639	Extremely belligerent	+12.565	Belligerent
S7.	+.227	Balanced	-.142	Nonbelligerent
S8.	+.780	Balanced firm	+.333	Nonbelligerent
S9.	+.950	Balanced firm	+.709	Nonbelligerent
S10.	+.986	Balanced firm	+.936	Nonbelligerent
S11.	+.811	Balanced firm	+.392	Nonbelligerent
S12.	+4.239	Extremely belligerent	+2.842	Belligerent
S13.	+.966	Balanced firm	-.225	Nonbelligerent
S14.	+.910	Balanced firm	+.938	Nonbelligerent
S15.	-.547	Balanced flexible	+.700	Nonbelligerent
S16.	+.788	Balanced firm	+.695	Nonbelligerent
S17.	+.487	Balanced firm	+.398	Nonbelligerent
S18.	-.522	Balanced flexible	-3.497	Nonbelligerent
S19.	+.453	Balanced firm	+.018	Nonbelligerent
S20.	+2.331	Quite belligerent	+1.250	Belligerent

Period ended by major Soviet action	WESTERN BEHAVIOR		SOVIET BEHAVIOR (RESPONDER)	
	b/a[a]	Category	b/a	Category
S21.	+.574	Balanced firm	+2.528	Belligerent
S22.	-.740	Balanced flexible	+.061	Nonbelligerent
S23.	-3.790	Extremely accommodative	-5.693	Nonbelligerent
S24.	+.166	(Inconsistent)	-1.271	Nonbelligerent
S25.	-.465	Balanced flexible	+.271	Nonbelligerent
S26.	-.156	Balanced	-.144	Nonbelligerent
S27.	+.434	Balanced firm	-.513	Nonbelligerent
S28.	-.747	Balanced flexible	-2.367	Nonbelligerent
S29.	-2.661	(Inconsistent)	-4.034	Nonbelligerent
S30.	+.308	Balanced	+.544	Nonbelligerent
S31.	-6.666	Extremely accommodative	-2.116	Nonbelligerent
S32.	-.421	Balanced flexible	-.190	Nonbelligerent
S33.	-1.360	Fairly accommodative	+.398	Nonbelligerent
S34.	-1.156	Fairly accommodative	-.401	Nonbelligerent
S35.	-.780	Balanced flexible	-.717	Nonbelligerent
S36.	-1.103	Fairly accommodative	-1.148	Nonbelligerent
S37.	-1.168	Fairly accommodative	-2.395	Nonbelligerent
S38.	-.402	Balanced flexible	-.265	Nonbelligerent
S39.	+6.320	Extremely belligerent	+6.912	Belligerent
S40.	-.184	Balanced	-.080	Nonbelligerent
S41.	-.387	Balanced flexible	-.244	Nonbelligerent
S42.	+1.485	Fairly belligerent	+1.306	Belligerent
S43.	-2.352	(Inconsistent)	+9.268	Belligerent
S44.	-1.248	Fairly accommodative	-1.623	Nonbelligerent

Period ended by major Soviet action	WESTERN BEHAVIOR		SOVIET BEHAVIOR (RESPONDER)	
	b/a^a	Category	b/a	Category
S45.	+1.929	Fairly belligerent	+1.290	Belligerent
S46.	+.012	Balanced	-.885	Nonbelligerent
S47.	-.407	Balanced flexible	-.033	Nonbelligerent
S48.	+.221	(Inconsistent)	+5.527	Belligerent
S49.	+.862	Balanced firm	+3.112	Belligerent
S50.	-.285	Balanced	+1.071	Belligerent
S51.	+1.020	Fairly belligerent	+1.453	Belligerent
S52.	-.835	Balanced flexible	-.804	Nonbelligerent
S53.	+.752	Balanced firm	+.769	Nonbelligerent
S54.	+.862	Balanced firm	-.157	Nonbelligerent
S55.	+2.425	Quite belligerent	+3.862	Belligerent
S56.	-.050	Balanced	+1.148	Belligerent
S57.	-.687	Balanced flexible	-.264	Nonbelligerent
S58.	-.240	Balanced	+.051	Nonbelligerent
S59.	+7.08	Extremely belligerent	+3.98	Belligerent
S60.	+5.33	Extremely belligerent	-.760	(Inconsistent)
S61.	+1.755	(Inconsistent)	-5.608	Nonbelligerent
S62.	-1.456	Fairly accommodative	-.478	Nonbelligerent
S63.	-.547	Balanced flexible	-.861	Nonbelligerent

Period ended by major Western action	SOVIET BEHAVIOR		WESTERN BEHAVIOR (RESPONDER)	
	b/a [a]	Category	b/a	Category
W1.	+.122	Balanced	+.186	Nonbelligerent
W2.	+4.997	Extremely belligerent	+2.231	Belligerent
W3.	-1.436	(Inconsistent)	+2.576	Belligerent
W4.	-1.105	Fairly accommodative	-.329	Nonbelligerent
W5.	+2.495	Quite belligerent	+1.515	Belligerent
W6.	+.322	Balanced	+.711	Nonbelligerent
W7.	-1.406	Fairly accommodative	-.557	Nonbelligerent
W8.	+.166	Balanced	+.702	Nonbelligerent
W9.	+1.135	Fairly belligerent	+1.626	Belligerent
W10.	+1.566	Fairly belligerent	+1.422	Belligerent
W11.	-.163	Balanced	+1.732	Belligerent
W12.	+1.767	Fairly belligerent	+1.271	Belligerent
W13.	+1.900	Fairly belligerent	+5.927	Belligerent
W14.	+.469	Balanced firm	+.792	Nonbelligerent
W15.	+1.130	Fairly belligerent	-.105	Nonbelligerent
W16.	+.777	Balanced firm	+.529	Nonbelligerent
W17.	+.024	Balanced	-.025	Nonbelligerent
W18.	+.185	Balanced	+.574	Nonbelligerent
W19.	+1.254	Fairly belligerent	+2.381	Belligerent
W20.	+2.044	Quite belligerent	+.979	Nonbelligerent
W21.	+3.844	Extremely belligerent	+2.837	Belligerent
W22.	+.307	Balanced	+1.354	Belligerent
W23.	-1.554	Fairly accommodative	-3.374	Nonbelligerent

Period ended by major Western action	SOVIET BEHAVIOR		WESTERN BEHAVIOR (RESPONDER)	
	b/a^a	Category	b/a	Category
W24.	-.785	Balanced flexible	-.316	Nonbelligerent
W25.	-.030	Balanced	-.377	Nonbelligerent
W26.	-.155	Balanced	-.164	Nonbelligerent
W27.	-1.322	Fairly accommodative	+.806	Nonbelligerent
W28.	-1.585	Fairly accommodative	-1.117	Nonbelligerent
W29.	-2.397	Quite accommodative	-.636	(Inconsistent)
W30.	+.326	Balanced	-.277	Nonbelligerent
W31.	-7.579	Extremely accommodative	-7.592	Nonbelligerent
W32.	+.039	Balanced	-.444	Nonbelligerent
W33.	-.109	Balanced	-.510	Nonbelligerent
W34.	+.844	Balanced firm	+1.350	Belligerent
W35.	-.675	Balanced flexible	-.152	Nonbelligerent
W36.	-1.156	Fairly accommodative	-.606	Nonbelligerent
W37.	-1.709	Fairly accommodative	-1.121	Nonbelligerent
W38.	-.104	Balanced	-.428	Nonbelligerent
W39.	-.017	Balanced	-.180	Nonbelligerent
W40.	+.119	Balanced	-.172	Nonbelligerent
W41.	+12.775	Extremely belligerent	+5.762	Belligerent
W42.	-.134	Balanced	-.401	Nonbelligerent
W43.	+7.872	Extremely belligerent	+10.035	Belligerent
W44.	-1.047	Fairly accommodative	-1.699	Nonbelligerent
W45.	-1.300	Fairly accommodative	-1.285	Nonbelligerent
W46.	+.238	Balanced	+.055	Nonbelligerent

Period ended by major Western action	SOVIET BEHAVIOR		WESTERN BEHAVIOR (RESPONDER)	
	b/a^a	Category	b/a	Category
W47.	−.110	Balanced	−.514	Nonbelligerent
W48.	+4.882	Extremely belligerent	−.129	(Inconsistent)
W49.	+3.740	Extremely belligerent	+.591	Nonbelligerent
W50.	+.902	Balanced firm	+1.335	Belligerent
W51.	+1.343	Fairly belligerent	+.336	Nonbelligerent
W52.	+.353	Balanced firm	+.474	Nonbelligerent
W53.	+.297	Balanced	+.214	Nonbelligerent
W54.	−.665	Balanced flexible	+.396	Nonbelligerent
W55.	−.261	Balanced	+2.062	Belligerent
W56.	+.315	Balanced	+.426	Nonbelligerent
W57.	+3.445	Extremely belligerent	+2.054	Belligerent
W58.	+.161	Balanced	−.122	Nonbelligerent
W59.	+.669	Balanced firm	−.176	Nonbelligerent
W60.	−23.291	Extremely accommodative	+13.439	Belligerent
W61.	−.679	Balanced flexible	−.350	Nonbelligerent
W62.	−2.270	Quite accommodative	−2.133	Nonbelligerent

[a] *Belligerent/accommodative score.*

GLOSSARY OF FREQUENTLY USED TERMS

Accommodative behavior. A coalition's overall pattern of behavior in some specified time period, characterized by a high level of conciliatory activity and a low level of refractory activity.

Aggressive behavior. An interpretation of predominantly belligerent patterns which follows from the assumptions contained in certain belief systems.

Balanced pattern. A coalition's overall pattern of behavior in some specified time period, characterized by an even mixture of both conciliatory and refractory activity.

Belief system. A set of basic assumptions about the goals and world-view of a coalition. These assumptions specify (1) the coalition's strategic goals, (2) its image of how its strategic goals are perceived by its adversary, and (3) its perception of its adversary's strategic goals.

Belligerent pattern. A coalition's overall pattern of behavior in some specified time period, characterized by a high level of refractory activity and a low level of conciliatory activity.

Coalition. A group of nations that coordinate their resources in interaction with some common adversary.

Conciliatory action. Any action by one coalition which has the effect of decreasing disagreement with the other coalition or of making existing disagreement less salient.

Consolidationist (abbreviation: *C*). A coalition whose strategic goals involve holding on to what it has and making more secure its influence in areas where some influence has already been established. Its characteristic orientation is defensive.

Decision model. A set of assumptions about the decision process by which a coalition translates its strategic goals and world-view into specific responses to different patterns of adversary behavior. Hence, a set of rules for translating a belief system about a coalition into specific predictions about how that coalition will respond to its adversary's behavior.

Destructionist (abbreviation: *D*). A coalition whose strategic goals involve the elimination of its adversary as a serious competitor in the international arena. Its characteristic orientation is exploitative.

Disagreement-relevant action. Any action by either coalition that either increases or decreases disagreements between the two coalitions.

Expansionist (abbreviation: *E*). A coalition whose strategic goals involve the expansion of its own influence by increasing its control in areas where it presently has little or no influence. Its characteristic orientation is opportunistic.

211

Inconsistent pattern. A coalition's overall pattern of behavior in some specified time period, characterized by quite high and roughly equal levels of both conciliatory and refractory activity.

Interaction unit. An ordered pair of descriptions that brings together the behavior of both coalitions and serves as the basic unit of analysis. Each interaction unit contains a description of one coalition's pattern of behavior in some specified time period *and* a description of the other coalition's major action ending this time period.

Lax behavior. An interpretation of predominantly accommodative patterns which follows from the assumptions contained in certain belief systems.

Major action. An exceptionally refractory or conciliatory action — one whose impact on disagreement is so great that it exceeds a specified threshold and thereby qualifies to form the second half of an interaction unit.

Parameter. A basic and stable property of a coalition which can assume different theoretical values (e.g., a coalition's strategic goals). A belief system consists of assumptions about the values of three parameters. (*See* belief system.)

Receptive behavior. An interpretation of predominantly accomodative patterns which follows from the assumptions contained in certain belief systems.

Reflected image. A short-hand term that refers to a coalition's image of how its own strategic goals are perceived by the adversary.

Refractory action. Any action by one coalition which has the effect of increasing disagreement with the other coalition or of making existing disagreement more salient.

Responder-belligerent. A belligerent behavior pattern of a *responding* coalition in the period prior to its major action.

Responder-nonbelligerent. A nonbelligerent behavior pattern of a *responding* coalition in the period prior to its major action.

Responding coalition. The coalition whose major action marks the end of a given interaction unit.

Rough strategic parity. A situation in which neither side can inflict devastating losses on the other with impunity.

Soviet coalition. The Soviet Union and its allies. More precisely, a group of largely socialist nations that look to the Soviet Union for leadership and that meet the criteria for membership in a coalition described in Chapter One, page 8.

Strategic goals. A politically operative end state that guides a coalition in its choice of courses of action.

Tactically contingent action. An action by one coalition that is contingent on the behavior of the opposing coalition; that is, an action in which the decision calculus includes what the other side has done or might do as one important element.

Time period. The chronological period spanned by a single interaction unit. Hence, a segment of time, bounded at the end by a major action of one coalition and bounded at the beginning by the initiation of the other coalition's preceding pattern of behavior. (*See* interaction unit.)

Western coalition. The United States and its allies. More precisely, a group of largely Western nations that look to the United States for leadership and that meet the criteria for membership in a coalition described in Chapter One, page 8.

BIBLIOGRAPHY

Acheson, Dean. 1969. *Present at the Creation*. New York: W. W. Norton.

Alperovitz, Gar. 1965. *Atomic Diplomacy: Hiroshima and Potsdam*. New York: Simon and Schuster.

Aspaturian, Vernon V. 1966. "Internal Politics and Foreign Policy in the Soviet System." In R. Barry Farrell, ed., *Approaches to Comparative and International Politics*. Evanston, Ill.: Northwestern University Press, pp. 212–287.

————. 1968. "Foreign Policy Perspectives in the Sixties." In Alexander Dallin and Thomas B. Larson, eds. *Soviet Politics Since Khrushchev*. Englewood Cliffs, N.J.: Prentice-Hall, pp. 129–162.

Ball, George W. 1968. *The Discipline of Power*. Boston: Atlantic-Little, Brown.

Barnet, Richard J. 1963. "Initiative and Response in Soviet Foreign Policy." *World Politics* 16 (October):173–187.

Barnet, Richard J. 1968. *Intervention and Revolution*. New York: World.

Bell, Daniel. 1958. "Ten Theories in Search of Reality: The Prediction of Soviet Behavior in the Social Sciences." *World Politics* 10 (April):327–365.

Bishop, Donald G., ed. 1952. *Soviet Foreign Relations*. Syracuse, N.Y.: Syracuse University Press.

Blackmer, Donald L. M. 1968. "Scholars and Policymakers: Perceptions of Soviet Policy." Paper delivered at the 1968 Annual Meeting of the American Political Science Association, Washington, D.C.

Bloomfield, Lincoln P., Clemens, Walter C., Jr.; and Griffiths, Franklyn. 1966. *Khrushchev and the Arms Race*. Cambridge, Mass.: M.I.T. Press.

Bouscaren, Anthony Trawick. 1962. *Soviet Foreign Policy: A Pattern of Persistence*. New York: Fordham University Press.

Brody, Richard A. 1966. "Cognition and Behavior: A Model of International Relations." In O. J. Harvey, ed. *Experience, Structure, and Adaptability*. New York: Springer, pp. 321–348.

Bronfenbrenner, Urie. 1961. "The Mirror-Image in Soviet-American Relations." *Journal of Social Issues* 17, 3:45–57.

Brumberg, Abraham, ed. 1962. *Russia Under Khrushchev: An Anthology from Problems of Communism*. New York: Frederick A. Praeger.

Brzezinski, Zbigniew. 1960. "Communist Ideology and International Affairs." *Journal of Conflict Resolution* 4 (September):266–290.

Chinese Government Spokesman. 1963. *Peking Review*. 6, no. 33 (August 16), p. 7.

213

Coombs, Clyde H. 1964. *Theory of Data.* New York: Wiley.

Dallin, Alexander. 1963. "Russia and China View the United States." *Annals of the American Academy of Political and Social Science* 349 (September):154–162.

Dallin, David J. 1961. *Soviet Foreign Policy after Stalin.* Philadelphia: J. P. Lippincott.

Dexter, Byron. 1950. "Clausewitz and Soviet Strategy." *Foreign Affairs* 29 (October):41–55.

Dutt, Clemens, ed. 1960. *Fundamentals of Marxism-Leninism.* Moscow: Foreign Language Publishing House.

Eckhardt, William, and White, Ralph K. 1967. "A Test of the Mirror-Image Hypothesis." *Journal of Conflict Resolution* 11 (September):325–332.

Edelman, Murray M. 1964. *Symbolic Uses of Politics.* Urbana, Illinois: University of Illinois Press.

Etzioni, Amitai. 1962. *The Hard Way to Peace.* New York: Crowell-Collier.

Fleming, D. F. 1961. *The Cold War and Its Origins.* Garden City, N.Y.: Doubleday.

Floyd, David. 1964. *Mao Against Khrushchev.* New York: Frederick A. Praeger.

Fontaine, Andre. 1968. *History of the Cold War.* New York: Random House.

Fromm, Erich. 1961. *May Man Prevail?* Garden City, N.Y.: Doubleday, Anchor Edition.

Fulbright, J. William. 1966. *The Arrogance of Power.* New York: Random House.

Gamson, William A. 1964a. "Experimental Studies of Coalition Formation." In Leonard Berkowitz, ed., *Advances in Experimental Social Psychology,* vol. 1, pp. 81–110. New York: Academic Press.

————. 1964b. "Evaluating Beliefs about International Conflict." In Roger Fisher, ed., *International Conflict and Behavioral Science.* New York: Basic Books, pp. 27–40.

Gamson, William A., and Modigliani, Andre. 1963. "Tensions and Concessions: The Empirical Confirmation of Belief Systems about Soviet Behavior." *Social Problems* 11 (Summer):34–48.

————. 1965. "Soviet Responses to Western Foreign Policy, 1946–53." *Papers, Peace Research Society* 3 (November):47–78.

————. 1968. "Some Aspects of Soviet-Western Conflict." *Papers, Peace Research Society* 9 (November):9–24.

Garthoff, Raymond L. 1962. *Soviet Strategy in the Nuclear Age.* New York: Frederick A. Praeger.

George, Alexander L. 1967. "The 'Operational Code': A Neglected Approach to the Study of Political Leaders and Decision-Making." The Rand Corporation, Santa Monica, Cal., Memorandum RM-5427-PR.

Glaser, William A. 1956. "Theories of Soviet Foreign Policy." *World Affairs Quarterly* 27 (July):128–152.

Guttman, Louis. 1969. "A Structural Theory for Interpersonal Beliefs and Action." *American Sociological Review* 24:318–328.

Halle, Louis J. 1967. *The Cold War as History.* New York: Harper and Row.

Hayter, Sir William. 1964. "The Cold War and the Future." In Evan

Luard, ed., *The Cold War: A Re-Appraisal*. New York: Frederick A. Praeger, pp. 307–328.

Herz, Martin F. 1966. *Beginnings of the Cold War*. Bloomington, Indiana: Indiana University Press.

"Historicus." 1949. "Stalin on Revolution." *Foreign Affairs* 27 (January): 175–214.

Hoffman, Stanley. 1968. *Gulliver's Troubles, or the Setting of American Foreign Policy*. New York: McGraw-Hill Book Co.

Holsti, Ole R.; North, Robert C.; and Brody, Richard. 1968. "Perception and Action in the 1914 Crisis." In J. David Singer, ed., *Quantitative International Politics*. New York: The Free Press, pp. 123–158.

Horelick, Arnold L., and Rush, Myron. 1966. *Strategic Power and Soviet Foreign Policy*. Chicago, Ill.: University of Chicago Press.

Horowitz, David. 1965. *The Free World Colossus*. London: MacGibbon and Kee.

Horowitz, David, ed. 1967. *Containment and Revolution*. London: Anthony Blond Ltd.

Hudson, G. F. 1967. *The Hard and Bitter Peace*. New York: Frederick A. Praeger.

Jecker, J. D. 1964. "Attitudes Toward Political Defection." Paper delivered at the Midwestern Psychological Association, St. Louis, Mo.

Jones, Edward E., and Gerard, Harold B. 1967. *Foundations of Social Psychology*. New York: John Wiley.

Kautsky, John H. 1965. "Myth, Self-Fulfilling Prophecy, and Symbolic Reassurance in the East-West Conflict." *Journal of Conflict Resolution* 9 (March):1–17.

Keep, John, ed. 1964. *Contemporary History in the Soviet Mirror*. New York: Frederick A. Praeger.

Kennan, George F. ["X"]. 1947. "The Sources of Soviet Conduct." *Foreign Affairs* 25 (July):566–582.

Kissinger, Henry A. 1961. *The Necessity for Choice*. New York: Harper.

Leites, Nathan. 1953. *A Study of Bolshevism*. Glencoe, Ill.: The Free Press.

Levine, Robert A. 1963. *The Arms Debate*. Cambridge, Mass.: Harvard University Press.

Luard, Evan, ed. 1964. *The Cold War: A Re-Appraisal*. New York: Frederick A. Praeger.

Lukacs, John. 1966. *A New History of the Cold War*. Garden City, N.Y.: Doubleday, Anchor Edition.

MacIntosh, J. Malcolm. 1963. *Strategy and Tactics of Soviet Foreign Policy*. New York: Oxford University Press.

Mamatey, Victor S. 1964. *Soviet Russian Imperialism*. Princeton, N.J.: D. Van Nostrand.

McLellan, David S. 1966. *The Cold War in Transition*. New York: Macmillan.

Mills, C. Wright. 1958. *The Causes of World War Three*. New York: Simon and Schuster.

Moses, Lincoln E.; Brody, Richard A.; Holsti, Ole R.; Kadane, Joseph B.; and Milstein, Jeffrey S. 1967. "Scaling Data on Inter-Nation Action." *Science* 156 (May 26):1054–1059.

Neal, Fred Warner. 1960. "The Sources of Soviet Conduct." In Devere E. Pentony, ed., *Soviet Behavior in World Affairs*. San Francisco: Chandler, pp. 145–157.

Nordheim, Erik V., and Wilcox, Pamela B. 1967. "Major Events of the Nuclear Age: A Chronology to Assist in the Analysis of American Public Opinion." Oak Ridge National Laboratory.

Oglesby, Carl. 1967. "Vietnamese Crucible: An Essay on the Meanings of the Cold War." In Carl Oglesby and Richard Shaull, *Containment and Change*. New York: Macmillan.

Osgood, Charles E. 1962. "Reciprocal Initiative." In James Roosevelt, ed., *The Liberal Papers*. Garden City, N.Y.: Doubleday, Anchor Edition, pp. 155–228.

Oskamp, S. 1963. "Attitudes Toward U.S. and Russian Actions: A Double Standard." Paper delivered at the California Psychological Association.

Quester, George H. 1971. *Nuclear Diplomacy: The First 25 Years*. New York: Dunellen.

Reshetar, John S., Jr. 1955. *Problems of Analyzing and Predicting Soviet Behavior*. Garden City, N.Y.: Doubleday.

Roberts, Henry L. 1956. *Russia and America: Dangers and Prospects*. New York: New American Library, Mentor Books.

Robertson, Charles L. 1966. *International Politics Since World War II*. New York: John Wiley.

Scott, Andrew M. 1967. *The Functioning of the International Political System*. New York: Macmillan.

Seton-Watson, Hugh. 1960. *From Lenin to Khrushchev*. New York: Frederick A. Praeger.

———. 1962. *Neither War Nor Peace*. New York: Frederick A. Praeger.

Sharp, Samuel L. 1958. "National Interest: Key to Soviet Politics." *Problems of Communism* (March–April).

Shulman, Marshall D. 1963. *Stalin's Foreign Policy Reappraised*. Cambridge, Mass.: Harvard University Press.

———. 1966. *Beyond the Cold War*. New Haven: Yale University Press.

Siegel, Sidney. 1956. *Non-Parametric Statistics*. New York: McGraw-Hill.

Singer, J. David. 1960. "International Conflict: Three Levels of Analysis." *World Politics* 12 (April):453–461.

Singer, J. David, ed. 1968. *Quantitative International Politics: Insights and Evidence*. New York: The Free Press.

Smith, Howard K. 1949. *The State of Europe*. New York: Alfred A. Knopf.

Spanier, John W. 1968. *American Foreign Policy Since World War II*. New York: Frederick A. Praeger.

Steel, Ronald (1967) *Pax Americana*. New York: Viking.

Stimson, Henry L. 1947. "The Challenge to Americans." *Foreign Affairs* 26 (October):5–14.

Strausz-Hupé, Robert; Kintner, William R.; and Possony, Stefan T. 1961. *A Forward Strategy for America*. New York: Harper.

Triska, Jan F. 1958. "A Model for Study of Soviet Foreign Policy." *American Political Science Review* 52 (March):64–83.

Tucker, Robert C. 1963. *The Soviet Political Mind*. New York: Frederick A. Praeger.

Ulam, Adam B. 1968. *Expansion and Coexistence: The History of Soviet Foreign Policy, 1917–67*. New York: Frederick A. Praeger.

Warburg, James. 1962. "A Re-examination of American Foreign Policy." In James Roosevelt, ed., *The Liberal Papers*. Garden City, N.Y.: Doubleday, Anchor Edition, pp. 49–96.

Whiting, Allen S. 1960. *China Crosses the Yalu.* New York: Macmillan.

Williams, William Appleman 1959. *The Tragedy of American Diplomacy.* Cleveland, Ohio: World.

Wolfe, Bertram D. 1962. "Communist Ideology and Soviet Foreign Policy." *Foreign Affairs* 41 (October):152–170.

Wolfe, Thomas W. 1964. *Soviet Strategy at the Crossroads.* Cambridge, Mass.: Harvard University Press.

Wolfson, Murray. 1968. "A Mathematical Model of the Cold War." *Papers, Peace Research Society* 9:107–123.

Zimmerman, William. 1968. "Soviet Perceptions of the United States." In Alexander Dallin and Thomas B. Larson, eds., *Soviet Politics Since Khrushchev.* Englewood Cliffs, N.J.: Prentice-Hall, pp. 163–179.

———. 1969. *Soviet Perspectives on International Relations.* Princeton, N.J.: Princeton University Press.

Zinnes, Dina A. 1968. "The Expression and Perception of Hostility in Prewar Crisis: 1914." In J. David Singer, ed., *Quantitative International Politics.* New York: The Free Press, pp. 85–119.

INDEX

219

DATE DUE